YOU DON'T
HAVE TO TAKE IT ANYMORE,
BECAUSE YOU ARE ...

DRESSED TO KILL

A BIBLICAL APPROACH
TO SPIRITUAL WARFARE AND ARMOR

RICK RENNER

TEACH ALL NATIONS

A book company anointed to take God's Word
to you and to the nations of the world.

a division of
RICK RENNER MINISTRIES

Dressed To Kill
A Biblical Approach to Spiritual Warfare and Armor
ISBN: 978-0-9779459-0-0
Copyright © 1991 by
Rick Renner
P.O. Box 702040
Tulsa, Oklahoma 74170-2040

Published by Teach All Nations
P.O. Box 702040 • Tulsa, OK 74170-2040

New Edition 2007
6th Printing

Editorial Consultant: Cynthia Hansen
Text Design: Lisa Simpson, www.SimpsonProductions.net
Graphic Design: Debbie Pullman, Zoe Life Creative Media
design@ZoeLifeCreative.com

Printed in the USA.

DEDICATION

I dedicate this newest version of *Dressed To Kill* to the pastors, churches, organizations, businesspeople, and partners from every walk of life who financially support our ministry. Denise and I, along with our family and our God-called team, are called to do the work of the ministry on the frontlines of the mission field. However, it is the grace of God and the faithful financial support of all our partners that empowers us to stay here and fulfill this nation-changing assignment from Heaven. We love every one of you, and we thank God for joining us together with you in the work of the Kingdom!

Rick Renner

TABLE OF CONTENTS

Acknowledgments...13

CHAPTER ONE
Spiritual Warfare Mania 17
    Spiritual Hostages...20
    Spoiling Principalities and Powers 22
    Ridiculous and Unscriptural Behavior.........26
    Why the Preoccupation With Spiritual Warfare? 28
    Nothing New Under the Sun............................30
    What About Witches?..38
    Biblical Spiritual Warfare 39
    How Real Warfare Begins.................................42
    Dealing With the Wind and the Waves
        in Your Life 46
    Spiritual Warfare: A Mental Condition 50
    A Warning About Spiritual Warfare 54

CHAPTER TWO
Fleshly Weapons vs. Spiritual Weapons............................59
    Bloodthirsty, Daring, and Committed
        Men of War...61
    Spiritual Weapons and Spiritual Strategies 63
    The Futility of the Flesh.................................66
    Weak and Silly Weapons of Flesh 67

What Does the Bible Say
  About the Purpose of Tongues? 70
Touch Not, Taste Not, Handle Not 73

CHAPTER THREE
Resting in Our Redemption.......................**81**
Satan's Slave Market.....................................83
Dominated by 'the Course of This World'...........85
Who Is Working Behind the Scenes? 88
Demonically Energized..................................92
Purchased 'Out of' Slavery 94
Paying the Demanded Price 96
Restored to Full Status 97
Translated Out of Satan's Kingdom 99

CHAPTER FOUR
Why Does the Battle Still Rage? **103**
Spiritual Warfare and Renewing the Mind 107
A Lifelong Commitment...............................111

CHAPTER FIVE
A Menace From Heaven **115**
An Opportune Moment for the Devil To Attack........116
Demonic Attacks That Backfire! 118
A Closed Door Does Not Mean Failure............122
If You've Been Gaining New Ground,
  Get Ready To Be Challenged! 125
Attacks Against Churches and Ministries.........130
A Pattern of Strife and Discord 133
Heavily Dressed, Trained Killers 136

CHAPTER SIX

An Important Message To Remember............................143

    Spiritually Lopsided Believers...........................146

    Comrades in the Fight 151

    Soldiers Who Are Worthy of Your Association...........154

CHAPTER SEVEN

Be Strong in the Lord......................................159

    Superhuman Power for a Superhuman Task 163

    Where To Get This Power................................165

    It's Yours for the Taking..............................166

    Evidence of the Holy Spirit's Power 169

    Kratos Power...171

    God's Mighty Arm!.....................................176

CHAPTER EIGHT

The Wiles, Devices and Deception of the Devil..............181

    A New Set of Clothes...................................185

    How Do You Put On the Whole Armor of God?........187

    Maintaining a Strategic Position
       Over the Battlefield of Your Life and Mind.............192

    An Eyeball-to-Eyeball Confrontation!...................195

    Taking a Stand Against the Wiles of the Devil..........196

    The Devices of the Devil 198

    The Deception of the Devil.............................201

    An Example of Demonic Intimidation....................204

    The Hard Facts of Spiritual Warfare 209

    The Flesh Counts for Nothing 211

    Moving Beyond the Flesh................................217

Prevailing Over the Philistines in Your Life 221
The Devil's Mode of Operation 223

CHAPTER NINE
Wrestling With Principalities and Powers **227**
The Survival of the Fittest 231
Principalities and Powers 233
The Devil's Rank-and-File Forces 235
Revealing Names, Symbols, and Types
    of the Devil in the Bible 239
Satan's Destructive Bent 241
Satan's Perverted Nature 242
Satan's Desire To Control 245
Satan, the Mind Manipulator 246
A Roaring Lion 248
A Prerequisite to Spiritual Warfare 251

CHAPTER TEN
The Loinbelt of Truth **257**
Paul's Expanded Version of Spiritual Armor 258
For Review 260
The Most Important Weapon 261
A Visible Piece of Armor 263
The Difference Between *Logos* and *Rhema* 264
The Only Way To Succeed Spiritually 266
How To Walk in Righteousness 268
How To Walk in Peace 269
How To Walk in Strong Faith 270
The Helmet and the Sword 271

Winning or Losing Is *Your* Choice.....................275
The Reproductive Ability of God........................276
The Major Mistake Believers Make.....................278
The Psalmist Who Understood the Centrality
   of the Word 280
The Key to Victory and Success 281
The Word's Best Advice 283
The Way To Win 286

CHAPTER ELEVEN
The Breastplate of Righteousness **291**
The Beauty of the Breastplate 293
Someone Wants To Hurt You 294
The Correct Attitude for Warfare 297
Scriptures on Righteousness..............................299
A New Source of Confidence 301
Powerless Religion vs. Powerful Religion 303
Righteousness: A Defensive Weapon 305
Righteousness: An Offensive Weapon 307

CHAPTER TWELVE
Shoes of Peace **313**
Two Kinds of Peace..317
Dominating Peace 319
Peace: A Defensive Weapon 320
How Peace Protects You....................................324
Protection From the Devil's Attacks 325
How To Set a Guard Around Your Heart.....................327
Spikes for Standing Firmly 328

How To Have Immovable Faith 332
Peace: An Offensive Weapon 333
It's Time To Do Some Walking! 336
What Does 'Shortly' Mean? 337

CHAPTER THIRTEEN
The Shield of Faith **343**
    The Shield of Faith 346
    How To Care for Your Shield of Faith 349
    What Does 'Above All' Mean? 352
    The Purpose of the Shield of Faith 355
    The Fiery Darts of the Wicked 356
    Fire That Stirs the Vilest Passions 358
    Who Is Responsible for Failure? 359
    Quenching, Extinguishing, and Ricocheting Faith........362
    Corporate Faith in the Local Church 365
    Does Your Shield Have Cracks? 366
    If Your Faith Needs an Anointing...........................367
    In Conclusion 368

CHAPTER FOURTEEN
The Helmet of Salvation **373**
    The Helmet of Salvation 374
    God's Most Gorgeous Gift...................................375
    Armed and Dangerous 379
    Playing Mind Games With the Devil.........................380
    What Is a Stronghold?.....................................381
    Two Kinds of Strongholds 385
    What Is Oppression? 389

Salvation Protects Your Mind 390
What Is a Sound Mind? 392
What Does the Word 'Salvation' Mean? 395
A Transformed Mind 396

CHAPTER FIFTEEN
The Sword of the Spirit **403**
The Swords of the Roman Soldier 404
What Is a *Rhema*? 406
The Sword and the Loinbelt 408
What Is a Two-Edged Sword? 415
Meditation and Confession 418
How To Hear From God 422
When Jesus Needed a Sword 425
A Sure-Fire Guarantee! 430

CHAPTER SIXTEEN
The Lance of Prayer and Supplication **435**
Various Kinds of Lances 436
Various Kinds of Prayer 439
How Often Should We Pray? 442
Six Kinds of Prayer for the Believer 443
A Final Word 462

ACKNOWLEDGMENTS

I wish to express my deepest gratitude to the late Rev. Kenneth E. Hagin for his public support of this book and for encouraging me in the work of the Lord. At the 1991 Winter Bible Seminar, Brother Hagin used and referred to this book often as he taught on biblical spiritual warfare. This was a great encouragement to me personally. There are no words sufficient to express my thanksgiving for his words of support and for the many truths imparted to my life through his ministry.

Let me also thank Tony Cooke for being used of God to pass the original manuscript of this book along to Brother Hagin. I appreciate you, Tony. You are a dear friend and fellow soldier, and I am grateful that we have known each other all these years. I highly value you.

I also wish to thank Cindy Hansen for her work of reediting this newest release of *Dressed To Kill*. You are among the best editors I know. What makes you most valuable as an editor is not only your editorial abilities but also your spiritual insights and comments, which are very appreciated.

Most importantly, I want to thank my precious wife, Denise, for believing in me and my ministry and for faithfully releasing the godly fragrance of Jesus Christ into our home and into our personal lives. You are such a treasure to my life. Thank you for being the godly example you are as a wife, mother, and grandmother. I love you dearly, Denise. My heart beats with thanksgiving to Jesus for calling you to be my wife.

Rick Renner

DRESSED TO KILL

A BIBLICAL APPROACH
TO SPIRITUAL WARFARE
AND ARMOR

CHAPTER ONE

SPIRITUAL WARFARE MANIA

*F*rom time to time, the subject of spiritual warfare becomes a popular, almost faddish focus for the Body of Christ. When this happens, it is taught with such enthusiasm that a newcomer to Christ might assume spiritual warfare is a brand-new revelation, even though it is not. There have even been many moments in history when this subject has become the rage in the Charismatic sector of the Body of Christ. Any person who has been in touch with the national pulse of the Church would quickly agree that at times, the Body of Christ experiences what I have come to call a "spiritual warfare mania."

This emphasis on spiritual warfare is *good* in that it causes us to become familiar with our adversary, the devil, and how he operates. Once we understand his mode of operation, we can then foil his attacks against us. This is the very reason Paul told the Corinthians concerning the devil and his mode of operation, "...We are not ignorant of his [Satan's] devices" (2 Corinthians 2:11).

On the other hand, an overemphasis on spiritual warfare has the potential of having a very *bad* effect on the Church. If spiritual warfare is not taught properly, it can be devastating, for this subject has a unique way of captivating people's attention so completely that they eventually think of nothing *but* spiritual warfare. This is a favorite trick of the devil to make believers magnify his power to a greater degree than it deserves. If this trick works, these imbalanced, devil-minded believers begin to imagine that the devil is behind everything that occurs, thus becoming paralyzed and incapable of functioning normally in any capacity of life. In this way, the enemy eliminates them from future usefulness in the Kingdom of God. Unfortunately, this has been the outcome in the lives of too many people who have focused on the issue of spiritual warfare in years past.

Don't misunderstand what I am saying: I am *not* opposed to spiritual warfare. *Spiritual warfare is real!* We are commanded in Scripture to deal with the unseen, invisible forces that have been marshaled against us. We are commanded to "cast out devils" (Mark 16:17) and to "pull down the strongholds" of the mind (2 Corinthians 10:3-5). This is a part of our Christian responsibility toward the lost, the oppressed, and the demonized.

> We are commanded in Scripture to deal with the unseen, invisible forces that have been marshaled against us.

In my own ministry, I have had to deal with demonic manifestations on occasion. For instance, I remember a time years ago when a young teenage Satanist approached me at the end of one of my meetings in a large church. During the meeting, he realized that Satan's powers had taken his mind captive, so he came forward to receive prayer in the prayer line.

As I continued through the prayer line, praying for first one and then another, I could visibly see from a distance that this particular young man was sending forth spiritual signals of a very strong, evil presence. As I came nearer to him, I sensed that he had been involved in some type of occult activity.

When I finally reached the young man, he looked up through eyes that were tightly squeezed together like little slits in the front of his head. I looked into his eyes, and it was as if a demon was looking back at me from behind his face. When I saw this, I knew that this young man was serious about being helped. It had taken a great deal of determination for him to shove aside that manipulating force and forge his way down to the front of the church auditorium.

As I laid my hands on the young man that night, his body began to react violently to the power of God. Trembling under the weight of God's power, he crumbled to the floor, landing in a heap next to my feet. Lying there engulfed in the electrifying power of God that was surging up and down his body, the young man quietly moaned, "I'm afraid to leave them [the satanic group in which he was involved]. They said they would kill me if I left the group!"

I leaned over to pray for him a second time, and as I did, the horrible demonic influence that had held his mind captive immediately released him and fled from the scene. Oh, yes, I *definitely* believe in genuine spiritual warfare!

SPIRITUAL HOSTAGES

There are multitudes of people in the world today who are held hostage by the devil in their minds. First John 3:8 says, "...For this purpose the Son of God was manifested, that he might destroy the works of the devil."

The word "destroy" is taken from the Greek word *luo*, and it refers to *the act of untying or unloosing something*. It is the exact word we would use to picture a person who is untying his shoes. In fact, the word *luo* is used in this exact way in Luke 3:16, when John the Baptist says, "...But one mightier than I cometh, the latchet of whose shoes I am not worthy *to unloose....*"

Thus, Jesus Christ came into the world to *untie* and *unloose* Satan's binding powers over us. At the Cross, Jesus unraveled Satan's power until His redemptive work was finally complete and our liberty was fully purchased.

Furthermore, Peter told the household of Cornelius, "How God anointed Jesus of Nazareth with the Holy Ghost and with power: who went about doing good, and healing all that were oppressed of the devil; for God was with him" (Acts 10:38).

We know from both of the above verses that setting people free from Satan's power is a primary concern of Jesus Christ. Since this is His concern, it should be ours as well.

In order to free people from demonic oppression, we must learn how to recognize the work of the enemy and how to overcome his attacks against the mind, *for the mind is the primary area he seeks to attack.* Satan's goal is to plant a stronghold of deception in some area of an individual's mind. If he is successful, he can then begin to control and manipulate the person from that lofty position.

> Setting people free from Satan's power is a primary concern of Jesus Christ. Since this is His concern, it should be ours as well.

The Holy Spirit is obviously speaking a strong message about spiritual warfare to us in these days. Christian leaders and churches all across the nation are awakening to this reality. In light of this, we must give heed to what the Spirit is saying to the Church *and proceed with the Word of God as our guide and foundation.*

As we seek to engage in spiritual warfare, we must be very careful to walk in balance. For one thing, we need to realize that this subject involves more than just dealing with the devil. Other major elements of spiritual warfare have to do with *taking control of our minds* and *crucifying the flesh.* We must not forget that these latter elements of spiritual warfare are just as vital as the first.

The truth is, the devil's attacks against our lives wouldn't work if our flesh didn't cooperate. If we were truly mortifying the flesh on a daily basis (Colossians 3:5), living lives that are "dead to sin" (Romans 6:2) as we are commanded to do in Scripture, we would not respond to demonic suggestions and to fleshly temptation. Dead men are incapable of responding to *anything.* Thus, we see the power of a crucified life!

Living the crucified life is a critical part of spiritual warfare. If I wrote a book on spiritual warfare without mentioning this truth, I would do my faithful readers a great injustice by giving them a very unrealistic view of the subject.

A person can scream at the devil all day long, but if that person has willfully permitted some area of his mind to go

> **Living the crucified life is a critical part of spiritual warfare.**

unchecked and unguarded — if he is aware of an area of sin but has not been willing to deal with it — he has opened the door for an attack on himself. In that case, all his prayers against the devil will be to no avail because his real enemy is not the devil. Rather, it is his own carnal mind and flesh, which must be submitted to the control of the Holy Spirit in order to eradicate these attacks.

The bottom line is this: If people focus *only* on the devil as they pursue the subject of spiritual warfare and fail to consider other equally important areas, their emphasis on spiritual warfare can and will be very damaging to them.

SPOILING PRINCIPALITIES AND POWERS

Although spiritual warfare is real and we cannot ignore it, we must be careful to remember that the real battle with Satan was won at the Cross and the resurrection. Now this same victorious Christ who single-handedly defeated the devil lives in us in the Person of the Holy Spirit! This is why the apostle John tells us, "...Greater is he that is in you, than he that is in the world" (1 John 4:4).

Our view of spiritual warfare must begin with this basic understanding of Jesus' already accomplished victory over Satan. If we don't start out with this as our foundation, eventually we will be led to utterly ridiculous spiritual conclusions. The victory has already been won; there is nothing we can add to the destructive work Jesus did to Satan's domain when He was raised from the dead.

> We must be careful to remember that the real battle with Satan was won at the Cross and the resurrection.

In Colossians 2:15, Paul vividly portrays Jesus' victory and Satan's defeat. It says, "And having spoiled principalities and powers, he made a shew of them openly, triumphing over them in it." Especially notice the word "spoiled." This word is taken from the Greek word *apekdusamenos*, and it refers to *the act of stripping one's garments off to the point of complete nakedness.*

By using the word "spoiled," the Holy Spirit tells us that when Jesus Christ arose from the dead, He thoroughly plundered the enemy. Quite literally, He *"spoiled principalities and powers."* An even better translation could read, *"He completely stripped principalities and powers and left them utterly naked, with nothing left at their disposal to retaliate."*

Furthermore, Paul goes on to tell us that Jesus didn't stop when His mission was accomplished and His sacking and plundering of hell's powers was complete. Instead, Jesus rubbed this defeat in the devil's face by throwing the biggest party the universe had ever seen!

Colossians 2:15 continues, "And having spoiled principalities and powers, *he made a shew of them openly, triumphing
over them in it.*" The word "shew" is taken from the word
deigmatidzo, and it literally means *to display* or *to expose*
something. It was used in classical Greek writings to denote the
display of captives, weaponry, and trophies that were seized during war on foreign soil.

Once the war was over and the battle was won, the reigning
emperor would return home and victoriously *display* and *expose*
the treasures, trophies, weaponry, and captives he had seized
during his military conquest. This was a grand moment of
celebration for the victor — and a *very* humiliating experience
for the defunct foe!

Now the Holy Spirit has carefully chosen to use this same
word *(deigmatidzo)* to let us know what Jesus did after He was
finished plundering the enemy. When His resurrection was
complete and the enemy was stripped bare to the core, Jesus
then proceeded to publicly *display* and *expose* this defeated
spiritual foe and all his defective wares to the hosts of Heaven!

But wait — there is still more to Colossians 2:15 we must
understand. Paul goes on to tell us that "...he made a shew of
them *openly*...."

Especially pay heed to the word "openly." The word
"openly" is taken from the word *parresia*, which is used
throughout the books of the New Testament to denote *boldness*
or *confidence*.

By using the word *parresia*, Paul declares that when this heavenly party or celebration of Jesus' victory commenced, it was no quiet affair. Quite the contrary! Jesus *boldly*, *confidently*, and *loudly* exposed and displayed this now-defunct foe to Heaven's hosts!

Make no mistake about it — when Jesus made a "shew of them openly," it was *not* a quiet moment in Heaven. Jesus made a display of these defeated enemies and their defective wares *openly*, *boldly*, *confidently* — and, yes, even *loudly*! In other words, this was quite a *show*!

Then the verse continues: "...He made a shew of them openly, *triumphing over them in it*." The word "triumphing" is taken from the Greek word *triambeuo*, which is a technical word used to describe *a general or an emperor returning home from a grand victory in the enemy's territory*. The word "triumph" (*triambeuo*) was a word used to specifically describe the emperor's *triumphal parade* when he returned home. (For more on this, *see* Chapter Nine in my book, *Living in the Combat Zone*.)

Colossians 2:15 explicitly teaches that when Jesus' work on the Cross was finished, He descended into the lower places in order to take the enemy apart piece by piece. Jesus thoroughly "spoiled principalities and powers" through His death and resurrection. *They were so utterly plundered that they were "stripped to bare nakedness" and left with nothing in hand to retaliate!*

If our understanding of spiritual warfare does not begin with this as our foundation, we will eventually move into realms of teaching and experience that are not doctrinally sound. Therefore, we *must* approach warfare from this perspective.

RIDICULOUS AND UNSCRIPTURAL BEHAVIOR

The term "spiritual warfare" creates all kinds of images in our minds. Certainly it rightly makes us think about our ongoing conflict with unseen, demonic powers, for this is indeed what spiritual warfare is all about. As Ephesians 6:12 tells us, "For we wrestle not against flesh and blood, but against principalities, against powers, against the rulers of the darkness of this world, and against spiritual wickedness in high places."

> If we do not have a solid, biblical understanding of the devil — of our Christ-imparted authority over him and our divinely empowered weaponry to be used against him — we are left wide open to all kinds of wrong thinking, vain imaginations, fears, and unfounded methods of opposing our enemy.

But the mind also has the ability to dream up some very wild, unfounded, unbiblical ideas about the devil and our warfare against him. If we do not have a solid, biblical understanding of the devil — of our Christ-imparted authority over him and our divinely empowered weaponry to be used against him — we are left wide open to all kinds of wrong thinking, vain imaginations, fears, and unfounded methods of opposing our enemy.

This is precisely the reason I stated that an emphasis on spiritual warfare is both *good* and *bad*. It is *good* because it teaches us how our adversary operates.

In no way do I intend to convey the idea that all teachings about spiritual warfare are bad; in fact, some are *exceptionally* good! But as we approach this topic, we must guard against superstitious, homemade remedies about spiritual warfare. It is our responsibility to base our teachings and actions firmly on what the Word of God has to say rather than on exciting "hype" that stirs the emotions or the wild imaginations that temporarily thrill a frenzied crowd of novice believers.

For instance, some years ago, some so-called leading spiritual warfare specialists taught that since demon spirits lived in "high places" in the Old Testament and Satan is called the "prince of the power of the air" (Ephesians 2:2), believers must find a way to get as high as possible in order to do serious damage to the devil. Some of these "specialists" in spiritual warfare even suggested that the fortieth, fiftieth, or sixtieth floors of tall skyscrapers were the best places to hold prayer meetings and wage spiritual warfare!

Should victory still elude a person after he had ascended to these particular "high places" to battle the enemy, these same "specialists" often offered an additional suggestion: Perhaps that person needed to rent a plane or helicopter to go up even higher — right up to the actual "high places" where demons dwell — so he could wage spiritual warfare even more effectively!

When I first heard this teaching years ago, I was dumbfounded by its stupidity. I wanted to ask these so-called specialists how the Lord Jesus Christ ever took authority over evil forces. After all, He had no 60-floor buildings in which to hold His meetings, and no planes or helicopters were available to Him so He could get up high enough to do the devil damage. *Yet somehow, in some miraculous way, Jesus was still able to fully carry out His earthly ministry according to the will of His Father!*

This kind of teaching excites a crowd and sells books, but it is *not* based on the Bible. Ignorance of God's Word always leaves the Body of Christ in a vulnerable position. This is why Hosea 4:6 says, "My people are destroyed for lack of knowledge...."

> **Ignorance of God's Word always leaves the Body of Christ in a vulnerable position.**

Where ignorance is rampant concerning the Word — especially concerning the devil and our authority over him — superstition nearly always prevails. This results in all kinds of "spiritual hocus-pocus" in order to "shoo away the devil."

Unfortunately, much of what is called spiritual warfare often falls into this embarrassing category of ridiculous and unscriptural behavior. Yet spiritual warfare is real, and we must not ignore this truth. Rather, we must proceed into this subject with the Word of God as our guide.

WHY THE PREOCCUPATION WITH SPIRITUAL WARFARE?

Someone recently wrote me and asked, "Why does it seem that people from time to time become so preoccupied with the subject of spiritual warfare? Why does it periodically become the hot topic everyone talks about?"

In response to this question, I began to do some research. I spoke to many national Christian leaders about the subject of spiritual warfare, specifically asking them, "Why do you believe spiritual warfare often becomes such a central issue?"

The answers I received fit into three different categories. The first group of leaders I spoke with suggested that Satan is unleashing new hordes of demon spirits against the Church in these last days — perhaps more demon spirits than ever before. Therefore, they believe that this thrust on spiritual warfare is God's way to teach us how to overcome these masses of innumerable, uninvited nuisances that have been released to destroy the Church in these last days.

The second group of leaders suggested that there has been a new infiltration of demons into the Church in these last days. These demons have been specifically assigned to destroy individual churches and ministries from within. In fact, some leaders even expressed their strong belief that this is the reason so many ministers have failed morally and have fallen into immorality in recent times.

Because these Christian leaders believe that demon spirits are working around the clock to wreak havoc within the Church leadership at large, they say we must learn right now — at this very crucial time — how to combat these foul creatures of darkness that have come to carefully scheme the demise of great men and women of God.

The third group of leaders believe that the reason for this new emphasis on spiritual warfare is that witches and Satanists are uniting together in satanic prayer to cast curses upon the Church of Jesus Christ. These leaders believe that in order to combat these curses, the Holy Spirit is bringing to the Body of Christ a new awareness about the necessity of spiritual warfare.

Whether any of these three scenarios is right or wrong, it is still true that spiritual warfare has recently come to the forefront of the Body of Christ. Regardless of *why* this strong emphasis has occurred, the fact remains that we need to know what the Word of God has to say on these issues of spiritual warfare and spiritual armor.

NOTHING NEW UNDER THE SUN

It is clear from history that innumerable masses of demon spirits were released to attack and victimize the Church of Jesus Christ in its infancy during the first, second, and third centuries. (For a display of ancient Roman coins depicting the Roman caesars and emperors who ruled during the first 300 years of the Church, *see* centerfold insert, pages 1-16.)

Because we are the ones living in these contemporary times, it is natural for us to think that our problems are far worse than those of any preceding generation. But even with all these present problems and the potential difficulties still to come, our problems we face today are really no greater than those of the preceding generations of believers who have gone before us.

When the Church of Jesus Christ first emerged on the scene on the Day of Pentecost, it was born into a world very similar to ours. Nations were in revolt; national boundaries were disappearing; violence in entertainment was popular; and godly morals in the Roman world were nearly nonexistent.

The Roman army was quickly conquering the entire civilized world of that day. Homelands were being seized, plundered, and occupied by this invading army from Italy. The world was being united both politically and economically by the prevailing government of Rome. Meanwhile, the occultic paganism of the hour was far worse than any historian could ever state.

Satan used all these factors as a part of his plan to destroy the Church of Jesus Christ before it could destroy him. Nevertheless, his plan to destroy the Church miserably failed, for God had another plan! Rather than being destroyed, the Early Church arose in the power of the Spirit to meet the challenge — just as we will arise in our own day to meet any challenge the enemy would attempt to put before us!

Equipped with "the whole armor of God" (Ephesians 6:10-18), these early believers lived victoriously for the Lord in the midst of the worst predicaments — predicaments much worse than anyone reading this book has ever known. *Satan buffeted the Early Church with unimaginable torture and outward persecution, but he could not destroy her!*

> **Rather than being destroyed, the Early Church arose in the power of the Spirit to meet the challenge — just as we will rise in our own day to meet any challenge the enemy would attempt to put before us!**

"The whole armor of God" that worked so effectively for these early believers is the identical set of spiritual armor worn by the Church of Jesus Christ today. Just as these early Christians were fully equipped with the whole armor of God for the troubles of *their* day, we also have the whole armor of God to live victoriously for Jesus Christ in *our* day. And this armor still works just as effectively as it did then!

Each element of God's spiritual armor — the loinbelt of truth, the breastplate of righteousness, the shoes of peace, the shield of faith, the helmet of salvation, the sword of the Spirit, and the lance of prayer and supplication — are still vital, effective, and powerful weapons for the Body of Christ today.

Second Corinthians 10:4 talks about these spiritual weapons: "(For the weapons of our warfare are not carnal, but mighty through God to the pulling down of strong holds)." With these "weapons of our warfare" in hand, we are more than able to defeat any foe or demonic stronghold that would challenge our faith!

The "strongholds" these early believers faced were very real. They really knew what strongholds were all about! Christians in the Early Church lived in an environment of paganism, demonism, and idol worship to a measure we cannot fathom. They were forced to live with *religious, social,* and even *political* opposition.

The opposition of the pagan Roman society was so furious that Christians were regularly attacked and physically assaulted by witches, astrologers, and mediums. In fact, it was in this type of circumstance that Timothy, Paul's disciple and the pastor of the Ephesian church, was brutally murdered.

Intense hatred for Christians grew rapidly under the reign of Nero. Believers were burned to death at the Circus Maximus in Rome; they were eaten alive by wild beasts in the Coliseum; and they were publicly mutilated to death by gladiators in the amphitheaters. In fact, the gruesome, terrible, and grotesque deaths of Christians provided the Romans with the most popular form of entertainment of that time.

The violent deaths of believers became so popular with the Romans that the seating capacity of the Coliseum was expanded. This expansion was necessary in order to accommodate the massive crowds that would assemble for an entire afternoon of Christian martyrdom. Wild beasts would be released into a series of tunnel-like passages. Then Christians were placed into these same passages to be hunted down by ferocious wild animals. They were chased by these hungry beasts until caught; then they were eaten alive before tens of thousands of cheering people.

At first such murderous events only took place once a year — usually during the month of January as a dedication to the gods. However, during the demented rule of Nero, the number of such afternoons of entertainment at the Coliseum increased greatly.

Nero used nearly every excuse he could come up with to see additional Christians die in the Coliseum — whether it was his birthday, the anniversary of his becoming emperor, the anniversary of his predecessors' birthdays, his mother's birthday, a special religious day, or simply a normal Roman holiday.

Any of these was enough reason for Nero to fill the Coliseum to the brim with spectators who would sit on the edge of their seats to watch Christians die in the Coliseum.

Christians were considered of so little worth in the Roman world that when the construction of the Appian Way (a road leading from Rome to southern Italy) required road workers to labor into the night, the dead bodies of martyred Christians were strung on poles along the road and set on fire to serve as huge "lanterns" by which the road workers could continue working and building!

Demonic activity in Rome was rampant! All Roman emperors from this period consulted astrologers and occult priests for important decisions. These high-ranking mediums were considered to be so vital to the fulfillment of governmental affairs that they actually held official positions in the administration and were held in the highest esteem by the reigning emperor.

In addition to these high-ranking occult spiritualists who held especially prominent positions in the government, hundreds of other lower-class occult priests were on the payroll of Rome and served as priests for the official religion of Rome. There is no doubt that these official governmental witches, astrologers, soothsayers, and mediums must have influenced Nero's sentiments about God-fearing believers.

There were also other brands of religion besides the official religion of Rome. The city of Pergamos, the most famous of all Asian cities and the official seat of the Proconsul of Rome, was a city filled with idolatry and paganism.

High upon a mountaintop above the city of Pergamos sat a great altar to the goddess Athena. Directly in front of this temple to Athena was yet another idolatrous statue. A huge, polished marble altar built in the shape of a giant throne, it protruded out on a ledge that was visible to the entire city below and glistened in the sunlight every afternoon. This was the altar of Zeus.

From every section of Pergamos, citizens could look upward and see the smoke of burning incense billowing out into the sky from this demonic altar. This is the reason Jesus told the Pergamene believers, "I know thy works, and where thou dwellest, *even where Satan's seat is...*" (Revelation 2:13).

But wait — there is still more! In addition to this idolatrous worship of Athena and Zeus, the city of Pergamos was also the citadel of the cult of Asklepios, a demon spirit that took the outward form of a large serpent.

This particular cult boasted that Asklepios, the serpent spirit, had the power to heal the sick. The supernatural manifestations of this serpent spirit eventually became so well known that people traveled from all over the world in order to consult with the priests of Asklepios and be healed. Massive altars to Asklepios were erected all over the city. Literally hundreds of mediums were employed as priests in this dark, demonic cult.

As for the morality of Rome — *there was none*! Even non-Christian historians and scholars agree that Nero carried on an active homosexual relationship with many of the men who were close to the imperial throne. Bisexuality was completely acceptable by the standards of the day. Nero was himself a married man when he was cavorting with men.

Like the entertainment industry today, the theater was blatantly sensuous and sexual, full of vulgarities and lewdness. It was even common for sexual scenes to be fully acted out on stage in front of a carnal Roman audience. Female believers who fell into the hands of Nero's government and refused to renounce their faith in Jesus Christ were often forced to work in Rome's perverted burlesque as a form of mental and spiritual persecution.

Satan tried to destroy the Church of Jesus Christ at its inception — and it is certain that he will try to attack and victimize the Church as we approach the coming of the Lord. The devil knows that if he is going to do damage to the plan of God, this is his last opportunity and he must do his damage quickly.

> Satan tried to destroy the Church of Jesus Christ at its inception — and it is certain that he will try to attack and victimize the Church as we approach the coming of the Lord.

It is emphatically clear that the Early Church, just like the modern Church today, had to contend with many demonic attacks. But just as the Early Church arose in the power of the Spirit to meet the challenge, we will also conquer the world around us as we go forth, *equipped with the whole armor of God*, to live victoriously for Jesus Christ in these last days. As the apostle John told us, "For whatsoever is born of God overcometh the world: and this is the victory that overcometh the world, *even our faith*" (1 John 5:4).

The spiritual condition of the world cannot possibly be any worse today than it was back then. Have any of your friends been burned at the stake recently? Have you seen any of your Christian friends eaten alive by wild, hungry beasts? Have you been imprisoned for your faith?

Although spiritual opposition is as real today as it was during the days of the Early Church, it definitely isn't worse. This is the same lost world it has always been; this world system is still ruled by the same "prince of the power of the air" that has always sought to dominate it; and our battles are the same battles the Church has been fighting since its infancy. Satan has always sought to destroy the Church through his army of invisible, wicked, lawless spirits. This is not a new phenomenon at all!

Because the devil did this in the past, it should be no great surprise if he tries to do it again in these last days. But remember, his early attack upon the Church failed miserably. The harder the devil hit the Early Church, the faster the Church of Jesus Christ grew and multiplied. If the devil does send forth a new army of innumerable wicked spirits against the Church in these last days, as some have suggested, the Church will once again grow, thrive, multiply, and *overcome*!

WHAT ABOUT WITCHES?

The idea of witches and Satanists corporately uniting to cast curses on the people of God is not a new idea either. In First

Kings 18:17-40, the Bible tells us that 400 prophets of Baal corporately assembled to release their demonically energized power against the prophet Elijah.

Although Elijah stood physically alone on Mount Carmel that day, he single-handedly confronted the prophets of Baal with the power of God and subsequently witnessed their total destruction. These Old Testament Baal worshipers were the equivalent of today's witches and Satanists. Yet these Old Testament devil worshipers, who genuinely did possess strong satanic powers, did not prevail over the power of God.

In light of this, we can joyfully declare that the outcome would be the same even if modern-day witches and Satanists try to repeat this same scenario again. Regardless of how many of them show up to cast curses upon a specific local church, a specific ministry, or the Body of Christ at large, they will fail miserably, just as the prophets of Baal in the Old Testament did.

Even with all the planning and scheming of evil men — even with their incontestable diabolical assistance from Satan — no evil force has ever prevailed over the power of God or the people of God, *and none ever will*! Every world leader who has attempted to destroy the Church of Jesus Christ has himself been destroyed. Every dark period in the past 2,000 years of history has eventually succumbed and given way to the overwhelming, conquering light of Jesus Christ and His Church.

Satan has raged loudly like a ferocious beast on many occasions, but he has never devoured the Church — and according to the Lord Jesus Christ, he never will. In Matthew 16:18, Jesus said in reference to the Church, "...and the gates of hell shall *not* prevail against it."

> No evil force has ever prevailed over the power of God or the people of God, and none ever will!

In regard to the casting of curses upon believers, Proverbs 26:2 declares, "As the bird by wandering, as the swallow by flying, so the curse causeless shall not come." What does this verse mean? Just as a bird might fly around without finding a place to build a nest, so a curse may flutter all around a believer but will not find a resting place in that person's life. And just as a swallow migrates to another place when the season changes, so will the curse eventually return to those who sent it.

Witches and Satanists can cast curses, use potions, and recite incantations and magic spells until they are blue in the face. But no matter how hard they try, their power will *never* prevail over the people or the power of God!

BIBLICAL SPIRITUAL WARFARE

The Old Testament is replete with illustrations of spiritual warfare, such as the battle of Jericho, Jehoshaphat and his singers, and David and Goliath. Nevertheless, the words "war" or "warfare" only occur *five times* in the entire New Testament. That is pretty remarkable when you consider how much talk there is today about spiritual warfare.

These Old Testament true-life stories that tell us how God's army, Israel, defeated both natural and spiritual adversaries were written down for our instruction and admonition. This is Paul's message in First Corinthians 10:11: "Now all these things happened unto them for ensamples: and they are written for our admonition, upon whom the ends of the world are come."

Certainly it is true that by studying the battles of Old Testament Israel, we can ascertain much-needed revelation about conquering the invisible foes that attack and try to destroy the Church of Jesus Christ. However, since the terms "war" and "warfare" are used so often today in the Body of Christ, it is imperative for us to build a doctrinal understanding of how these words were used in the New Testament.

It is significant to note that of the five times the words "war" and "warfare" (taken from the Greek word *stratos*) are used in the New Testament, they are *never once* used in connection with the devil. For instance, both words are used in Second Corinthians 10:3-5 to denote *mental bondages* that must be "pulled down."

It is true that these bondages and strongholds in the mind may have first attached themselves to us in the past when we were still under Satan's control. However, we must keep these verses in their proper context. *In context, these verses are referring to a person making an immovable decision to take charge of his mind and take the thoughts of his mind captive!*

The word "war" is used in First Timothy 1:18 in connection with a prophetic utterance that was spoken over Timothy. Paul commanded Timothy to remember the prophecies that had been spoken over him so that by those prophecies, he might "war a good warfare."

By using the words "war" and "warfare" in this verse, Paul intended to admonish Timothy to stay in the fight of faith and to be faithful to the call of God on his life. *Once again, the words "war" and "warfare" in this verse have nothing to do with the devil!*

In Second Timothy 2:4, Paul uses the word "warreth" once again, saying, "No man that warreth entangleth himself with the affairs of this life; that he may please him who hath chosen him to be a soldier."

The word "warreth" in this verse has nothing to do with the devil either! Rather, Paul is exhorting Timothy to *keep his life clear of clutter*; *to be single-minded*; and to *stay committed to the call of God on his life, regardless of the cost.*

Then in James 4:1, the word "war" is used again — this time to describe the flesh, not the devil. According to James, "spiritual warfare" is primarily concerned with fighting fleshly *lusts* that come to destroy spiritual growth and development.

Peter uses the word "war" in the same way to vividly describe "...fleshly lusts, which war against the soul" (1 Peter 2:11). Once again the word "war" is used not to describe the activity of the devil, but rather to describe *the flesh's attempt to conquer and subdue the mind.*

In light of this, it is abundantly clear that the New Testament usage of the words "war" and "warfare" primarily has to do with conquering the flesh and taking charge of our minds. Yes, the devil may attack the mind, and he may attempt to energize the flesh to work against us. However, if we will keep our minds and our flesh under the control of the Holy Spirit, most of the spiritual warfare we encounter in life will have already been settled!

HOW REAL WARFARE BEGINS

Most believers who have fallen in recent times would *not* have fallen if they had not given the devil some kind of foothold in their minds. These people would be the very first to tell you that they left a door open for demonic attack somewhere along the way by not dealing with an unseen, private area of their lives.

Demon spirits have absolutely no power to bring about destruction unless they can find an open door into a person's mind. But if they can locate such an entrance into the mind, from this lofty position they can then begin to introduce evil influences and launch their attacks upon the individual.

The Holy Spirit is faithful to convict us of any areas in our lives that leave us vulnerable to attack. He will urge us to repent and change before the devil builds strongholds in our thinking. However, it is still up to us to see that these opened doors are slammed shut and forever closed.

But what happens if we ignore the Holy Spirit's pleading? What if we allow sin, willfully permitted temptation, or wrong attitudes to persist in our lives, unconfessed and unchanged? In that case, we are leaving gaping holes through which the enemy will seek to undo us. The truth is, most spiritual destruction is avoidable, but only if we will reverently listen to the pleading of the Holy Spirit and obey His warnings to us.

Again, demon spirits cannot destroy without an open door into a person's soul — and such an entrance can only be given by way of permission.

Evil forces may try to buffet and hinder us, as they tried to buffet and hinder the apostle Paul (2 Corinthians 12:7; 1 Thessalonians 2:18), but they cannot destroy you or me unless there is something already wrong in us to which they can latch hold and twist to our destruction.

> Demon spirits cannot destroy without an open door into a person's soul — and such an entrance can only be given by way of permission.

The tendency of flesh has always been to blame personal failure on someone else or on some external circumstance that is beyond our control. In fact, *shifting blame is as old as the Garden of Eden.* Remember, it was Adam (the natural father of us all) who shifted the blame for his own moral failure to Eve. Rather than acknowledge that he had committed sin when he ate freely of the forbidden fruit of the Garden, Adam told God, "...The woman whom thou gavest to be with me, she gave me of the tree, and I did eat" (Genesis 3:12).

Likewise, a Christian is shifting blame that rightfully belongs to him when he says, "The devil made me do it" or "I failed because witches are praying against me." Regardless of how many demon spirits have been assigned to destroy a believer, that person must cooperate with the enemy's

> Regardless of how many demon spirits have been assigned to destroy a believer, that person must cooperate with the enemy's suggestions before temptation can overtake him and ruin his witness.

suggestions before temptation can overtake him and ruin his witness.

This means that ultimately, *you are responsible* for your own failure or success in obeying God in this life. You cannot shift the blame to anyone else. You can't even shift the blame for your failure to demonic attack. In order for that demonic attack to work effectively, you had to cooperate in some way — either through ignorance, through deliberate cooperation, or through negligence by refusing to deal with some unseen, private area of your life. For instance:

- You can scream that the devil is after your money until you are blue in the face. But if you failed to balance your checkbook or were irresponsible in paying your bills, you opened the door to that financial attack.

- You can declare that the enemy is attempting to afflict you with sickness. But if you abuse your body by eating wrong, overworking, and pushing your body beyond its capabilities, you have opened the door for your body to be attacked.

- You can cry out that your marriage is under attack. But if you often speak harshly to your spouse, never spend any time with him or her, and have not made your marriage a priority in your life, you have thrown open the door for the enemy to come in and destroy your marriage.

- And the list goes on and on.

Certainly there are genuine surprise attacks from the demonic realm that catch believers off guard. Sometimes the devil really does attack their finances — especially if they are using their finances for the Kingdom of God. It is absolutely true that at times the enemy comes to steal, kill, and destroy a person's health. And it is similarly true that the enemy may try to orchestrate failure in a marriage.

In my own ministry, the enemy has struck viciously to destroy from time to time. I know the reality of a genuine demonic attack. These attacks have usually come at critical points in our ministry when we were about to do something important in the Kingdom of God. Each was a clear attempt to thwart the plan of God.

Many years ago, when my book *Living in the Combat Zone* was about to be published, my own ministry was thrust into a financial combat zone. For some strange reason we could not explain, no offerings came into the ministry and our partners stopped writing. In a matter of days, all our income dried up.

The enemy knew that God was going to use that book in a great way. Therefore, he wanted to stop it before it ever got into the hands of our readers. Obviously, the devil's attack failed and the power of the Cross prevailed!

Dealing With the Wind and the Waves in Your Life

Anytime you are on the frontlines of battle and are doing something significant for the Kingdom of God, the enemy's attacks against your life will escalate. Even Jesus came under such an attack when He was preparing to cast a legion of demons out of the demoniac of Gadara (Mark 4:35-41).

> Anytime you are on the frontlines of battle and are doing something significant for the Kingdom of God, the enemy's attacks against your life will escalate.

Violent and destructive winds seemed to come from out of nowhere to capsize Jesus' boat and drown Him and His disciples in the middle of the lake. Verse 37 says, "And there arose a great storm of wind, and the waves beat into the ship, so that it was now full."

Notice that it says, "And *there arose.* ..." The phrase "there arose" is taken from the Greek word *ginomai*. The word *ginomai* is used more than 200 times in the New Testament; hence, its primary meaning is well documented. The word *ginomai* normally describes *something that happens unexpectedly* or *something that catches one off guard*.

For instance, the word *ginomai* is used in Acts 10:9,10 to describe how Peter received his vision revealing that salvation had become available for the Gentiles.

On the morrow, as they went on their journey, and drew nigh unto the city, Peter went up upon the

housetop to pray about the sixth hour: and he became very hungry, and would have eaten: but while they made ready, he FELL INTO a trance.

Especially notice the words "fell into." This phrase is derived from the Greek word *ginomai*. Because Luke uses the word *ginomai*, we know that Peter didn't expect this visitation to occur that afternoon. He was waiting on dinner when suddenly — *unexpectedly* — he "slipped into" a trance. This was an encounter with God that caught him off guard.

When John tells us how he received the book of Revelation in Revelation 1:10, he also uses the word *ginomai*: "*I was* in the Spirit on the Lord's day...." The phrase "I was" is also taken from the word *ginomai*. Therefore, we know from the usage of this word that John was not expecting to have a visitation that day. The vision came unexpectedly, taking him completely off guard as he looked up and found himself standing in the realm of the Spirit.

Now this same word, which contains an element of surprise, is used in Mark 4:37 to plainly tell us that Jesus and His disciples didn't expect bad weather that night. These winds overtook them *unexpectedly*.

Many of Jesus' disciples were fishermen before they were called into the ministry, so they knew the weather of the sea. If a natural storm had been brewing that night, these men would never have taken their little boat out into the middle of that sea. Therefore, you can be sure that when they began their journey that night, it was a perfect night for sailing.

But suddenly and unexpectedly, "there arose" a great storm of wind. Notice that Mark tells us it was "a *great* storm of wind." The word "great" is taken from the word *mega*, which denotes *something of magnificent proportions*. It is where we get the idea of "megabills," "megawork," "megatired," and "megaphone." By using this word, we know that this was a *megastorm*!

And notice what kind of storm it was. Mark doesn't say that it was a thunderstorm or a rainstorm; he tells us that it was "a great storm *of wind*."

The word "wind" is taken from the word *lalaipsi*, and it describes *a turbulence* or *a terribly violent wind*. Therefore, the storm that came against Jesus that night was an unseen storm. A person couldn't see this storm, but he could feel the effects of it.

This was an attempt of the enemy to destroy Jesus and His crew before they reached the other side. On the other side, in the country of the Gadarenes, Satan had a prized possession: the demoniac of Gadara. The devil knew that if Jesus' ship reached the other side, he would lose his prized possession and Jesus would perform one of the greatest miracles of His ministry.

So when Jesus was on the edge of a breakthrough, this unexpected attack of *violent and destructive turbulence* came down upon Him and His disciples to kill and destroy. The devil didn't want Jesus to arrive at the country of the Gadarenes. *This was a preemptive strike of the devil to undo the work of God.*

This was also a great opportunity for the disciples to learn that Jesus Christ is Lord of the wind and the waves! After He exercised authority over this unseen turbulence and spoke to the waves of the sea, the Word says that "...the wind ceased, and there was a great calm" (Mark 4:39).

The fact that this attack came just as Jesus was on the brink of a major miracle is not uncommon. In fact, this is normally the time when genuine demonic attacks occur. If such attacks came against Jesus, we can be sure that the enemy will attempt to do this to us as well. Therefore, we must mentally and spiritually prepare ourselves to deal with demonic attacks. We are to "put on the whole armor of God" and take authority over the wind and the waves that come against our lives, our families, our businesses, or our bodies — just as Jesus took authority over the wind and the waves that came against Him.

So what do you do if you come under a demonic attack? First, make sure you know that you have been diligent to cover all your bases by obeying the Holy Spirit's promptings in the various areas of your life. Make sure also that, to the best of your knowledge, you have left no doors open for an attack. Then just like the Lord Jesus Christ, you must rise up to take authority over the wind and the waves. This is your golden opportunity to see a demonstration of God's power in your life!

Let me also stress another important point: When the wind and the waves ceased that night, the Word says that "...there was a *great* calm" (v. 39). Verse 37 previously told us that this storm had been a *great* storm. So when everything was said and done, Jesus had matched a *great storm* with a *great calm*!

If the enemy has created a great financial problem in your life, Jesus Christ wants to match it with a great financial blessing. If the adversary has created a great sickness in your body, Jesus Christ wants to match it with a great healing. If the devil has created a horrible marital mess in your life, the Lord Jesus Christ wants to match that marital crisis with a great marital blessing. *Whatever the devil does, Jesus Christ wants to match that attack with an even greater blessing in your life!*

> Most battles are fought because we were unfaithful to heed the Holy Spirit's warnings to deal with some area of our lives before it got out of control.

However, we must be honest with ourselves when it comes to these attacks. The majority of battles that we fight in life do not fall into this category of "surprise attacks." *Most battles are fought because we were unfaithful to heed the Holy Spirit's warnings to deal with some area of our lives before it got out of control.*

SPIRITUAL WARFARE: A MENTAL CONDITION

Spiritual warfare is not a momentary gust of emotion to temporarily frighten away the devil. Quite the opposite! Real spiritual warfare is a specific condition of the mind that involves a lifelong commitment. *It is not so much an action as it is a determined and committed attitude of the mind.*

The apostle Paul understood this truth about spiritual warfare. After being outwardly buffeted by demonic forces who had come against his ministry, Paul prayed three times and asked the Lord to remove the messenger of Satan that had been sent to "buffet" him (2 Corinthians 12:7) and to keep him from moving into higher realms of revelation.

Yet the buffeting was never removed. In response to Paul's request that God would deliver him from this buffeting, the Lord answered, "...My grace is sufficient for thee..." (2 Corinthians 12:9).

Why did God answer Paul in this way? Because Paul had made a request that was *unrealistic.* As long as Paul was being effective for God, as long as he was doing damage to the realm of darkness, he would be opposed by demonic forces. Rather than offer Paul false promises that he could achieve a life free from opposition, the Lord promised instead to give him the grace and power he needed to conquer each of these attacks as they came.

Paul's outward circumstances were a constant challenge. Invisible spiritual opposition stirred up horrible community hatred toward him everywhere he went. The government of the day stood in his way and sought to block the Gospel message. Yet despite all the opposition he endured, Paul was never destroyed by any of these outward attacks. As he himself said in Second Corinthians 4:8 and 9, "We are troubled on every side, yet not distressed; we are perplexed, but not in despair; persecuted, but not forsaken; cast down, but not destroyed."

From Paul's own personal testimony in Second Corinthians 11:24-28, we know that his outward opposition was extremely intense. For instance, in verse 24, he tells us, "Of the Jews five times received I forty stripes save one."

As if this was not enough for Paul to endure, he continues in verse 25: "Thrice was I beaten with rods, once was I stoned, thrice I suffered shipwreck, a night and a day I have been in the deep."

Without going into great detail about all the methods of persecution that Paul underwent, we can quickly summarize what the Word tells us. We know that his feet were beaten with rods on three different occasions; his head was crushed at least once; he endured three separate shipwrecks; and at some point in his ministry, he spent a night and a day in the deep — an entire 24 hours treading water in order to stay alive! (For more details on the methods of persecution and the afflictions that Paul endured, *see* pp. 60-95 in my book, *If You Were God, Would You Choose You?*).

After mentioning these extremely harsh afflictions, Paul continues to speak more generally about other lesser afflictions he has endured.

> **In journeyings often, in perils of waters, in perils of robbers, in perils by mine own countrymen, in perils by the heathen, in perils in the city, in perils in the wilderness, in perils in the sea, in perils among false brethren; in weariness and painfulness, in watchings often, in hunger and thirst, in fastings often, in cold and nakedness.**
>
> **2 Corinthians 11:26,27**

Yet with all these challenges and forms of opposition — and with all his mental fatigue and physical exhaustion — Paul never fell into any kind of immorality or any type of moral failure. He never rationalized failure by saying:

- "I failed because demons were assigned to destroy me."

- "I failed because witches were meeting in covens and casting curses on me."

- "The devil trapped me and made me do this!"

It is true that the majority of demonic attacks and tragedies occur because of some *omission* on the part of a believer. For instance, many tragedies occur in Christians' lives because of doors left open to the enemy through anger, bitterness, wrath, or slothfulness. Nevertheless, it is also true that the devil can strike a believer who is walking in faith and in the Spirit. These "sneak attacks" are real.

As I stated before, as long as a believer seeks to do God's will and to obey His Word, the devil will try to thwart the plan that God desires to accomplish through that believer. However, surprise attacks from the demonic realm will not find success if the believer's shield of faith is in place to protect him and to cause those attacks to ricochet back to where they originated. *Demon spirits cannot destroy a person unless there is already an area of sin in his life they can grab hold of and twist to that person's destruction.*

There were no such vulnerable areas in Paul's life — *nothing* that the devil could use to destroy him. *Therefore, Paul's personal consecration to the Lord was his greatest defense against the enemy.*

Although Paul was outwardly buffeted, he was never attacked to the point of personal failure. He lived the crucified

> Paul's personal consecration to the Lord was his greatest defense against the enemy.

life and was thus dead to sin. *Nothing in him cooperated with the devil's devices and temptations.* Thus, Paul's personal holiness paralyzed the devil's ability to make him fail morally.

We can thus conclude from a study of Paul's life that *it is very difficult, if not entirely impossible, for the devil to completely destroy a person who lives a sanctified and consecrated life.* Most attacks would be totally avoided if sin and wrong attitudes were not permitted to have a place in the believer's life.

A WARNING ABOUT SPIRITUAL WARFARE

Because of the unscriptural approach to spiritual warfare that some have taken in times past, many seasoned and respected Spirit-filled Christian leaders have felt compelled to urge the Body of Christ to come back into a proper balance on this issue of spiritual warfare. These are men and women of God who understand that *there is a real spiritual adversary that must be opposed with genuine spiritual weapons.*

Spiritual warfare is most definitely a reality we must all learn to face at some point in our lives. However, we must also realize that the devil, who is himself a very cunning strategist, would love to sidetrack us and prevent us from doing any real damage to him. One way he tries to do this is by getting us off track with silly spiritual tactics — making weird noises, violently screaming at the devil, or engaging in other extremely unfounded, unscriptural, so-called "spiritual warfare" nonsense.

People tend to look for cure-all solutions that do not make them look at their own flaws or deal with their flesh. This is often why they flock to teachings and methods that offer relatively simple solutions to difficult, lifelong problems. Holding fast to God's Word and applying its principles to their lives seems to take too long and be more difficult to do. After all, the Word of God requires a person to live a crucified life. It demands that he repent of a wrong thought life. It insists that he seek to conform to the image of Jesus Christ.

> The thought of an instant cure is very alluring to the uncommitted and spiritually immature who are looking for a "quick fix" to change their deeply rooted, habitual, and often self-imposed problems.

Therefore, the thought of an instant cure is very alluring to the uncommitted and spiritually imma-ture who are looking for a "quick fix" to change their deeply rooted, habitual, and often self-imposed problems.

Again, no one — including this author — would doubt the reality of *genuine spiritual warfare*. We have all come face to face with the enemy at some point in our lives, and we can be certain that we will face him again at some point in the future. At the time of this printing, I live in a part of the world that is often hostile to the work of the Gospel. I know from personal experience that spiritual warfare is a very real force that fre-quently assails God's people!

The fact is that as long as we seek to live in God's will and obey His Word for our lives — as long as we seek to drive back the forces of darkness and shine the light of the Gospel where it has not been shined before — the devil will do his best to oppose and thwart the plan that God wishes to accomplish through us. It is for this cause that God has given us a complete set of spiritual armor. (In Chapters Ten through Sixteen, we will study what the Bible says about this spiritual armor, verse by verse and word by word.)

Once this powerful set of invisible armor is in position in our lives, we are ready for the fight. With this weaponry at our disposal, we are *DRESSED TO KILL*!

QUESTIONS FOR PERSONAL GROWTH OR GROUP DISCUSSION

1. In what ways can an emphasis on spiritual warfare be both *good* and *bad* for the Church? What can you do to avoid the pitfalls that some believers have experienced as you study the subject of spiritual warfare?

2. What is the enemy's primary target when he plans his attack against someone? How does that knowledge help you in dealing with the devil's attacks in your own life?

3. Why is crucifying the flesh such a critical part of true spiritual warfare? What happens if you *don't* take this vital step when attempting to overcome the enemy's strategies against your life?

4. What is the foundational starting point in developing a correct view of spiritual warfare?

5. What can we learn from studying the early believers' response to intense persecution and demonic attacks? How can we apply these lessons to our daily walk with God?

NOTES:

CHAPTER TWO

FLESHLY WEAPONS VS. SPIRITUAL WEAPONS

*L*et me say right from the start that some people will love this chapter and others will despise it. Yet because of the various kinds of teachings on spiritual warfare that are circulated periodically throughout the Christian community, I am compelled by the Holy Spirit to include this chapter in this book.

Instead of magnifying the victorious work of Jesus Christ over Satan and our deliverance from Satan's power, much of what is taught today implies that the work of the Cross is unfinished — that Jesus' blood saved us but didn't really free us completely from Satan's power. Although this may not be the intent of some of those who teach on spiritual warfare, it is often the message that is perceived.

> Much of what is taught today implies that the work of the Cross is unfinished — that Jesus' blood saved us but didn't really free us completely from Satan's power.

The fruit of this teaching is a new form of spiritualized legalism. In other words, what Jesus Christ did was not enough by itself; therefore, you must now do additional "things" in order to gain additional freedom from the devil's control. In reality, this is the equivalent of trading one form of bondage for another — and the second bondage is much more dangerous. It comes in the guise of spirituality and, at least at first, is very difficult to discern.

In regard to such manmade fleshly weapons and fleshly techniques, Paul has this to say: "For though we walk in the flesh, we do not war after the flesh: (For the weapons of our warfare are not carnal, but mighty through God to the pulling down of strong holds;)" (2 Corinthians 10:3,4).

Notice how Paul begins: "For though we walk in the flesh...." The word "walk" is taken from the word *peripateo* and is a compound of the words *peri* and *pateo*. The word *peri* means *around*, and the word *pateo* means *to walk*. When the two words are compounded together (*peripateo*), the new word simply means *to walk around* or *to habitually live and carry on in one general vicinity*.

By using the word *peripateo*, Paul is sending a very strong message about his humanity. The word carries this idea: *"Nearly everything I do, I do in this realm of flesh: I eat in the flesh; I recreate in the flesh; I sleep in the flesh; I think in the flesh; I study in the flesh. My life primarily consists of this earthly realm."*

In fact, the Greek tense used here is *the locative sphere of influence*. This is extremely important! Quite literally, this meant that Paul knew he was "locked into" his fleshly body and could not get out of it, nor could he trade it for another! He was "body-bound." This state of being "body-bound" would never change until death, when his carnal, natural body would be gloriously transformed into a spiritual body.

The very fact that Paul said, "...We do not war after [or according to] the flesh" tells us that he was aware of the weakness and futility of his own natural man. Paul knew there was no hope of accomplishing anything good through his carnal man; therefore, he turned toward the spirit realm where supernatural assistance was available.

BLOODTHIRSTY, DARING, COMMITTED MEN OF WAR

Paul continues by telling us that there is one thing he does not do with his carnal, fleshly, natural body: "...We do not *war* after the flesh." The word "war" is taken from the word *strateomenos*, and it refers to the *militant attitude of a trained soldier*. It was particularly used to denote the committed attitude of a heavily dressed, trained-to-kill Roman soldier.

There is no doubt that Roman soldiers were the finest military machines of their day and among the most skilled soldiers in the history of the world. These men were trained killers. In fact, they were so thoroughly trained in the acts of murder and mutilation that such acts of war had become instinct to them. Professionals in the weapons of war, Roman soldiers knew how to use those weapons against adversaries very effectively. You might say that these particular soldiers had *a taste for blood*.

Furthermore, especially good soldiers requested to be placed on the frontlines of battle. Their insatiable desire to draw the blood of their adversaries was so ingrained into their disposition that they were not content to wage war from behind the lines, where only minimal action was taking place. These soldiers would request to be placed out on the frontlines of battle so they could see the enemy first and have *the first opportunity to strike*.

In addition, extremely brave soldiers frequently volunteered to go on dangerous missions that others didn't want to undertake. The notions of penetrating an enemy's camp and invading dangerous foreign soil were thrilling prospects to these special types of soldiers. *They were bloodthirsty, daring, and committed men of war.*

All these graphic images are conveyed in the word "war" that Paul now uses in Second Corinthians 10:3. Therefore, when Paul says, "...We do not war after the flesh," he is making several powerful statements to the Church.

First, Paul tells us that, spiritually speaking, his own mental attitude is much like that of a Roman soldier: He is so committed to experiencing victory that he wants to draw the enemy's blood himself. Furthermore, he wants to be placed out on the frontlines of battle so he will have the opportunity to strike first. And he is so spiritually brave that he is willing to go where no other soldier will go!

This was Paul's mental attitude, and it was one of the reasons he declared that he wanted "to preach the gospel in the regions beyond..." (2 Corinthians 10:16). Paul's desire was to go and minister in places where no other men would go! This is the reason he was willing to go into cities like Ephesus and Corinth, which were citadels of sensuality and demonic activity. Paul was a frontline soldier of the Lord!

But Paul tells us something else that is also very important in this verse. In addition to possessing this committed and determined mental attitude and resolve, he says, "...We do not war *after the flesh.*"

Remember, Paul was an educated and impressive man, naturally speaking. Yet when it came to dealing the enemy a blow, he knew that his intelligence and his education did not count. *Paul's flesh, regardless of how impressive it looked or how loud it roared, would be no match for a spiritual foe.* Fleshly weapons simply are not suited to fight spiritual adversaries, and they never will be!

> **Fleshly weapons simply are not suited to fight spiritual adversaries, and they never will be!**

SPIRITUAL WEAPONS AND SPIRITUAL STRATEGIES

Paul continues in verse 4: "(For the weapons of our warfare are not carnal, but mighty through God to the pulling down of strong holds;)." Pay special heed to the words "weapons," "warfare," and "carnal" in this all-important verse about spiritual warfare.

In the first place, Paul tells us that we *do* have weapons at our disposal — but they are *spiritual* weapons. These weapons, both offensive and defensive, can be found in Ephesians 6:13-18. (We will thoroughly cover these weapons in Chapters Ten through Sixteen.)

Second, notice that Paul goes on to say, "For the weapons of our *warfare*...." The word "warfare" provides another major key to defeating the attacks of the enemy. It is taken from the word *stratos*, and it is where we get the word "strategy." By choosing to use this word, the Holy Spirit has told us some very important things about spiritual warfare.

In the first place, the word *stratos* tells us that in order for spiritual weapons to work effectively, they must be accompanied with a divine *strategy* on how to use them. If we have weapons but no battle plan, our defeat will be assured.

> In order for spiritual weapons to work effectively, they must be accompanied with a divine strategy on how to use them.

This, in fact, is the primary reason most believers don't experience victory in their personal lives. It isn't that they lack the proper weaponry — *God has given them all that they need!* However, they *don't* have a strategy that tells them *how* to attack. Hence, their weapons are to no avail.

Weapons without a strategy always spells failure. Imagine an army that is fully equipped with weapons of warfare but has no strategy for using those weapons against the enemy! Even with all those weapons and artillery at their disposal, this kind of an army will utterly fail.

Likewise, many believers boast of having "the whole armor of God" but have no idea how that spiritual armor should be used practically and experientially in their lives. Until God gives these believers clear direction and a battle plan is conceived in their hearts, these weapons will do little to drive back the forces of hell that come against them.

Just as God graciously dressed you in spiritual armor when you were born again, He now wants to graciously give you a *strategy* on how to pull down the devil's lies and deceptions that have dominated your mind so they can no longer control you.

In order for you to receive this divine strategy, you must hear from the Spirit of God. This mandates that you spend time praying in the Spirit, reading the Word, and seeking the mind of God. By yourself, you will never conceive a plan that will deliver you.

> When strongholds become deeply rooted in the mind, only the Holy Spirit can give you a strategy on how to pull them down.

When strongholds become deeply rooted in the mind, only the Holy Spirit can give you a strategy on how to pull them down. He will show you how to use your God-given weapons, and He will instruct you on *when* and *what* to attack!

THE FUTILITY OF THE FLESH

We now come to the next point in this verse. Paul continues, "For the weapons of our warfare *are not carnal*...."

The word "carnal" is taken from the word *sarkos*, which is the Greek word for "flesh." By electing to use this word, Paul tells us that real spiritual weapons do not come from the flesh realm. In fact, Paul takes a hard stand on this subject. *He emphatically declares that spiritual weapons have absolutely nothing to do with the flesh or the activity of the flesh.*

> Spiritual weapons have absolutely nothing to do with the flesh or the activity of the flesh.

Although Paul lived, functioned, and walked in the flesh, just as we do today, he did not rely on the flesh or on fleshly techniques to defeat spiritual adversaries. In order for him to reinforce the victory that Jesus won through the Cross and the resurrection, Paul would be required to use *spiritual* weapons. *Flesh can fight flesh, but flesh is no match for the spiritual realm.*

Even though Paul was extremely educated:

- Neither his education nor his marvelously genius mind were a match for the devil.

- His notoriety as a well-known Christian leader did not scare or impress the devil.

- His manner of speech and his vocal style of preaching were not wonderful enough to rid him of the devil's assaults.

Regardless of how good the flesh looks or how loud the flesh roars, it was never intended to fight a spiritual foe.

This is the reason God has so graciously given us spiritual weapons, such as "the loinbelt of truth," "the breastplate of righteousness," "the shoes of peace," "the shield of faith," "the helmet of salvation," "the sword of the Spirit," and "the lance of intercession." Without these weapons, we stand naked and defenseless before the adversary!

> Regardless of how good the flesh looks or how loud the flesh roars, it was never intended to fight a spiritual foe.

WEAK AND SILLY WEAPONS OF FLESH

Nevertheless, far too many believers try to use outward, physical, fleshly techniques in their attempt to defeat the work of the adversary in their lives and to do so-called "spiritual warfare." Rather than rest in the redemptive work of Jesus Christ and use the weapons that are provided in Scripture (Ephesians 6:13-18), these believers move over into a mode of "spiritual warfare" that is totally foreign to any teaching of the New Testament, where they must do additional "things" in order to free themselves from the devil's control.

But outward, physical, fleshly techniques are not what struggling believers need! Such methods are not only ineffective — they will eventually become a new form of legalism in the lives of people who rely on them to do battle against the devil. Thus, in addition to fighting real strongholds that the devil has sown in their minds, these believers will also have to struggle with feelings of condemnation for not gaining victory through the so-called "spiritual warfare techniques" that were taught to them!

This legalism of doing so-called "spiritual things" in order to obtain freedom has painfully come to the forefront of many groups throughout the years. I feel this tragedy deeply in my heart, for I am called of God to minister to people. Therefore, when I see sincere people swallowed up in works of the flesh that, in reality, add nothing to their freedom, it grieves me deeply.

I can't help but sorrow for believers who constantly and habitually try to set themselves free from demon possession when Jesus Christ has already set them free. For instance, I feel so sorry for the group of Christians who started teaching several years ago that believers have to deliver themselves from demonic control by deliberately making themselves vomit, day after day, week after week — as though vomiting alone would somehow remove demonic powers! They saw this purging as proof that demon powers had exited people's bodies.

In the past few decades, it has also been unfortunate to see so many Christians physically abusing their bodies and hurting their throats with a teaching called "warring tongues" — a teaching that grew in popularity some time ago. People who held to this teaching believed that by screaming, screeching, and violently praying in throat-ripping, loud prayer, they could exert more power against the devil.

Some even teach that if you pray quietly, you might as well find something better to do with your time. In their distorted view, prayer exerts no spiritual power unless it is done loudly at an ear-deafening volume. Somehow they believe their authority is attached to the volume of their voice!

But when you are dealing with the devil, the issue is not the sound level or the volume of your voice. The devil is not afraid of noise. Remember, he has created all kinds of horrendous, loud, screaming music in these modern times. Noise obviously does not bother the devil.

A policeman doesn't yell and scream to stop a crime; he simply pulls out his gun and waves it in front of the offender. There is no need for the policeman to scream, yell, and holler. All the screaming in the world wouldn't stop the offender! On the other hand, that officer's gun carries *great* authority. With gun in hand, he can whisper to the offender, and the offender will gladly obey.

Likewise, it is the authority resident within your spirit that causes the devil to obey. If you know who you are in Jesus Christ and how to use that Christ-imparted authority against the devil, you can whisper ever so faintly to him and he will flee. *The issue is not the volume level of your voice; it is the authority contained in your spirit.*

> It is the authority resident within your spirit that causes the devil to obey.

The whole idea behind screaming violently in tongues is that the heavenlies are full of demonic powers and believers are physically under that dark, demonic cloud. Therefore, they must try to *pierce* the heavenlies with their loud, screaming noises in an attempt to break their way through that hellish barrier. Thus, sincere brothers and sisters are led to believe that they must scream violently at the devil for hours on end, day after day and week after week, in order to gain freedom for their personal lives.

Having heard of these meetings, I personally attended one years ago. As I listened to the message that night, I could hardly believe my ears. For an entire hour, the speaker instructed the people how to yell, scream, "go into weepings" (self-imposed crying), and "go into purgings" (self-imposed vomiting). My heart ached to learn what sincere believers were doing in the name of the Holy Spirit and to hear what they thought was genuine spiritual warfare.

I have no question as to the sincerity of these fellow believers, nor do I doubt their true desire to defeat the work of the devil in their personal lives and in the lives of others. Their zeal is admirable, but their actions are not scripturally based or "according to knowledge" (Romans 10:2).

Never once does the Bible teach that we are to yell and scream endlessly against the devil — and the Scriptures absolutely must be the foundation of all we believe, teach, and do.

WHAT DOES THE BIBLE SAY ABOUT THE PURPOSE OF TONGUES?

Because some have inferred in times past that praying in tongues is *the* major tool we are to use against the devil, it is important for us to know what the Bible says about praying in tongues and its God-given purpose. This is the only way we can know exactly what tongues are intended for in our lives.

In First Corinthians 14:2, the apostle Paul talks about praying in tongues. He says, "For he that speaketh in an unknown tongue speaketh not unto men, *but unto God.....*" Notice that when Paul writes about praying in tongues, he makes no mention at all about the devil. In fact, First Corinthians 14:2 says that the purpose of praying in tongues is not to speak to the devil, but on the contrary, *to speak mysteries unto God*!

Paul goes on to say, "He that speaketh in an unknown tongue *edifieth himself...*" (1 Corinthians 14:4). Thus, we see that the end result of praying in tongues is for personal, faith-building edification.

By praying in the Spirit, our faith is built up to help us stand against the devil's schemes when necessary. But praying in tongues was never meant to be something we use to "speak at the devil," as many in the Christian community have claimed from time to time.

There is no scripture for this claim. Therefore, this popular teaching has no basis in Scripture, and those who teach it are *wrong*.

If we do choose to pray loudly, let us clarify *why* we are doing it. It is *not* because we are "warring" with the devil. On the contrary, we are warring with *the flesh*, trying to break through the strong lusts and desires of the flesh so God can have His way and speak to our spirits, bringing us divine revelation.

I must admit that there have been times in my own life when I have prayed very loudly. However, I haven't done this to defeat the devil, but rather to rise above the cries of my own flesh as it tried fiercely to war against my soul.

Wrong teachings about this subject stem from a deliberate attempt of the adversary to enslave believers in spiritual nonsense and drag them into legalism — where they will never be able to do enough to satisfy their sense of guilt or find the freedom they desire. It is only a matter of time before they will have to do something else in order to procure more freedom — and then they'll have to do something else. There is no end to where legalism will take people.

One dear brother whom I knew personally became a victim of this kind of doctrinal error. He became involved in an off-base "spiritual warfare" group that required these kinds of fleshly works in order to combat the devil. He was attracted to these believers because of their great zeal — but it wasn't long before he had swapped the joy of his salvation for a life of spiritual bondage.

It didn't matter how much this man did — it was never enough. If he prayed for hours on end, *it wasn't enough.* If he screamed like the others did, even until he lost his voice, *he didn't scream long enough.* If he induced vomiting to rid himself of demon spirits as did others in his group, *he never seemed to rid himself of all the demons.* There was *always* more for him to do. Enough is never enough with legalism.

In the end, the man sank into deep despair and became a shattered and broken man, convinced that he could never do enough to gain complete freedom in Jesus Christ.

All of these are merely doctrines of men that are not based on Scripture. Every one of these teachings tries to add to the already completed, redemptive work of Jesus Christ as though His work were not enough. As Paul so correctly asked the Galatian believers: "Are ye so foolish? having begun in the Spirit, are ye now made perfect by the flesh?" (Galatians 3:3).

TOUCH NOT, TASTE NOT, HANDLE NOT

Legalism — adding one's own works to the already completed, perfect work of Christ — was trying to attach itself to the Church in the region of Galatia. Paul knew that legalism is a killer that eventually saps spiritual strength and joy out of people. So he commanded the Galatians, "Stand fast therefore in the liberty wherewith Christ hath made us free, and be not entangled again with the yoke of bondage" (Galatians 5:1).

The Galatians were being tempted to go back under the Old Testament law. After they had *freely* received Jesus Christ and the promise of the Holy Spirit, erroneous teaching was now coaxing them back into the Old Testament rules and regulations from which they had been delivered.

The Galatians' thinking was, *Yes, we received Jesus Christ freely. But now in order to maintain and keep that salvation we so freely received, we must do our part to "keep" our salvation.*

Therefore, we must place ourselves back under Old Testament Law to keep its rules and regulations.

For similar reasons, Paul wrote the Colossian church and told them:

> **Let no man therefore judge you in meat, or in drink, or in respect of an holyday, or of the new moon, or of the sabbath days....**
>
> **...If ye be dead with Christ from the rudiments of the world, why, as though living in the world, are ye subject to ordinances, (Touch not; taste not; handle not; which all are to perish with the using;) after the commandments and doctrines of men?**
>
> **Colossians 2:16,20-22**

Then Paul continued, "Which things have indeed a shew of wisdom in will worship, and humility, and neglecting of the body; not in any honour to the satisfying of the flesh" (Colossians 2:23).

These outward things do indeed have an outward show of self-abasement, humility, and hardness on the flesh. The religious nature of man loves that outward show! The religious person wants to believe that, by his own work and merit, he can somehow attain a perfection that makes himself acceptable to God.

> The religious person wants to believe that, by his own work and merit, he can somehow attain a perfection that makes himself acceptable to God.

This is precisely why Far Eastern religions such as Buddhism and Hinduism require their adherents to live a life of self-denial, abasement, and humility.

It is a disguised pride of the flesh that says, "I can do this on my own" or "Thanks for Your help, God, but I also need to help out in this."

This same religious nature also tries to attach itself to believers in this matter of spiritual warfare. The old flesh nature says:

- "Let me do something to merit my freedom!"

- "Christ's work alone surely cannot be enough!"

- "Let me scream for my freedom!"

- "Let me purge myself of demon spirits!"

To all of these, we must answer, "Not by works of righteousness which we have done, *but according to his mercy he saved us...*" (Titus 3:5)!

We can add absolutely nothing to what Jesus did at the Cross of Calvary. It was a total, perfect, and completed work! And in that glorious work of redemption (which we will cover in Chapter Three), Jesus also purchased our complete and total deliverance from the powers of the evil one!

> We can add absolutely nothing to what Jesus did at the Cross of Calvary.

In Hebrews 2:3, the writer of Hebrews declares that our salvation is a "*great* salvation." But how "great" is this salvation if Satan's power still controls us? How "great" is this salvation if we are still under his heavy hand and must fight our way out from under him day after day? How "great" is this salvation if we must scream, yell, or vomit in order to maintain our freedom? I trust that you see how utterly ridiculous the work of the flesh really is!

If it is true that we must do all these outward, fleshly, physical things, it would seem that Jesus' death and resurrection did not really effect a permanent change in the spirit realm and that our salvation is not so "great" after all. How "great" can a salvation be that doesn't completely and thoroughly deliver?

But there is good news! Our salvation IS a "great salvation"!

By His work at the Cross and His victorious resurrection from the dead, Jesus Christ completely broke the dominion of Satan and the bondage of sin over us. Then in the new birth, He released all of His creative powers in *us* as we passed from the realm of death over into the realm of life (1 John 3:14)!

Our goal in life now is not to fight for our deliverance; rather, it is to freely accept our deliverance that has already been procured for us. In fact, Scripture commands us to cease from our own works and "...enter into that rest..." (Hebrews 4:11), where we may enjoy the wonderful provision that God has made available on our behalf. Entering into that "rest" — that is, learning to accept and rest in Jesus' finished redemptive work — is what the faith walk is all about!

> Our goal in life now is not to fight for our deliverance; rather, it is to freely accept our deliverance that has already been procured for us.

To enable us to enjoy our salvation and its benefits (healing, soundness of mind, preservation of mind, and deliverance from bondages), God has graciously supplied us with the faith to believe. But He didn't stop there. God has also given us His Word to enlighten us to our inheritance by virtue of the Cross.

Yes, Satan will try to wage warfare against us after we have experienced the new birth. He will try to afflict us with past bondages, afflictions, or poverty. He will use every kind of demonic weapon he can to pull us back under his control. But we have been given divinely empowered weapons to resist the enemy's attacks and maintain the blessings of our salvation.

> We have been given divinely empowered weapons to resist the enemy's attacks and maintain the blessings of our salvation.

These spiritual weapons are not the fleshly weapons that so many try to use to overcome the devil's attacks. On the contrary, the weapons God has provided for us are of *spiritual* substance — and according to the apostle Paul, they are "...mighty through God to the pulling down of strong holds" (2 Corinthians 10:4)!

QUESTIONS FOR PERSONAL GROWTH OR GROUP DISCUSSION

1. Why is it impossible for us to succeed when we "war after the flesh" in our dealings with the devil?

2. What must be combined with the spiritual weapons God has provided for us in order for us to achieve victory in any given situation?

3. How can you discern the difference between fruitless, fleshly techniques used to combat the devil and true spiritual warfare?

4. What is legalism? How does a legalistic attitude keep you from receiving the benefits of deliverance from all the power of the enemy?

5. What are some examples of legalistic methods that some believers have used to wage war against the devil?

NOTES:

_____

_____

_____

_____

_____

_____

_____

_____

_____

_____

_____

_____

_____

_____

_____

_____

_____

_____

_____

_____

_____

_____

_____

CHAPTER THREE

RESTING IN OUR REDEMPTION

*B*efore we begin to study what the Bible has to say about spiritual armor in Ephesians 6:10-18, we must first back up for a moment and see what the Bible has to say about redemption. A correct view of redemption will clear up many wrong ideas about the devil and spiritual warfare.

There are four different words used to denote "redemption" in the Greek New Testament: *agoridzo, exagoridzo, lutroo,* and *apolutrosis.* All four of these words are extremely important for us to understand as we approach this issue of spiritual warfare.

> **A correct view of redemption will clear up many wrong ideas about the devil and spiritual warfare.**

Agoridzo, the first of these four words, was a technical term that was used to describe *the marketplace.* It was most frequently used to specifically describe *the slave market.*

The slave market was a dreadful and deplorable place. Such places should have never been permitted. Human beings were paraded in front of potential buyers and were then placed on the trading block where they were auctioned off like animals, old furniture, or unwanted junk.

The slaves' value was determined primarily by the condition of their teeth. If they had good teeth, they were probably in good shape and were therefore more expensive. If they had rotten teeth, they probably could be bought rather cheaply.

So before the nauseating process of buying, selling, and trading human debris began, potential buyers were allowed to check out the "merchandise." The slaves' heads were shoved up and backward; their mouths were forcibly jerked open; and their teeth were inspected to see if they were rotten or in fairly good shape.

As if this wasn't inhumane and degrading enough, slave-buying customers were also encouraged to kick and hit the "merchandise" in order to determine the slave's level of physical fitness.

To discover the slave's temperament, buyers slapped them, cursed at them, and spat in their faces. If a slave could swallow his pride, grit his teeth, and hold his temper during such humiliating abuse, the buyer assumed he could be used to the point of abuse without giving his owner any kind of trouble.

In short, slaves had no personal worth. They were viewed to be no better than animals. According to the thinking of the day, they were just another kind of workhorse and had no real human value. Their only purpose in the world was to serve the demands that their current owners exacted of them.

With all this in mind, we can see that the Holy Spirit has told us something extremely important by using the word *agoridzo* to describe "redemption."

SATAN'S SLAVE MARKET

When Jesus Christ came into the world, the world had become an utterly deplorable place.

The beautiful paradise that God had originally created in Eden was gone; not even a hint of it remained. In its place, the world had become a global "slave market," where Satan had gripped the hearts of men and filled their natures with violence and destruction. With each successive generation after Adam, spiritual death drove people of all nations, tribes, and ethnic groups deeper and deeper into slavery and total depravity.

> The world that Jesus Christ was born into nearly 2,000 years ago was a world of complete captivity. Through Adam's disobedience, spiritual death had seized the nature of all mankind.

Thus, the world that Jesus Christ was born into nearly 2,000 years ago was a world of complete captivity. Through Adam's disobedience, this spiritual death had seized the nature of all mankind. As Paul said, "Wherefore, as by one man sin entered into the world, and death by sin; and so death passed upon all men, for that all have sinned" (Romans 5:12).

By using the word *agoridzo*, we unmistakably know that when Jesus Christ first came to the earth, He came into a disgusting, nauseating spiritual *slave market* where human beings lived their entire lives on this earth as *slaves* to Satan and to the negative effects of sin.

Our bondage at that time was so complete that Paul states we were "sold under sin" (Romans 7:14). The word "sold" is from the Greek word *piprasko*, and it literally describes a *transfer of property*. By using this word, Paul clearly tells us that mankind had been transferred from the hands of God into the hands of a new owner. This, of course, is the picture of Satan's total ownership of us before Jesus Christ came into our lives.

Like slaves in the slave market, we stood helpless before the devil as he slapped our lives around — hitting us, kicking us, spitting upon us, and abusing us in every way he possibly could. Our "slaveowner" tried to damage our self-image, kill our bodies with various kinds of sin and vices, and mar us emotionally. When he was finished using one form of bondage and death on us, he would place us back on the trading block to be auctioned off again. Soon another form of bondage would overtake us and begin to make its own destructive mark on our lives.

Thus, we were passed from one bondage to the next in a never-ending cycle of defeat. Each day we lived, whether we were aware of it or not, this hellish ownership took us further downward and ever deeper into the captivity of sin and total depravity — lock, stock, and barrel, from the inside out, from the beginning to the end, every inch from head to toe, backward and forward and up to the brim.

The Bible says that this was our condition before the grace of God touched our lives. This is the very reason Paul repeatedly tells us in Scripture that we were previously "the servants of sin" (Romans 6:17,20).

The word "servant" is taken from the word *doulos*, which is the most abject term for *a slave* in the Greek language. One expositor has explained that the word *doulos* describes *one whose will is completely swallowed up in the will of another.*

This means that prior to our salvation experience, we were "swallowed up" in the will of Satan. We intellectually thought that we were in charge of our lives and that we were the ones calling the shots. But in reality, we were abject slaves to sin and our destinies were being orchestrated by an unseen, diabolical spirit that wanted to destroy us.

> Prior to our salvation experience, we were "swallowed up" in the will of Satan.

Our prior slavery to the devil was so deep-seated that our nature became intrinsically meshed together with the seed of rebellion, which is at the very core of Satan's nature. Rebellion against God ran deep in our blood and became ingrained in our human disposition. Eventually the gulf between God and us was so vast that Scripture declares we became "alienated and enemies" in our minds through wicked works (Colossians 1:21).

DOMINATED BY 'THE COURSE OF THIS WORLD'

This pervading demonic presence in our lives and in the world around us was absolute and supreme. Paul describes it this way: "Wherein in time past ye walked according to the course of this world, according to the prince of the power of the air, the spirit that now worketh in the children of disobedience" (Ephesians 2:2).

Notice that Paul says, "Wherein in time past ye walked *according to* the course of this world...." The phrase "according to" is taken from the word *kata*. This word portrays something that is *forceful* or *dominating*.

By choosing to use this word, Paul tells us that before we met the Lord, we were not just *influenced* by "the course of this world." The word *kata* emphatically means that we were completely *dominated*, *manipulated*, and *controlled* by it!

The word "course" is taken from the Greek word *aiona*. This is a simple word that describes *a specific, allotted period of time*, such as *an age, a specific era*, or *a generation*. For instance, each decade of a century (e.g., the 1950s, 1960s, 1970s, 1980s, 1990s, 2000s, and so on) is technically an *aiona — a specific, allotted period of time*. You could say that this word denotes *the influence of one particular generation* or *a short-lived period of time*.

But there is still more to this! The word *aiona* signifies not only a time period, but also the *spirit* of that period. For instance, the spirit of the 1920s was typified as the "roaring twenties." With the advent of rock-n-roll, the 1950s was typified as a "rebellious period." The spirit of the 1960s and 1970s, because of drugs and war, was typified as a time of "experimentation and questioning of the status quo." Each of these individual decades (*aiona*) had a flavor of its own that was unique to its particular time and place in history.

So when Paul declares that we "...walked according to the course of this world...," the word "course" conveys the idea of being dominated by the popular thinking of our own particular time and generation. Paul is saying that when we were still lost and without God in this world, we had no eternal perspective and no constant biblical standard to live by. As a result, we were dominated entirely by these *fluctuating philosophies and ideas* that come and go very quickly.

> When we were still lost and without God in this world, we had no eternal perspective and no constant biblical standard to live by.

The word "world" is from the Greek word *kosmos*, and Paul uses the word *kosmos* to convey the ideas of *order* and *arrangement*. Scientists use *kosmos* to describe the universe because, although huge, diverse, and ever-expanding, the universe is a perfectly ordered and arranged system.

The word *kosmos* was also used during the early Greek period to describe *society*. At least in a measure, society is a system that possesses *order* and *arrangement*. When *kosmos is* used to depict society, it also carries with it the ideas of *fashion* and *sophistication*. This is exactly the idea that Paul presents in Ephesians 2:2.

Before we met the Lord, we were so short-sighted and temporal-minded that Scripture says we were totally dominated, manipulated, and mastered by the society and the day in which we lived.

We could paraphrase the verse this way: *"...You walked around completely dominated by the whim of the times...."* Or we could translate it: *"...You walked around controlled by the fashion of the day and the thinking of the hour...."*

Who Is Working Behind the Scenes?

Paul isn't finished yet! Now he is going to tell us *who* is manipulating the lost world system that is dominating and controlling lost men and women! In addition to being controlled by the society and world in which we lived, Paul adds that we also formerly walked *"...according to the prince of the power of the air..."* (Ephesians 2:2).

The phrase "according to" is once again taken from the word *kata*, the same Greek word that has already been used once in this verse to convey the ideas of *domination, manipulation*, and *control*.

Thus, to the same extent our lives were formerly controlled by the trendsetters of the world (Hollywood, fashion, the music industry, the educational system, etc.), Paul says we were also dominated by "the prince of the power of the air."

Scripture tells us three things about Satan in this verse:

1. He is a prince.

2. He has genuine authority.

3. His power base is located in the lower regions of the air.

Let's look at each of these points one at a time.

First, this verse tells us that Satan is a "prince."

The word "prince" is taken from the word *archonta*, and it refers to *one who is in first place* or *one who is in a ruling position*. It describes *a potentate, ruler, chief*, or *prince*.

This shouldn't surprise us! In Matthew 9:34, the Bible tells us that Satan is "the prince of the devils" and even ascribes a real kingdom to him called "the power [or the kingdom] of darkness" (Colossians 1:13). In John 12:31, Jesus calls Satan "the prince of this world."

In Second Corinthians 4:4, the apostle Paul specifically states that Satan is "the god of this world." Paul continues in this verse to tell us that as "the god of this world," Satan has "...blinded the minds of them which believe not..." so they cannot see the truth.

In addition to these well-known scriptures that identify Satan as a "prince," Ephesians 6:12 also tells of an entire ordered demonic system that is under Satan's domain. Satan himself is lord over these demonic hosts.

Therefore, Satan is a real prince over demon spirits and exercises real authority over the affairs of lost men and women whom he has blinded.

Second, this verse tells us that Satan has "power."

Paul designates Satan as "the prince of the *power* of the air." The word "power" is derived from the word *exousia*. The word

> Satan is a real prince over demon spirits and exercises real authority over the affairs of lost men and women whom he has blinded.

exousia would be more accurately translated "authority." Since Satan is a real prince over a real kingdom, it should not surprise us that his dark kingdom has real authority to back up his wicked reign.

During Jesus' 40-day temptation in the wilderness, the Bible says, "And the devil, taking him up into an high mountain, shewed unto him all the kingdoms of the world in a moment of time. And the devil said unto him, All this power [*exousia*, meaning *authority*] will I give thee, and the glory of them: for that is delivered unto me; and to whomsoever I will I give it" (Luke 4:5,6).

Please pay attention to the fact that the Lord Jesus never argued about Satan's claim to possess authority. It is obvious from this passage that Jesus had no argument with the devil's claims. He knew that Satan did indeed possess a measure of authority over the deteriorating world system and over lost humanity.

Praise God, the authority of the devil over believers was eternally broken through Jesus' death and resurrection! However, lost humanity is still being dominated by "the prince of the power of the air."

Third, Satan's power base is located in the "air."

> Praise God, the authority of the devil over believers was eternally broken through Jesus' death and resurrection!

The word "air" is taken from the word *aer*, and it was used by the classical Greek writers to describe *the lower, denser regions of the earth's atmosphere* — as opposed to the word *aither*, which was used to describe *the purer, cleaner air that resided high above the mountaintops.*

Why is this important? Because it explicitly tells us that Satan's power base is not "high up in the air" as some have suggested in their spiritual warfare teachings from time to time. Just the opposite! The air that is *high above the mountaintops* represents the cleanest and purest atmosphere that we know.

You don't have to go out into outer space in order to locate the devil's power base. Satan's power base is located in the lower, denser environment that engulfs the earth. He isn't interested in controlling uninhabited planets and expanses of the universe that are devoid of human beings. He wants to own, control, dominate, and manipulate *man*!

This is the reason Satan is called "the prince of this world" (John 12:31) and "the god of this world" (2 Corinthians 4:4). He doesn't want the moon. He doesn't want Mars or Jupiter. He doesn't want Venus, Neptune, or Pluto. The devil wants to be "the god of *this world*"!

DEMONICALLY ENERGIZED

Paul continues to tell us that Satan is "...the spirit that now worketh in the children of disobedience" (Ephesians 2:2).

What a shocking discovery this is — to find out that before our life in Jesus Christ, we were demonically energized by the power of Satan himself. Yet this is precisely what this scripture teaches!

> Before our life in Jesus Christ, we were demonically energized by the power of Satan himself.

The verse says Satan is "the spirit that now *worketh*." The word "worketh" is from the word *energeo*, and it denotes *a power that is operative or energizing*. This is where we get the word "energy."

Therefore, in this verse the Holy Spirit vividly portrays how destitute our spiritual condition was before we were born again. *This verse declares that prior to our salvation, we were "energized" by demon spirits.* The devil himself was at work in us, energizing us and working through us to accomplish his destructive will in our lives. This was our condition before Jesus Christ touched us and totally set us free!

It was into this stinking, deteriorating, sinking, death-permeated, demonically energized world, where all of humankind was being auctioned off by the devil into various kinds of slavery and bondage, that Jesus Christ came 2,000 years ago. And God sent His Son into the enemy's "slave market" with one purpose in mind: *so Jesus could secure man's deliverance from Satan's bondage once and for all!*

> God sent His Son into the enemy's "slave market" with one purpose in mind: so Jesus could secure man's deliverance from Satan's bondage once and for all!

Agoridzo, translated "redemption" in the New Testament, denotes this horrible, deplorable, abject slavery in Satan's slave market where we used to live. But, thank God, we don't live there anymore!

The word *agoridzo,* fully understood in the context of "redemption," means that Jesus came to redeem us from this miserable state of bondage. As Paul told the Corinthians, "For ye are *bought* with a price..." (1 Corinthians 6:20). The word "bought" in this verse is the word *agoridzo.*

Regarding this same redeeming work of Jesus, Paul said again later, "Ye are *bought* with a price; be not ye the servants of men" (1 Corinthians 7:23).

The word "bought" is once again derived from the word *agoridzo.* Paul's admonition could be paraphrased: *"Since Jesus paid the price to deliver you from bondage and slavery to Satan, do not now turn around and make yourselves slaves to people!"*

When the 24 elders fall before the throne of God and begin to worship, they sing a song about Jesus' work of *redeeming* us from Satan's slave market: "And they sung a new song, saying, Thou art worthy to take the book, and to open the seals thereof: for thou wast slain, and hast *redeemed* [*agoridzo*] us to God by thy blood out of every kindred, and tongue, and people, and nation" (Revelation 5:9).

It is imperative for us to understand the word *agoridzo.* This important word adequately portrays our spiritually bankrupt condition in the "slave market" of the world before Jesus Christ set us free, as well as Jesus' redemptive work to remove us from that terrible place.

This leads us to the second word for "redemption" that is used in the New Testament.

PURCHASED 'OUT OF' SLAVERY

The second Greek word for "redemption" is derived from the word *exagoridzo*. The word *exagoridzo* is a compound of the words *ex* and *agoridzo*.

The word *ex* is a preposition that means *out* and, as we have already discussed, the word *agoridzo* described *a slave market*. When *ex* and *agoridzo* are combined, they form the word *exagoridzo*, which pictures *one who has come to purchase a slave OUT OF the slave market*.

Exagoridzo conveys the idea of *removal*. Therefore, it signifies *the purchase of a slave in order to permanently set that slave FREE from that heinous place, never to be put on the trading block of slavery again*. The word *exagoridzo* pictures a slave who has been liberated *out of* that stinking, nauseating, disgusting, depraved, and cursed slave market forever!

This word *exagoridzo* is used several times in Paul's epistles to paint a picture of Jesus' redemptive work *to remove us* from slavery. A perfect New Testament example of this word is found in Galatians 3:13, where Paul says, "Christ hath *redeemed* us from the curse of the law...."

By using the word *exagoridzo* in connection with Jesus *redeeming* us from the curse of the Law, Paul is telling us plainly that Jesus' sacrificial death not only paid the penalty for our sin, but His death also *removed us* from living under the curse from henceforth!

Paul continues to tell us that it was for this work of redemption that Jesus came into the world: "But when the fulness of the time was come, God sent forth His Son, made of a woman, made under the law, *to redeem them* that were under the law, that we might receive the adoption of sons" (Galatians 4:4,5).

This is what we must understand about God's plan of redemption: His purpose in sending His Son was not just to inspect our condition of slavery and to locate us in our depravity. His ultimate plan, which He accomplished in Jesus Christ's death and resurrection, was to *buy us out of* that miserable condition and to make us His own sons and daughters — forever removed from under the curse of sin and the Law.

However, slaves did not come cheaply. If the auctioneer knew that a buyer really wanted a particular slave, he could demand unbelievably high prices. We must therefore ask, "What price did Jesus pay for our freedom from Satan's power?"

This leads us to the third word for "redemption" that is used in the New Testament.

PAYING THE DEMANDED PRICE

The third Greek word used to describe "redemption" in the New Testament is taken from the word *lutroo*.

The word *lutroo* means *to set a captive free by the payment of a ransom*. In order for a buyer to secure the slave of his choice, a very high price had to be paid. If he greatly desired a certain slave, the auctioneer could demand unreasonably high ransoms.

In using the word *lutroo* to denote the redemptive work of Jesus Christ on our behalf, Paul reminds us that our freedom was not really free. Quite the contrary! Our freedom from Satan's power was *extremely expensive*.

> **What was the ransom that Jesus paid in order to procure our freedom from Satan's ownership? His own blood!**

In fact, the price Jesus paid for us was the highest price ever paid for a slave in the history of mankind.

What was the ransom that Jesus paid in order to procure our freedom from Satan's ownership? His own blood!

- Ephesians 1:7 says, "In whom we have redemption *through his blood....*"

- Colossians 1:14 says, "In whom we have redemption *through his blood....*"

- Colossians 1:20 says, "And, having made peace *through the blood* of his cross...."

- Hebrews 9:12 says, "...But *by his own blood* he entered in once into the holy place, having obtained eternal redemption for us."

- First Peter 1:18,19 says, "Forasmuch as ye know that ye were not redeemed with corruptible things, as silver and gold...but with the *precious blood of Christ....*"

It was the shedding of Jesus' own blood that guaranteed our deliverance and lasting freedom from demonic powers that previously held us captive. The word *lutroo* unmistakably means that Jesus paid the ransom that set you and me free! *He bought us with His own blood!*

Titus 2:14 declares that Jesus gave *Himself* as the ransom in order to set us free: "Who gave himself for us, that he might *redeem* us from all iniquity, and purify unto himself a peculiar people, zealous of good works." The word "redeem" used in this verse is taken from the word *lutroo*. According to Titus 2:14, a price had to be paid, and Jesus paid it with His own life and His own blood on the Cross.

But wait! There is yet a fourth word that describes Jesus' work of "redemption."

RESTORED TO FULL STATUS

The fourth word for "redemption" that is used in the New Testament is taken from the word *apolutrosis*.

The word *apo* means *away*, and it often conveys the idea of *a return*. In this particular case, *apo* would be better translated "back," as in something that is being *returned back*. The second part of *apolutrosis* is taken from the word *lutroo*, which we just covered. The word *lutroo* means *to set a slave free by the payment of a ransom.*

This fourth word for "redemption" tells us God's ultimate purpose in redeeming us from Satan's slave market. The word *apolutrosis* ("redemption") most assuredly means that Jesus paid the ransom in order to *return* us to the condition we were in before our captivity began. In the plainest of language, this means that Jesus paid the price to permanently set us free and to *restore* us to the full status of sons!

Paul uses the word *apolutrosis* in this very way in Ephesians 1:7 when he says, "In whom [Christ] we have *redemption* through his blood, the forgiveness of sins, according to the riches of his grace."

By choosing to use the word *apolutrosis* ("redemption"), Paul declares that we were forever delivered from Satan's power — we were forever removed from that dreadful place — and now we have been *fully restored* by the blood of Jesus Christ and *placed back into a state of rightstanding with God.* We are fully restored and fully set free from Satan's former grip over us!

This is why Galatians 4:7 declares, "Wherefore thou art no more a servant, but a son; and if a son, then an heir of God through Christ." Romans 8:17 proclaims that we are so entirely restored through the blood of Jesus that we have now become "joint-heirs" with Jesus Christ Himself!

- The first word for "redemption" (*agoridzo*) tells us that Jesus Christ came to earth to *locate us* in our depravity and to personally inspect our slavery to Satan.

- The second word for "redemption" (*exagoridzo*) declares that Jesus came not only to inspect our condition but to permanently *remove us* from Satan's power.

- The third word for "redemption" (*lutroo*) tells us that Jesus was so dedicated to delivering us from Satan's dominion that He was willing to pay *the ransom price* of His own blood in order to break the devil's ownership over us.

- The fourth word for "redemption" (*apolutrosis*) tells us that, in addition to permanently setting us free from Satan's hold, Jesus also *restored* us to the position of "sons of God." Now we are fully restored and made joint-heirs with Jesus Christ Himself (Romans 8:17).

This is what *redemption* is all about!

Translated Out of Satan's Kingdom

What do all four of these words for "redemption" have to do with spiritual warfare and spiritual armor? *Everything!*

These truths explicitly let us know that the real purpose of spiritual warfare is *not* to fight for freedom from Satan's control over us. This has already been accomplished by the death of Jesus Christ on the Cross and by His triumphant resurrection from the dead. *We are already free!*

Ephesians 2:6 states that we are not under Satan's power *but are rather above it*: "And [Christ] hath raised us up together, and made us to sit together in heavenly places in Christ Jesus" (Ephesians 2:6).

Accordingly, Colossians 1:13 teaches that we do not need to break away from Satan's dreadful dominion over us *because we have already been translated out of it*: "Who hath delivered us from the power of darkness, and hath translated us into the kingdom of his dear Son."

Because of Jesus' redemptive work, we are seated with Jesus Christ in the heavenly places and have been elevated "far above all principality, and power, and might, and dominion, and every name that is named, not only in this world, but also in that which is to come" (Ephesians 1:21).

> **Through the blood of Jesus, we have been utterly and completely set free from Satan's control!**

Therefore, Satan has no legal right to control us, our bodies, our families, our businesses, or our money. Although we once genuinely belonged to him (Ephesians 2:2), *we are no longer his to manipulate or dominate*. Through the blood of Jesus, we have been utterly and completely set free from Satan's control!

QUESTIONS FOR PERSONAL GROWTH OR GROUP DISCUSSION

1. Why would a fuller understanding of what *redemption* means help us in our stance against Satan's strategies in our lives?

2. What does the Greek word *agoridzo*, translated "redemption," tell us about our spiritual condition before the grace of God touched our lives?

3. How does a revelation of our utter spiritual bankruptry before we received Jesus as our Savior help in understanding true spiritual warfare?

4. What does Satan's name "prince of the power of the air" teach us about our enemy? How does this knowledge help us when confronted with a demonic attack in our own lives?

5. Why is the ransom price for our redemption such a crucial key to our victory against the enemy in every situation?

NOTES:

CHAPTER FOUR

WHY DOES THE BATTLE STILL RAGE?

Someone may ask, "If Jesus' death and resurrection really broke the authority of the devil over our lives, why does the battle still rage?"

"If we have been truly translated out of Satan's kingdom, why does his kingdom still seem to exert influence upon our lives?"

"If Jesus genuinely spoiled principalities and powers as Colossians 2:15 declares, why do so many believers still have to deal with horrible strongholds in their minds?"

Several years ago, the police called a friend of mine in the middle of the night, informing him that one of his animals, a goat, had gotten out of his property and had been hit and killed by a car. My friend quickly put on his jacket and rushed to the place where the dead goat was supposed to be lying.

However, when he arrived at the scene, he discovered that the goat wasn't dead at all. Someone had stolen the goat, tied up its legs with rope so it couldn't move, and then dumped the goat along the side of the road.

My friend reached over, untied the rope that held the goat captive, and then slapped it and said, "Get up!" But the goat just lay there as though it was still bound and unable to move. Once again, he slapped the goat and said, "Get up!" But the goat continued to lie on its side as if it were incapable of moving.

The man began examining the goat, looking for a wound that was possibly keeping it from getting up. Then he noticed that the animal's legs were still tightly clinging to each other as though they were still tied with ropes. The problem then became clear: The goat thought it was still bound!

So my friend bent over and picked up the goat, set it on its feet, and slapped it again, telling it to "Get up!" Finally, the goat realized its feet were no longer bound and began to jump and leap in its newfound freedom.

Most of us are just like the goat in this story. We were previously bound by Satan's destructive power. He tied us up in total slavery and then dumped us, waiting for destruction to completely ruin us.

Then when we heard the Gospel message and were born again, Jesus Christ came to "untie" Satan's hold on our lives! Through Jesus' redemptive work at the Cross, He legally removed the bondages that held us captive, including every stronghold that held us hostage in our minds. However, even though this freeing work has already been done, we often don't fully perceive that we have really been set free.

Jesus looks at us and says, "Get up!" Yet we lie on our sides, bound up in our scars, our pains, and our mental hang-ups, not realizing that we have really been set free. And even when someone finally comes along and points out our freedom to us, we still have to maintain our Christ-bought, Christ-imparted freedom by renewing our minds. Freedom becomes a way of life only as we replace our wrong thinking and wrong believing with what the Word of God declares about our new condition.

> Freedom becomes a way of life only as we replace our wrong thinking and wrong believing with what the Word of God declares about our new condition.

Any pastor can verify that people who have just been saved must work to overcome the emotional and mental scars they received when they were still in the world under the devil's control. Although the inner man has been born again and made new, the mind and the body must still be conformed to the image of the inner man.

These newly saved individuals received much abuse while they were members of Satan's "slave market," held captive by the negative consequences of sin. Perhaps they struggled with a bad marriage, a drug problem, a sexual perversion, a lying spirit, a mental hang-up, or some other type of scar that was inflicted on their souls before they met the Lord.

If these "residual areas" from the past are not removed through the renewing of the mind by the Word of God, these strongholds can and will continue to exert power in the life of a

Christian. Moreover, if these "residual areas" are not dealt with according to the Word, these are the very areas that Satan will use to wage warfare against that person's new life.

When the adversary locates an area in our lives that has never been surrendered to the sanctifying work of the Holy Spirit, he will try to seize that unsurrendered area in our minds or emotions and energize it — filling it with a brand-new vitality. Then the enemy will begin to use that stronghold to work against the growth and development of our new freedom in Jesus Christ. *This is why our refusal to deal with specific areas of sin in our lives is where the majority of spiritual warfare stems from!*

Satan knows precisely where to look to find weak areas in our lives to use against us as he tries to rob us of the legitimate freedom we now possess in Jesus Christ. Here are some of the most common "open doors" he looks for to gain access into our lives:

- Wrong thinking

- Wrong believing

- Memories of terrible experiences that happened before we knew the Lord that we still allow to dominate our emotions

- Fears that were transferred to us from our parents, family members, or friends

- Years of incorrect doctrine taught to us in our former churches that we must now "unlearn" and overcome

Notice that with all of these, *the mind* is the strategic center where spiritual warfare with the "god of this world" takes place!

SPIRITUAL WARFARE AND RENEWING THE MIND

The enemy knows very well the importance of the mind. He knows that your mind is the key to controlling your life.

Satan knows that if he can take control of one small area of your mind, he can then begin to expand outward into other weak areas that need to be strengthened by the Holy Spirit and the Word of God. By poisoning your mind with unbelief and lying strongholds, the devil can manipulate your mind, your emotions, and your body. Moreover, he can use you to pour the same kind of unbelief and lying strongholds into the minds of others around you.

> The mind is the strategic center where spiritual warfare with the "god of this world" takes place.

There is no doubt about it — the mind is the strategic center for spiritual warfare!

By nature, the condition of the mind is hostile toward God and is bent on destruction. We were all born with an innately rebellious mind and a rebellious nature that was against God. This is why:

- Romans 8:7 says, "...The *carnal mind* [the natural mind] is enmity against God...."

- Colossians 1:21 says that prior to your salvation experience, you were "...alienated and enemies in *your mind* by wicked works...."

- Ephesians 4:17,18 says that unbelievers walk "...in the vanity of *their mind*, having the *understanding* darkened, being alienated from the life of God through the *ignorance* that is in them, because of the *blindness* of their heart."

- Second Corinthians 4:4 says, "...The god of this world hath *blinded the minds* of them which believe not...."

- And in Romans 1:28, Scripture teaches that the natural mind is so completely contrary to God that it can become "*reprobate.*"

Hence, we were initially born into this world with a nature that was bent toward self-annihilation and was fully capable of developing strongholds by itself. The natural mind is contrary toward God and has always sought to fulfill itself in the destructive lusts of the flesh. This is why Paul said, "Among whom also we all had our conversation in times past in the lusts of our flesh, *fulfilling the desires of the flesh and of the mind; and were by nature the children of wrath...*" (Ephesians 2:3).

If you do not seek to renew your mind, your will, and your emotions to the truth of God's Word, the illusion of bondage will continue to dominate your life. Most often it is through these unrenewed areas of thinking that the devil continues to exert his foul influence upon you. He knows that if your mind is renewed to the truth, he cannot wage successful warfare against you or your family!

This is the reason the authors of the New Testament epistles earnestly plead with us to give serious attention to the condition of our minds. Throughout the epistles, we are commanded to renew our minds to the truth of God's Word:

- "...Be ye transformed by the renewing of your mind..." (Romans 12:2).

- "...Be renewed in the spirit of your mind" (Ephesians 4:23).

- "...Put on the new man..." (Ephesians 4:24).

- "...Put on the new man, which is renewed in knowledge after the image of him that created him" (Colossians 3:10).

- "Let the Word of Christ dwell in you richly..." (Colossians 3:16).

- "Wherefore gird up the loins of your mind..." (1 Peter 1:13,14).

Especially notice Peter's admonition to "gird up the loins of your mind." The picture Peter puts before us is that of a runner whose garments have fallen down and gotten entangled around his legs. He was running a good race and his stride was picking up until this encumbrance of dangling, loosely hanging clothing hindered his steps.

Likewise, we must "gird up the loins of our minds" by seeking to renew our thinking with the Word of God. The consistent renewal of our minds with the Word will eradicate wrong thinking, wrong believing, scars from the past, and hurtful, emotional memories that would exert their influence on our new life in Christ. *Otherwise, those loose, dangling, unsurrendered, and unrenewed areas of our minds will be used by the devil to wage warfare against us.*

> The consistent renewal of our minds with the Word will eradicate wrong thinking, wrong believing, scars from the past, and hurtful, emotional memories that would exert their influence on our new life in Christ.

The renewing of our minds doesn't add to the already completed work of Jesus Christ. It simply puts us in a mental state that enables us to better use our faith so we can enjoy the benefits of the redemptive work that Jesus accomplished for us!

Take heed! To deliberately allow wrong thinking and wrong believing to continue will impair your ability to enjoy your redemption. This is equivalent to a runner who deliberately allows his garment to hang down so it gets caught in his legs. Although he is still in the race, he certainly will not win the victory, nor will he experience much joy in running his race.

Therefore, Peter admonishes you to "gird up the loins of your mind." You must tighten up those areas that the devil would try to grab hold of and use against you!

A LIFELONG COMMITMENT

This is the reason I stress that spiritual warfare is a lifelong commitment and not just a gust of emotion that frightens away the devil for a few moments of time. Real spiritual warfare will take much longer than that, because *in addition to taking authority over demonic powers, realspiritual warfare also entails taking authority over your mind.*

> In addition to taking authority over demonic powers, real spiritual warfare also entails taking authority over your mind.

The Scriptures emphatically declare that the following are essential elements of genuine spiritual warfare:

- Renewing your mind

- Meditating on the Word of God until it gets into your heart and soul

- Learning to live a holy life

- Seeking to be conformed to the image of Jesus Christ on a day-to-day basis

- Learning how to walk after the Spirit

Real spiritual warfare requires a life of commitment, purity, and consecration. Any view of spiritual warfare that fails to include these requirements is *lopsided* and fails to meet the scriptural standard.

QUESTIONS FOR PERSONAL GROWTH OR GROUP DISCUSSION

1. Why do so many believers still struggle with strongholds in their minds, even though Jesus has already set them free?

2. What is the primary key to getting rid of residual areas of bondage from the past after a person is born again?

3. What is the consequence of *not* getting rid of these residual areas?

4. What does it mean to "gird up the loins of your mind"? What will the results be in your daily life when you make a practice of obeying this divine command?

5. What makes true spiritual warfare a lifelong commitment rather than a periodic act of taking authority over the devil?

NOTES:

_____

_____

_____

_____

_____

_____

_____

_____

_____

_____

_____

_____

_____

_____

_____

_____

_____

_____

_____

_____

_____

_____

_____

_____

_____

_____

CHAPTER FIVE

A MENACE FROM HEAVEN

*Y*ou can be assured that Satan was watching with great concern as the Holy Spirit's power came upon believers gathered in the Upper Room on the Day of Pentecost. With the emergence of the supernatural Church of Jesus Christ in Jerusalem, the devil knew — beyond any shadow of doubt — that his earthly domain was no longer secure. If Jesus could single-handedly defeat him so thoroughly, how could he now stand against multitudes of people filled with the same Spirit who raised Jesus from the dead?

Endued with supernatural power from on High, the believers in Jerusalem had been miraculously transformed into a divine army equipped with supernatural weaponry to execute the victory that Jesus had already achieved over this supernatural foe. *Satan's worst nightmare had become a reality.* His dark, demented, diabolical kingdom that had been secure for thousands of years before Jesus' birth had now been penetrated — first by Jesus, and now by the Church.

From the devil's perspective, a heavenly menace had entered his domain in order to execute the victory Jesus Christ won over him at the Cross and the grave and to demonstrate his defeat.

God's army, the Church, had been sent from Heaven's headquarters to take the dominion away from Satan and return it to the people of God!

The Kingdom of God had arrived! The Church began preaching, teaching, evangelizing, healing the sick, raising the dead, casting out demons, and driving back the forces of hell one step at a time. Satan's security was gone forever. The Church had arrived to execute judgment on him and his perverted hosts.

> Satan's security was gone forever. The Church had arrived to execute judgment on him and his perverted hosts.

Satan was desperate to avert his total collapse of power in the affairs of the lost world system. Therefore, he released all his fury in an effort to destroy this heavenly menace from Heaven before it could fully execute the judgment already declared concerning him.

AN OPPORTUNE MOMENT
FOR THE DEVIL TO ATTACK

When Paul wrote the book of Ephesians in the year A.D. 64, Satan's strategy to destroy the Church was already in full motion.

Paul — a powerful, faithful father and general of the Christian faith — was imprisoned in the imperial city of Rome, charged with allegedly helping to plan the huge fire that had burned down 12 sections of Rome the year before. In reality, it was Nero, the current reigning emperor, who had planned this arson.

Nero actually believed in his own deity — a delusion that was encouraged by his demonically influenced mother, Agrippina. So in A.D. 63, Nero went before the Roman Senate and requested a reconstruction of a large part of Rome — which, of course, would include idols of himself positioned throughout the city. That way, he argued, good Roman citizens could worship him at any given point on any day of the week.

When the Senate refused to grant Nero's request, he returned home. Tradition says he then placed torches in the hands of his servants and ordered them to burn the imperial city to the ground. Nero's demented thinking was, *If they won't let me tear it down, I'll burn it down!*

After surveying the city of Rome when the fire was finally extinguished, it became obvious to members of the Senate that Nero had planned this arson. The only section of Rome that didn't burn was the district where Nero was working on the construction of his new, famous palace. Upon discovering this convincing evidence, the Senate members realized that Nero was behind the devastating blaze that had severely burned their beloved city and immediately began to plan Nero's trial and execution.

It was then that Nero, empowered and inspired by the devil himself, began to publicly allege that Christians had burned down the imperial city (for more on this, *see* Chapter One in my book, *Living in the Combat Zone*). Because of Paul's notoriety as a Christian leader, he was captured and imprisoned for his alleged part in this fire that Nero had orchestrated. This wasn't the first time Paul had been imprisoned, but this time he would spend the remainder of his life chained to a heavily armed Roman soldier in a prison cell in Rome.

This attack against the Church was a part of Satan's plan to thwart the plan of God. At that time, the Church was growing at an unprecedented rate. It was growing numerically; it was growing doctrinally; and it was growing spiritually. So before the entire empire could fall from Satan's hands into the control of God's victorious army, the Church, the enemy struck quickly and viciously to abort the work of God.

As always is the case, this demonic attack, which was meant to destroy the Church, did not ultimately succeed. In the end, it actually helped to further the advancement of the Gospel.

DEMONIC ATTACKS THAT BACKFIRE!

None of Satan's strategies to destroy the Church have ever succeeded. By studying Church history, it becomes evident very quickly that each attack the enemy has waged against the Church has ultimately helped to further the cause of Jesus Christ. *Two thousand years of experience emphatically tell us that the devil has absolutely no winning strategies. He simply does not know how to win!*

By having Paul imprisoned for his faith, the devil thought he could

> By studying Church history, it becomes evident very quickly that each attack the enemy has waged against the Church has ultimately helped to further the cause of Jesus Christ.

destroy Paul's ministry. But this was not a winning strategy for the devil at all. By imprisoning Paul, the devil made the horrible mistake of placing Paul in a situation where he had nothing to do except listen to the Holy Spirit. *This strategy of Satan utterly failed!*

During his various confinements in prison, Paul received some of the most outstanding revelations in the entire New Testament — *the books of Galatians, Ephesians, Philippians, Colossians, Second Timothy, and Philemon.* All of the revelations contained in these epistles are a result of Paul's time spent in prison! Thus, we see the reason Paul said, "Wherein I suffer trouble, as an evil doer, even unto bonds; *but the word of God is not bound*" (2 Timothy 2:9).

Had Paul never been bound in prison, he may not have written these vital books of the New Testament. Can you imagine how hectic his ministry outside those prison walls must have been? His ministry was perhaps more demanding than any other ministry in history!

As an apostle, Paul had been consumed with establishing new churches, discipling new leaders, and helping to correct problems in the local church. Outside those prison walls, his ministry was extremely effective and damaging to the domain of darkness. By binding Paul in chains and throwing him in jail, the devil calculated that his effectiveness would be destroyed. But the devil was *wrong* — Paul's effectiveness increased!

History is full of the devil's miscalculations. Another example is found in the story of the apostle John.

The devil inspired Domitian, the Roman emperor, to imprison John on the isle of Patmos. By putting John on this foreboding little island out in the middle of the Mediterranean Sea, Satan thought he could destroy John's effectiveness in ministry. This was yet another horrible mistake! By isolating John on the isle of Patmos, the devil helped position John to receive the Book of Revelation!

How about the miscalculation the devil made regarding Aquila and Priscilla? This is another extremely dramatic illustration of how Satan's strategies always backfire!

The earliest Church records reveal that Aquila and Priscilla founded the church of Rome. In fact, the church in Rome actually met in their home when it was first being established. Then the massive persecution against Jews commenced during the reign of Emperor Claudius. Like many other believers who lived in the Jewish colonies of Rome, Aquila and Priscilla were driven out of the city.

Imagine how heart-rending it must have been for this couple to leave their church family behind! They had founded the church in Rome and had led many of those people to the Lord. They had helped the people get filled with the Holy Spirit and had taught them, discipled them, and watched them grow in their relationship with the Lord. The church family of Rome was precious and dear to the hearts of Aquila and Priscilla. But now, against their wills, they were being forced to leave it all behind.

You can be sure, just on the basis of human nature alone, that Aquila and Priscilla thought it was all over for them when they were expelled from Rome. Just think how devastated and crushed their hearts must have been as they packed their belongings and said farewell to their remaining church family in Rome. Surely they must have thought that they were all "washed up" in the ministry.

Yet this couple's greatest ministry began *after* they left Rome! Once expelled from Rome, Aquila and Priscilla traveled eastward and settled in the city of Corinth, where they took up the trade of tent-making and later met Paul. On Paul's subsequent trip to Ephesus, he brought Aquila and Priscilla with him. There the couple met Apollos, an extremely influential and educated Jew from Alexandria who had come to visit Ephesus. It was during Apollos' visit to this city that Aquila and Priscilla "...expounded unto him the way of God more perfectly" (*see* Acts 18:24-26).

Apollos eventually became the pastor of the Corinthian Church. Had Aquila and Priscilla been allowed to stay in Rome, they might never have met Apollos and led him to the Lord. This attack that came to destroy their ministry actually positioned them to help further the Gospel of Jesus Christ.

Likewise, had Aquila and Priscilla stayed in Rome, they might never have met the apostle Paul. It was only after they were driven out of Rome that they met him and joined him as one of his associates. This apostolic team ministered to churches all over Greece and Asia Minor for years and years to come.

So although the devil thought he was shutting down forever the powerful ministry of Aquila and Priscilla by expelling them from Rome, *he was actually positioning them to move up to a higher level of ministry than they had ever experienced!* Had the devil never attacked them and expelled them from their work in Rome, they might never have left Rome and entered into this greater mission field.

A CLOSED DOOR DOES NOT MEAN FAILURE

Regardless of what the devil tries to do to you, your family, your church, or your ministry, you must continue to stand in faith. As you do, God will turn around the enemy's attack so that it works for the advancement of His Kingdom!

Even if your finances are assaulted and the plan of God appears to come under siege in your life, God is able to take these wicked devices and turn them to work for your good. As Paul said, "And we know that all things work together for good to them that love God, to them who are the called according to his purpose" (Romans 8:28).

> If a door slams shut in your face and it looks like everything is over, hold tight and refrain from making a judgment call about the situation. What the devil did to hurt you, God will use to bless you!

A closed door does not mean failure! If a door slams shut in your face and it looks like everything is over, hold tight and refrain from making a judgment call about the situation. What the devil did to hurt you, God will use to bless you! *God may be preparing to open the largest, most effectual door of opportunity that has ever been made available to you!*

Paul had suffered many blows from the enemy that, naturally speaking, should have mortally wounded him. Yet when it was all said and done, he was still alive and well and thriving in the ministry. Having seen God's faithfulness on so many occasions, Paul confidently looked trouble in the face and declared, "Nay, in all these things we are more than conquerors through him that loved us" (Romans 8:37)!

Notice that Paul calls us "more than conquerors." The phrase "more than conquerors" is taken from the Greek word *hupernikos*, which is a compound of two words: *huper* and *nikos*. It appears that this is the first time the word *hupernikos* was ever used in Greek literature; it was coined by Paul himself.

Why is it important to know this? It tells us that there were no words strong enough in the Greek language to express what Paul wanted to say. Therefore, he made up his own word! By joining the words *huper* and *nikos* together into one word, Paul made one fabulous, jam-packed, power-filled statement!

The phrase "more than" (*huper*) literally means *over, above, and beyond*. It depicts something that is *way beyond measure*. We derive the word "super" from the word *huper*. As used in this passage, it conveys the idea of *superiority*. It means *greater; superior; higher; better; more than a match for; utmost; paramount; or foremost*. It also means *to be first-rate, first-class, top-notch, unsurpassed, unequaled, and unrivaled by any person or thing*!

Now Paul uses this word to denote what kind of conquerors we are in Jesus Christ. We are *huper-conquerors*! The word *huper* dramatizes our victory. It means that *we are greater conquerors, superior conquerors, higher and better conquerors. We are more than a match for any adversary or foe. We are utmost conquerors, paramount conquerors, foremost conquerors, first-rate conquerors, first-class conquerors, top-notch conquerors, unsurpassed conquerors, unequaled and unrivaled conquerors!* All of this is what the phrase "more than" means!

The word "conqueror" is from the word *nikos*. It describes an *overcomer, conqueror, champion, victor,* or *master.* It is the picture of *an overwhelming, prevailing force.* The word *nikos* is a dramatic word that depicts *one who is altogether victorious.* However, *nikos* alone wasn't strong enough to make Paul's point, so he joined the words *huper* and *nikos* together to make his point even stronger!

By calling us "more than conquerors," Paul tells us that in Christ Jesus, we are *overwhelming conquerors, victors paramount,* or *enormous overcomers.* This word is so power-packed that one could translate it *"a phenomenal, walloping conquering force"*!

In light of this, we can better see what Paul means when he says, "Nay, in all these things we are more than conquerors through him that loved us." He is not referring to a small victory; instead, he declares that we are *mighty* victors! We are "a phenomenal, walloping conquering force"!

With the power of Jesus Christ at our disposal, we can be certain that "...neither death, nor life, nor angels, nor principalities, nor powers, nor things present, nor things to come, nor height, nor depth, nor any other creature, shall be able to separate us from the love of God, which is in Christ Jesus our Lord" (Romans 8:38,39).

Regardless of what the devil has attempted to do to you in the past — regardless of the attacks that have come against you, your family, your business, or your ministry — in the end these attacks will utterly fail! Although the devil may try to abort the plan of God for your life, the Bible promises that "no weapon that is formed against thee shall prosper..." (Isaiah 54:17). Each attack that comes your way will ultimately work for your good, because you love God and are called according to His purpose (Romans 8:28).

Over the centuries, Satan's plan has not changed. He still hates the Church of Jesus Christ; he still despises the preaching and teaching of God's Word. He is still trying to prevent the Church from demonstrating Jesus' victory over him and from executing the judgment that the Word of God has declared over him.

> Each attack that comes your way will ultimately work for your good, because you love God and are called according to His purpose.

Satan still actively seeks to destroy us. *The Church is still a menace to his domain that he seeks to oppose with all of his might.*

IF YOU'VE BEEN GAINING NEW GROUND, GET READY TO BE CHALLENGED!

As you grow in your spiritual walk, you need to know that attacks on your life may begin to escalate. The good news is that your new growth and your knowledge of God's Word will help you come through each attack as the victor!

The adversary doesn't want you to grow. Spiritual growth in your life equals real trouble for him and his dark kingdom. He would much prefer that you remain infantile in your spiritual life so that you do him no serious damage.

Satan is well aware that your growth in the knowledge of God's Word and in the power of the Holy Spirit poses a grave threat to his domain. He will therefore attempt to make a preemptive strike against you to slow down your growth. *Do not be surprised by such preemptive strikes!*

Paul said, "There hath no temptation taken you but such as is common to man..." (1 Corinthians 10:13). In regard to these attacks from the devil, Peter said, "Whom resist stedfast in the faith, knowing that the same afflictions are accomplished in your brethren that are in the world" (1 Peter 5:9).

The devil may try to coax your flesh and emotions into believing that no one has ever suffered like you are suffering. He may whisper to your mind that no one else has ever gone through the difficulties that you are going through right now. *But you need to realize that this is a trick to make you fix your eyes on yourself.* If you allow this devilish strategy to work in your life, it will ultimately lure you into a maze of self-centeredness, where everything in life revolves around you — your problems, your difficulties, your fears, and so on.

Be assured that as you grow and your understanding of God's Word begins to increase, you will probably have *many opportunities* to use your faith and to resist the devil. I couldn't begin to count the times someone has told me, "I didn't have any health problems until I got the revelation that Jesus bore all my sicknesses! After I started believing and confessing that healing was in the Atonement, it seemed like I was hit with all kinds of sicknesses!"

> As you grow and your understanding of God's Word begins to increase, you will probably have many opportunities to use your faith and to resist the devil.

Others have said, "I had no financial woes until I believed what the Word of God has to say about tithes and offerings. Everything was fine financially until I started acting on the Word of God. When I began to give tithes and offerings to the Lord, everything seemed to fall to pieces!"

These are attempts of the adversary to drive you back from the land of promise. He doesn't want you to obey God's Word and experience blessing. This is exactly why the writer of Hebrews told his readers, "But call to remembrance the former days, in which, *after ye were illuminated, ye endured a great fight of afflictions*" (Hebrews 10:32).

> A fight nearly always follows illumination.

A fight nearly always follows illumination. (For more discussion on this, *see* Chapter Nine in *Living in the Combat Zone.*) When you have received revelation concerning some area of the Word of God, the enemy comes to attack almost immediately, trying to steal the Word you have just embraced.

Satan wants to make you doubt that Word so you are unable to confidently stand on it by faith.

That's why it's so important for you to realize that:

- An attack against your finances is not unique.

- An assault against your body is not unusual.

- A strike against your church is not an oddity.

This is just how the enemy works.

Satan comes to challenge you when you are gaining new ground. He waits until growth has begun; then he strikes with an unrelenting force to shove you back into spiritual despair. He wants you to retreat and back off from the frontlines of battle!

By knowing ahead of time how the enemy works, you will be mentally prepared to deal with such challenges. *Your knowledge of how and when Satan attacks will equip you to deal with these assaults more intelligently.*

> Your knowledge of how and when Satan attacks will equip you to deal with these assaults more intelligently.

In regard to these times of spiritual assault, James said, "My brethren, count it all joy when ye fall into divers temptations" (James 1:2). Notice that James doesn't say to count it all joy *if* you fall into diverse temptations. He says *when*.

The word "when" implies that these attacks *will* come. The Greek tense used here suggests that:

- These attacks normally come when you least expect them.

- They usually come from a direction you would have never dreamed of in a million years.

- They are specifically designed to catch you off guard and to take you by surprise.

From time to time, everyone comes under some type of assault. Regardless of whether the enemy's attack originates in the natural realm or the spirit realm, the important thing for you to know is how to respond when such an attack commences against you.

James doesn't warn us of this in order to inspire fear in us. Instead, he forewarns us of this reality so that when attacks do come, we will not be shocked and taken off guard and thus thrown into a state of confusion and discouragement. *We are to anticipate such attacks.*

The devil does not want you to make spiritual progress in your life, and he will try to stop you dead in your tracks! If nothing else, these attacks prove that you are making headway in your spiritual life and are becoming a threat to the security of the kingdom of darkness. Otherwise, these unseen enemies would leave you alone.

Thus, a large portion of spiritual warfare is mental preparation. If you are mentally prepared and alert to the way the enemy operates and to the potential of attack, you have already eliminated half the battle.

Constant mental preparation is the major key for dealing with potential attacks from the demonic realm. If we are

> If you are mentally prepared and alert to how the enemy operates and to the potential of attack, you have already eliminated half the battle.

mentally alert to this possibility, and if we understand that these attacks occur when we are becoming more illuminated concerning the Word and our place in Christ, we will be better positioned to guard against and to overcome these assaults.

Mental preparation removes the element of surprise. This will always give you the upper hand against the enemy.

ATTACKS AGAINST CHURCHES AND MINISTRIES

Consider these questions for a moment:

- How many local churches and independent ministries have been struck with destruction just when they were about to accomplish something significant for God?

- How many pastors have returned home from a time of vacation and relaxation, only to discover that sabotage occurred in the leadership of the church while they were away?

- How many local churches have been in the middle of a building program when suddenly the church family became divided by behavior that was completely out of character for that body of believers?

- How many ministries and churches have moved forward in faith toward the fulfillment of their God-given vision, only to have the finances of the ministry bottom out on them with no warning whatsoever?

Here is what we must understand: *As long as we do nothing for God, we can be confident that we will face no challenge from the enemy.* However, when we begin to do what God has called us to do and start experiencing a measure of success in it, we must stay mentally alert and aware! Countless churches have been split and destroyed right when they were on the verge of fulfilling their vision and accomplishing something important for the Kingdom of God.

> As long as we do nothing for God, we can be confident that we will face no challenge from the enemy.

The devil waits for an opportune moment to strike!

This is why Luke tells us that when Jesus' temptation in the wilderness was over, the devil "...departed from Him until an opportune time" (Luke 4:13 *NKJV*). The implication is that the devil would return to attack again — but he would wait for the moment when an attack was better suited for his purposes.

Remember, the violent winds that swept in to destroy Jesus and His disciples came at the very moment when Jesus' ship was headed toward the country of the Gadarenes (Mark 4:35-41).

Once Jesus reached the shores of the Gadarenes, He was going to cast a legion of demons out of the demoniac of Gadara. This would be one of the greatest miracles of His earthly ministry. Satan knew that Jesus was going to perform this miracle, and he knew he was about to lose a prized possession — *the demoniac.* Therefore, the enemy struck with all his fury to abort the miracle-working power of God.

In the same way, the devil loves to strike local churches and ministries when they are about to come to the shores of their own "Gadara," where the miracle-working power of God will be unloosed in the lives of the people involved. Satan doesn't want *any* ministry or church to move into the blessings of God!

Beware, therefore, when your vision is finally within your reach. Never let down your guard, for this may be the "opportune moment" when the devil seeks to deal a mortal wound to your church or ministry.

However, be confident in this: No matter what attack the devil levels against you — whether he attacks the church leadership, assaults the church finances, or causes strife and discord to erupt among church members — God is able to make all of these devastating devices work for your good.

For instance, the devil may incite spiritual sabotage among the church leadership while the pastor is away. Yet in the end, the devil has actually positioned the pastor to discover whom he can and cannot trust. It is good that this has occurred now rather than later when the damage could have been much more devastating. Thus, by acting to disrupt and destroy, *the devil overplayed his hand!*

Likewise, the enemy may have attacked your ministry with financial distress, causing you to put your plans of growth and expansion on hold. But even this wicked device will turn out in your favor! While things are on hold, God may reveal a far more expedient way to fulfill your vision. He may show you a method and a plan that will be easier for you to handle — one that will cost you less money in the end. You'll discover that once again, *the devil overplayed his hand!*

Satan hates the Church of Jesus Christ! In his view, we are a menace from Heaven that has invaded territory once secured by the domain of darkness. To discourage us and stop us from making further inroads into this earthly sphere, the devil will make every effort to attack and destroy the Church.

> Regardless of what the devil does in his attempts to hurt the work of God, we are called to remain faithful and to continue fighting "the good fight of faith."

But regardless of what the devil does in his attempts to hurt the work of God, we are called to remain faithful and to continue fighting "the good fight of faith." If we will do this, no attack of the enemy will ever find success in thwarting the plan of God. *God is able to make everything work for our good — even the weapons that the devil tries to use against us!*

A PATTERN OF STRIFE AND DISCORD

Attacks of strife and discord in the local church is a strategy that the enemy has universally used in the Christian community.

Concerning these types of demonic attacks, James says, "For where envying and strife is, there is confusion and every evil work" (James 3:16).

In the first place, notice that James mentions "envy." The word "envy" is from the Greek word *zelos*, and it denotes *a fierce desire to promote one's own ideas and convictions to the exclusion of everyone else's ideas*.

In order to disrupt the peaceable flow of things in the local church, the enemy may convince someone in the local church that he has a view that *must* be acknowledged and implemented by the leadership of the church. Many times this "fierce desire to promote one's own ideas and convictions to the exclusion of everyone else's ideas" becomes so strong that the person will not relent until the pastor succumbs and agrees with his point of view.

If this carnality persists, it will naturally lead to the next step in this horrible sequence of events. James says, "For where envy and *strife* is...." According to James, this "fierce desire to promote one's own ideas and convictions to the exclusion of everyone else's ideas" will naturally lead to "strife."

The word "strife" is taken from the word *eritheia*. It was used by the ancient Greeks to denote *a political party that had become entirely factioned*. This "factioning" eventually became so bad that the political party could no longer function as a whole. As a result of this internal strife, discord, and division, such divided political parties were usually deserted and abandoned. Thus, this word *eritheia* is often translated as a *party spirit*.

Why is this important to understand? It tells us that if this spiritual attack of "strife" is not dealt with severely and quickly, it is only a matter of time before the church family will be horribly divided and split by internal problems.

Ignoring the fact that the pastor is the God-appointed leader of the local church, a divisive person (not realizing he is operating under the outward influence of an evil spirit) begins to gather people around him who are willing to accept his view of things. This is the beginning of a "party spirit" inside the local church.

One group of people begins to take sides with one person's point of view as another group takes sides with someone else's point of view. Eventually the church becomes "factioned" into so many different points of view that, when all is said and done, this particular local body is no longer able to worship together.

This, then, leads to the next step in this sequence of events. James continues, "For where envying and strife is, *there is confusion....*"

The word "confusion" is taken from the word *akatastasia*. It was used in New Testament times to describe *civil disobedience, disorder, and anarchy* in a city, state, or government.

By choosing to use this word, James explicitly tells us what happens when situations of strife and discord are allowed to persist in the local church. As people begin to ignore or usurp the legitimate authority that God has given their pastor, they move into a dangerous type of lawlessness where anarchy, civil disobedience, and disorder begin to destroy the local church.

To make sure we understand where this kind of behavior will eventually lead us, James goes on to say, "For where envying and strife is, there is confusion and *every evil work*."

The word "evil" is from the word *phaulos*. The word *phaulos* describes something that is *terribly bad* or *exceedingly vile*. We derive the word "foul" from *phaulos*. When believers cooperate with this kind of divisive behavior, it always produces a "foul situation" in the local church.

Furthermore, if there is any question in your mind as to where this kind of behavior originates, James tells us! He says, "This wisdom descendeth not from above, *but is earthly, sensual, devilish*" (James 3:15).

But God has equipped us to successfully defeat these demonic attacks, whether leveled against us individually or against the local church body. He has provided us with *supernatural* weapons — everything we need to win every battle! As Paul declared, "For the weapons of our warfare are not carnal, but mighty through God to the pulling down of strong holds" (2 Corinthians 10:4).

HEAVILY DRESSED, TRAINED KILLERS

Rome, the city where Paul was held captive, was the most powerful political seat in the world at that time. It was also headquarters for the world's most highly developed, highly advanced military machine — *the Roman army*. Through this world-conquering military base, the entire civilized world had fallen prey to the Roman Empire.

Since Paul was surrounded by this huge military machine and bound to a heavily armed Roman soldier, it was therefore logical that his thoughts would turn toward the issue of spiritual warfare and spiritual armor. The environment was perfect for the Holy Spirit to begin speaking to Paul in such terms. There at Paul's side was a perfectly dressed and fully armed soldier who had been trained in the skill of warfare. This soldier was literally "dressed to kill"!

With this formidable image constantly at his side day and night, Paul began to receive exceptional spiritual insight from the Holy Spirit regarding our own spiritual weapons. He recorded this revelation for us in Ephesians 6:10-18. Yet this passage in Ephesians was not the first time Paul recorded his thoughts on the subject of spiritual armor.

About ten years earlier, when Paul was writing his first epistle to the Thessalonians around the year A.D. 54, he also wrote about spiritual weaponry. However, at that earlier time in his ministry, his understanding of spiritual armor was clearly undeveloped. At the time Paul wrote First Thessalonians, he mentioned only two pieces of spiritual weaponry: "But let us who, are of the day, be sober, putting on the breastplate of faith and love; and for an helmet, the hope of salvation" (1 Thessalonians 5:8).

It is plain to see that over the next ten years, the Holy Spirit continued to expand these ideas in Paul's heart and imparted even further revelation concerning the "weapons of our warfare" (2 Corinthians 10:4).

During his numerous imprisonments, Paul was frequently bound to a Roman soldier who kept constant watch over him. Hour after hour, day after day, and week after week, Paul lived side by side with this heavily dressed, trained killer.

As Paul sat and observed the durable loinbelt of the Roman soldier, the Holy Spirit must have begun speaking to him about the "loinbelt of truth." As his eyes moved toward the soldier's bright, shining, tightly woven breastplate of brass, the Holy Spirit began to illuminate his understanding regarding the "breastplate of righteousness."

When Paul's eyes turned downward toward the Roman soldier's dangerously spiked shoes and invincible greaves of brass, the Spirit began to open his eyes concerning the "shoes of peace." The apostle then caught a glimpse of the huge, oblong shield made of animal hide lying there at the soldier's side, and the Holy Spirit began to communicate to Paul about the "shield of faith."

As Paul looked upward and beheld the decorative helmet on the soldier's head, the Spirit of God began imparting revelation concerning the "helmet of salvation." Then turning his attention to the other side of the Roman soldier, Paul observed the man's broad, heavy, massive sword, and the Holy Spirit began to speak to him about the "sword of the Spirit."

During that ten-year period between A.D. 54 and A.D. 64, Paul's insight about spiritual armor had tremendously developed into an entire system of spiritual weaponry. Now in Ephesians 6, he tells us that, instead of having only two pieces of armor to use in our fight against the adversary, we have *six* pieces of weaponry, and perhaps even a *seventh*, since there is a possibility of an additional hidden weapon found in Ephesians 6:18.

Through his times of Roman imprisonment, Paul had become closely acquainted with the nature of the Roman soldier, who was a killer of the worst order. Once Roman soldiers retired from the military and returned to civilian life, it was not unusual at all for them to continue to kill. Murder and violence were ingrained in these men and had become a very integral part of their nature. Now Paul uses this very graphic, dangerous, and murderous example to show us what the spiritual weapons that God gives us can do to a spiritual foe.

On an average-sized Roman soldier, these pieces of weaponry (the loinbelt, breastplate, shoes with greaves, shield, helmet, sword, and possibly the lance) weighed approximately 100 pounds. The exact weight of a soldier's armor varied according to the physical stature of the soldier. If he was a large man, his armor was larger and heavier. If he was of smaller stature, his armor was proportionately smaller and therefore lighter. But regardless of their physical size, all Roman soldiers carried a very heavy amount of armor.

What kind of man would be required to wear this kind of weaponry? *A strong man!* No frail weakling would be able to stand, walk, run, or function to any degree in this kind of heavy armor. In order to wear this weaponry and to successfully wage warfare in it, the wearer would have to be extremely strong and physically fit!

> God has provided us with His supernatural power so we can effectively use the weapons of our warfare to contend with unseen, demonic powers.

Therefore, we will see that, before Paul goes into any detail about spiritual weapons, he first informs us that God has provided us with His supernatural power so we can effectively use the weapons of our warfare to contend with unseen, demonic powers. This mighty power infuses our inner man with the strength we need to reinforce Jesus' victory and demonstrate Satan's defeat in every situation of life!

QUESTIONS FOR PERSONAL GROWTH OR GROUP DISCUSSION

1. What is the primary role of the Church that makes her the devil's worst nightmare?

2. Can you think of other examples in history (besides the ones given in this chapter) where Satan's strategy to thwart God's purposes in a person's life backfired? Is there an example of this in your own life that stands out to you?

3. What is the wisest course of action for you to take when you're doing your best to follow God's will and a door slams shut in your face?

4. How did Paul respond when the devil tried to inflict a mortal wound on his life and ministry? What can you do the next time you face a seemingly insurmountable obstacle to follow Paul's example?

5. Can you think of a time in your life when the devil used strife to bring confusion and "every evil work" into the situation? How can you prepare *now* to thwart similar attacks in the future?

NOTES:

_____

_____

_____

_____

_____

_____

_____

_____

_____

_____

_____

_____

_____

_____

_____

_____

_____

_____

_____

_____

_____

_____

CHAPTER SIX

AN IMPORTANT MESSAGE
TO REMEMBER

*B*efore Paul launches into his detailed explanation of spiritual armor, he beseeches us, "Finally, my brethren, be strong in the Lord..." (Ephesians 6:10).

Notice that Paul begins this portion of Scripture about spiritual warfare and spiritual armor by saying, *"Finally...."* The word "finally" is one of the most important words in this passage. It is taken from the Greek phrase *tou loipou*, and it would be better translated *for the rest of the matter*; *in conclusion*; or *in summation.*

The phrase *tou loipou* is used in other secular Greek manuscripts of that same period to depict something so extremely important that it is held until the very end of the letter. Thus, the reader will be able to remember this one thing if he remembers nothing else of what was written.

In light of this, the word "finally" in Ephesians 6:10 carries this idea: *"In conclusion, I have saved the most important issue of this epistle until the end. That way if you remember nothing else of what I have said, you will remember this. I want this to stand out in your mind!"*

This is a remarkable statement! The book of Ephesians contains some of the most important truths and some of the most practical instructions given in the entire New Testament. The truths Paul writes to the Ephesian church are powerful, deep, detailed, and foundational to our view of Jesus Christ, the Church, ourselves, and the devil's defeated position. It is an epistle that demands our fullest attention!

For instance, in chapter 1, Paul covers some of the deepest and most-difficult-to-understand theological concepts in Christianity, such as:

- Election (1:4)

- Predestination (1:5)

- Adoption (1:5)

- The seal of the Spirit (1:13)

- The earnest of the Spirit (1:14)

- Our complete, glorified redemption (1:7,14)

And this is only in chapter 1!

Then there is chapter 2. In this powerful section of Scripture, Paul covers:

- The reality of spiritual death and its fruit (2:2,3)

- The intervention of God's rich mercy (2:4)

- The doctrine of grace versus man's works (2:8,9)

- The redemptive work of the Cross (2:11-18)

- The foundation of the apostles and prophets in the New Testament Church (2:19-22)

In chapters 3, 4, and 5, Paul deals with such profound subjects as:

- The mystery of Christ revealed (3:1-9)

- The eternal plan of God (3:10,11)

- The unity of one Spirit, one Lord, one faith, one baptism (4:4,5)

- The ministry gifts of apostles, prophets, evangelists, pastors, and teachers and their ultimate purpose (4:11-13)

- Renewing the mind and putting on the new man (4:23,24)

- Grieving the Holy Spirit (4:30)

- Being continually filled with the Spirit (5:18)

- God's plan for husbands and wives and the corresponding example of Christ and His Church (5:22-33)

Yet when you come to the end of this grand epistle that is so jam-packed with all these marvelous truths, Paul says, *"Finally..."*! He is telling us that, regardless of what we've already read, we better pay attention to what comes next in this letter!

SPIRITUALLY LOPSIDED BELIEVERS

Considering the powerful content contained in the first five chapters of Ephesians, you can surely see why I said it is so remarkable that Paul would say "finally" in Ephesians 6:10. This word indicates that he considered spiritual armor the most important subject discussed in his epistle to the Ephesian church!

At first, this fact perplexed me greatly. I asked myself:

How could the issue of spiritual armor be more important than the doctrine of election?

How could the issue of spiritual warfare be more important than the doctrine of predestination?

How is it possible that it could be more important than the doctrine of adoption?

Could understanding the subject of spiritual warfare possibly be more important than understanding the eternal plan of God?

Why would Paul save this section on spiritual armor and spiritual warfare to the very last of this powerful epistle — and then conclude that this subject is more important than any of these other truths? WHY?

Later I came to understand why Paul made this outrageous statement about spiritual warfare and spiritual armor. Generally speaking, these issues could *not* be more important than the other Bible doctrines Paul talks about in the book of Ephesians. These doctrines are *extremely important* for us to know and understand; they are *foundational* to all that we believe about the work of the Cross.

However, at this specific time and for the specific readers to whom Paul was writing, spiritual warfare and spiritual armor were *temporarily* more important for a very practical reason.

Like so many in the Church world today, the believers to whom Paul was writing had gathered together a vast accumulation of spiritual knowledge, information, and facts. Yet even with all this at their fingertips, they were still spiritually defeated in their personal lives. Although they could have answered nearly any Bible question you could have put before them, their personal lives were falling to pieces.

Ephesians 4:25-31 identifies a few of the problems that were afflicting Paul's readers. I'll mention just a few.

Paul commanded the Ephesian believers:

- "...Putting away lying, speak every man truth with his neighbour..." (4:25).

- "...Let not the sun go down upon your wrath" (4:26).

- "Neither give place to the devil" (4:27).

- "Let him that stole steal no more..." (4:28).

- "Let no corrupt communication proceed out of your mouth..." (4:29).

- "...Grieve not the holy Spirit of God..." (4:30).

- "Let all bitterness, and wrath, and anger, and clamour, and evil speaking, be put away from you, with all malice" (4:31).

Does this sound like Paul was talking to victorious people?

Do victorious people have to be told to stop lying?

Do victorious people give place to the devil in their personal lives and relationships?

Do victorious people permit corrupt communication to have a place in their conversation?

Do victorious people continuously grieve the Holy Spirit with bad attitudes such as bitterness, anger, clamor, and malice?

Naturally speaking, the churches that were situated in the Lycus Valley (one of which was the church of Ephesus) were more educated in regard to New Testament truth and doctrine than any other region during the first century. We know that the apostle Paul founded the church at Ephesus (Acts 19:1-20) and that, afterwards, he spent three years of his life raising up elders in that city (Acts 20:31). Furthermore, at some point after Paul's departure from Ephesus, Timothy arrived on the scene to serve as the pastor of the Ephesian church (1 Timothy 1:3).

If we stopped right here, this alone would have made the church of Ephesus the most unique local church in Church history. But there is more!

In addition to the roles of Paul and Timothy in the church of Ephesus, the apostle John was also a member of this church.

Moreover, when John moved his ministry base from Israel to the city of Ephesus, he moved Mary — the mother of Jesus — to the city with him, where he cared for her until her death. The mother of Jesus was a member of the church of Ephesus!

I think you can see from this how unusual the local church in Ephesus really was! You can also be certain that other great men and women of God came to minister there, since it was the largest church in existence during that day. Peter, Apollos, Aquila, and Priscilla had most assuredly ministered in this church at some point along the way.

Nevertheless, even with this abundance of excellent ministry and the accessibility of spiritual insight and knowledge, the Ephesian believers were not experiencing the overcoming, abundant life that Jesus Christ came to offer. On the contrary, their personal lives were in shambles!

Although Scripture doesn't specifically say *why* the Ephesian believers were experiencing turmoil and defeat in their personal lives, the fact that Paul reserved this text on spiritual warfare and spiritual armor for the end of his epistle implies the reason. It appears that the recipients of this letter were *spiritually lopsided.* They were mature in the realm of doctrine but had failed to develop in other critically vital areas.

The great bulk of these believers' time and energies had been spent developing doctrine and educating their minds with great and necessary scriptural truths. There was nothing wrong with this. Because of the newness of the Early Church at that time, it was very important for sound doctrine to be taught and analyzed.

In fact, studying the Word was an absolute necessity for these believers! As they began to record doctrine in those early days, it was imperative that they intensively searched and studied the Scriptures. (Anyone familiar with me or my ministry knows that I place the highest premium on the study of God's Word!)

However, while the Ephesian believers were growing in their intellectual understanding of the Word, they needed to *simultaneously* grow in their understanding of spiritual armor and spiritual conflict. They lived in a world very similar to ours today — a world full of conflict, violence, and upheaval. So even as the Early Church leaders developed, analyzed, and taught sound doctrine inside the Church at large, they also needed to equip the saints to deal with the hostile surroundings *outside* the Church.

> As the Early Church leaders developed, analyzed, and taught sound doctrine inside the Church at large, they also needed to equip the saints to deal with the hostile surroundings outside the Church.

These early Christians needed to start acting on the knowledge they had obtained.

- They had to learn how to take their intellectual understanding of the Word of God and turn it into a "sword of the Spirit."

- They desperately needed to grab hold of the faith they intellectually possessed and turn it into a "shield of faith."

- Their knowledge of salvation had to be forged into a "helmet of salvation."

- Their understanding of God's marvelous grace still needed to be transformed into a "breastplate of righteousness."

This was the backdrop against which Paul wrote his letter to the church at Ephesus. This is why Paul begins his text on spiritual warfare and spiritual armor by saying in essence, *"I've saved the most important part of this epistle for the end so that, if you remember nothing else, you will remember this!"*

Comrades in the Fight

As Paul continues on in Ephesians 6:10, he says, "Finally, *my brethren....*"

Now we come to the word "brethren." This is another very significant New Testament word that is overlooked and misunderstood. The word "brethren" is of tremendous importance to the issue of spiritual armor and spiritual warfare — so much so that we must back up for a moment and study this word before we go any further in Ephesians chapter 6.

The word "brethren" is taken from the Greek word *adelphos*, one of the oldest words in the New Testament. In its most frequent usage, *adelphos* simply means *brother*. However, the word "brethren" has a much deeper meaning than this.

In its very oldest sense, the word *adelphos* was used by physicians in the medical world to describe two people who were born from the same womb. So when the early Greeks addressed each other as "brethren," they meant to convey this idea: *"You and I are truly brothers! We came out of the same womb of humanity. We have the same feelings; we have similar emotions; and we deal with the same problems in life."*

At least in part, this was Paul's thinking when he addressed his readers as "brethren." By using this word, he was putting himself on the same level as his readers, identifying with both their personal struggles and their victories.

But this is not all there is to the word "brethren." Pay careful attention, because the following discussion will shed important light on the full meaning of this word.

The word "brother" (*adelphos*) wasn't used in a popular sense, as we use it today in the Body of Christ, until the time of Alexander the Great. During this time period, the word "brother" began to take on a new, militaristic twist to its meaning. Given that Ephesians 6:10-18 is a text about spiritual warfare and spiritual armor, there is no doubt that Paul also had this militaristic idea in his mind when he addressed his readers as "brethren."

Alexander the Great was irrefutably the finest soldier the world has ever known. By the age of 18, he had already conquered the entire eastern empire. By the time he was 33 years old, the western empire had also fallen into his hands. Alexander the Great had conquered nearly the entire civilized world of his day — from Europe to the northern end of Africa, reaching over into Greece, Turkey, and Asia, all the way to the western border of India. In a single military strike against the Persians, Alexander overcame 40,000 Persian aggressors, losing only 110 of his own fighting men.

The fame and notoriety of this young and powerful man of war was so widespread and revered that soldiers from all over his far-flung empire desired to have some kind of personal acquaintance with him. To know Alexander personally and to earn his recognition was the highest honor a military man could receive.

Therefore, on very special occasions, Alexander would host ceremonies. During these ceremonies, he would summon especially brave, hard-working soldiers onto a giant platform to stand at his side. Then Alexander would ceremonially give public recognition to these special soldiers who had fought so hard and had gone the extra mile in battle.

Before a large audience of adoring military men, Alexander would place his arm around individual faithful fighters one at a time and would publicly declare, "Let all the empire know that Alexander is proud to be the *brother* of this soldier." Thus, the word "brother," as it was used during Alexander's time, also carried the idea of *comrade* or *a fellow soldier*.

With this in mind, we know that the word "brother" portrays the picture of two soldiers who are fighting in the same fight and who share similar feelings, desires, and fears, just as two brothers born from the same womb do. Yet these brother soldiers have learned how to overcome their emotions and gain the victory in the midst of difficult attacks and confrontations.

If these men called someone a "brother," it meant that he was a true *comrade*. Through it all, these soldiers stayed together, united in the heat of the fray. Consequently, they achieved a special level of "brotherhood" that only soldiers know.

> "Like me, you are still in the fight and are giving it your best shot. Therefore, I am personally proud to be affiliated with people like you."

We can see, then, that Paul was imparting a powerful message to his readers when he addressed them as "my brethren." He was saying, *"We all came out of the same womb of humanity, and we share similar feelings, struggles, and emotions in life. Nevertheless, we have not been conquered by these things. Like me, you are still in the fight and are giving it your best shot. Therefore, I am personally proud to be affiliated with people like you. We are brothers!"*

SOLDIERS WHO ARE WORTHY OF YOUR ASSOCIATION

Even though the Ephesian believers were obviously struggling in their personal lives when Paul wrote them, they hadn't given up the fight! They were still in there, slugging it out and plodding along one step at a time.

This kind of ongoing commitment to stay in the battle is a key characteristic of believers who are worth knowing and affiliating with. Regardless of how well or how badly these believers are doing in the midst of their fight, *at least they still keep fighting*! Others have given up, but they have not. According to Paul, these are the very kind of people whom we should view as *comrades* in the faith!

This is particularly good news for you if you're going through a difficult time right now. The adversary may try to accuse you of being a spiritual failure because you haven't yet achieved total victory in your life. But as long as you remain faithful to the fight and refuse to relinquish your stance of faith against the enemy, you are *still* an exceptionally fine soldier! You are the very kind of soldier whom any believer should be happy to know and associate with!

> It isn't how well we fight that really counts in life. What really counts is that we keep on fighting.

So here is the bottom line regarding the word "brethren," used by Paul in this final, crucial section of his letter to the Ephesians: It isn't how well we fight that really counts in life. *What really counts is that we keep on fighting.* This "never-give-up" kind of attitude will eventually produce victory for us every time!

Questions for Personal Growth or Group Discussion

1. What are some of the common characteristics between the world of the early Christians and our modern world? What do these similarities tell us about the priority we should set on understanding the nature of true spiritual warfare?

2. In what way were the Ephesian believers spiritually lopsided? Can you think of an example of this same spiritual condition in the modern Church or in your own personal experience?

3. Why is it so important for us to develop a sense of unity as fellow comrades in this fight of faith?

4. What is a key characteristic that fellow believers should possess if you are going to closely associate with them?

5. Can you think of instances in your life that demonstrate the presence of this key characteristic in *your* life?

Notes:

_____

_____

_____

_____

_____

_____

_____

_____

_____

_____

_____

_____

_____

_____

_____

_____

_____

_____

_____

_____

_____

_____

CHAPTER SEVEN

BE STRONG IN THE LORD

efore Paul begins his message on our spiritual armor, he first urges us to receive supernatural power! Continuing in Ephesians 6:10, he says, "Finally, my brethren, *be strong in the Lord....*" In this chapter, we are going to see what Paul has to say about this supernatural power that God has made available to us.

So what exactly does it mean to be "strong in the Lord"?

First, the word "strong" is taken from the word *endunamoo*, which is a compound of the Greek words *en* and *dunamis*. The word *en* means *in* and the word *dunamis* means *explosive strength, ability, or power*. The word *dunamis* is where we get the word "dynamite."

When these two words are compounded together, the new word *endunamoo* describes *an empowering* or *an inner strengthening*. It conveys the idea of *being infused with an excessive dose of dynamic inner strength and ability*.

Because the first part of *endunamoo* means *in* or *into* and the second part depicts *explosive power*, it is easy to conclude that this word portrays *a power that is being deposited into something*, such as a container, a vessel, or some other form of receptacle.

The very nature of this word emphatically means that there necessarily must be some type of *receiver* for this *power* to be deposited *into*. This is where *we* come into the picture!

We are specially designed by God to be the receptacles for His divine power. This is the reason Paul urges us, "Finally, my brethren, *be strong....*" His words carry the idea, *"Receive a supernatural strengthening, an internal deposit of power into your inner man."* God is the Giver of this explosive power, and according to Ephesians 6:10, we are the receptacles *into* which this *power* is to be deposited.

> We are specially designed by God to be the receptacles for His divine power.

The Greek tense used in Ephesians 6:10 is the *present passive imperative*. This means Paul was not simply suggesting that they receive this power; he was *commanding* them to receive it and, furthermore, to receive it as soon as possible.

There is no question about Paul's intentions in this verse. The usage of the *present imperative tense* means he was urging them in the strongest of words; he was commanding them to open their hearts to receive a brand-new touch of God's power into their lives.

In addition to the *present imperative tense*, Paul also uses the *passive tense* in his command to "be strong." The *passive tense* describes the ongoing, lasting effect of this power upon a believer's life. This tense tells us that, although there is an immediate strengthening effect when God's special *endunamoo* power is released in a believer's life, it is more than a one-shot experience. This is a supernatural power that *continues* to strengthen that believer for a long, long time to come.

Paul knew that there is an ongoing experience with God's power that is available to all believers. Paul also knew we desperately need this special touch of supernatural power in order to successfully combat the attacks that the enemy brings against us in this life.

In light of these truths, Paul urges us to open ourselves to God — spirit, soul, and body — so we can receive His supernatural strength. In fact, Paul's desire for us to receive this power is so earnest that he uses the *present passive imperative tense*. Again, he is not *suggesting* that we receive this power; he is *commanding us* to receive it — and to receive it just as quickly as possible.

In a very strong, authoritative tone of voice, Paul commands all believers everywhere:

- *"Be infused with supernatural strength and ability."*

- *"Be empowered with this special touch of God's strength."*

- *"You must receive this inner strengthening!"*

Why was Paul so strong on this point? Because he knew that we need to receive this power before our fight with unseen forces commences. Without the supernatural power of the Holy Spirit operating in us, not one of us can ever be a match against Satan's wily schemes and devices or against the demon spirits that come to war against our souls.

Satan is intelligent, keen, brilliant, canny, cunning, quick, brainy, and shrewd. He is strong, capable, puissant, influencing, and determined. He is a wise strategist, orderly planning and arranging systematic assaults against humanity. He is the epitome of an opportunist, knowing exactly when to strike with his destructive power.

> Without the supernatural power of the Holy Spirit operating in us, not one of us can ever be a match against Satan's wily schemes and devices.

Naturally speaking, our physical strength doesn't even begin to compare with the devil's strength. Our intelligence doesn't begin to touch his brilliancy. Our wittiest moment is thoroughly deficient compared with the enemy's shrewd methods of thinking and operating.

Satan was a powerful, brilliant angel before he fell into his present perverted condition. And although fallen, he has still retained much of his former intelligence that was originally given to him by God.

It is true that Jesus stripped Satan of his *legal authority* over us; nevertheless, his *intelligence* remains intact. It is that cunning, keen, sharp, wily, brainy mind that the devil uses against us today. Satan's power is no match for the all-surpassing power of the Holy Spirit, and he knows it. Therefore, he seeks to outwit our natural minds with malevolent strategies that he has invented with his incredibly intelligent mind.

To stop these satanic strategies, we must receive God's special empowering from on High. When the Holy Spirit's supernatural strength is released within us, we are empowered to deal victoriously with this archenemy of the faith. That is why Paul commanded the Early Church to receive this special power — and now the Word of God gives us the same specific and urgent command: "Finally, my brethren, *be strong....*"

> When the Holy Spirit's supernatural strength is released within us, we are empowered to deal victoriously with this archenemy of the faith.

Remember, this is no suggestion on the part of Paul; this is a *direct command*.

SUPERHUMAN POWER FOR A SUPERHUMAN TASK

The word *endunamoo* ("strong") was frequently used by classical Greek writers to describe individuals who had been very carefully handpicked by the gods to perform extra-special, superhuman tasks.

For instance, writers from the classical Greek period would have said that the superhuman strength of the legendary character, Hercules, was the result of the pagan Greek gods' depositing *endunamoo* power into him. *Endunamoo* was perfectly suited to illustrate the kind of supernatural strength that Hercules supposedly possessed. Legend says that with this endowment from the pagan Greek gods, Hercules performed many extra-special, superhuman feats.

The apostle Paul was an exceptionally brilliant and educated man. From his own studies in classical Greek, he undoubtedly knew this historical usage of the word *endunamoo*. So when discussing the supernatural power that the Holy Spirit gives us to withstand the work of the adversary, Paul deliberately chose this word that had unmistakable connotations — denoting a power that turns mere men into champions who possess superhuman, supernatural strength.

Furthermore, *endunamoo* is a power that is bestowed on an individual *when he is called to perform a special task at hand that is beyond his natural abilities and that requires superhuman strength.*

Why did Paul begin this text on spiritual warfare and spiritual armor with this command to receive this *endunamoo* strength? The reason is clear: Paul assuredly believed that our only hope of reinforcing Jesus' victory and demonstrating Satan's defeat is by receiving the help of this special, supernatural power.

> **Our only hope of reinforcing Jesus' victory and demonstrating Satan's defeat is by receiving the help of this special, supernatural power.**

Paul knew emphatically — beyond any shadow of a doubt — that when God's power is released full force into the life of a believer, His supernatural flow of power will turn that normal believer into a spiritual giant! Therefore, Paul commands every believer in the strongest of terms:

- *"Be empowered!"*

- *"Receive this inner strengthening!"*

- *"Be infused with God's supernatural strength and ability!"*

WHERE TO GET THIS POWER

Paul continues, "Finally, my brethren, be strong *in the Lord....*"

The phrase "in the Lord" is grammatically called the *locative tense*. Simply put, this means that this special power (*endunamoo*) can be found only one place — and that is *"in the Lord."*

The fact that Paul wrote in the *locative tense* tells us that this power is "locked up" in the Person of Jesus Christ and that this power cannot be found anywhere else. We cannot obtain this special, supernatural power by reading books, listening to teaching tapes, or by any other such means. Thank God for good teaching tapes and books, but this special power can be obtained only through a personal relationship with the Lord Jesus Christ. This power is locked up *"in the Lord."*

The first chapter of Ephesians also uses the *locative tense*. In fact, this same locative tense is used seven times in Ephesians 1 to teach that we are "in Christ" (1:3,4,6,7,11,13). Doctrinally, this means that once we are redeemed by Jesus Christ, we are "locked up" in the Person of Jesus forever! As Paul told the Corinthians, "But he that is joined unto the Lord is *one spirit*" (1 Corinthians 6:17). Or as Paul told his audience on Mars Hill, "For in him we live, and move, and have our being..." (Acts 17:28).

> We are perpetually, endlessly, and infinitely "locked up" in the Person of Jesus Christ. He has become our realm of existence and habitation.

This wonderful locative tense is used seven times in Ephesians 1 to declare that we are perpetually, endlessly, and infinitely "locked up" in the Person of Jesus Christ. He has become our realm of existence and habitation. For all eternity, we are "in Him."

Now we can see why this special *endunamoo* power of God is so very accessible to you and me. Just as this divine power — this supernatural inner strengthening that turns normal people into spiritual giants — is gloriously "locked up" in the Person of Jesus Christ, *so are we!* As believers, we are locked up "in the Lord" — along with His special, divine power!

Although we may not always be mentally aware of it, we are constantly rubbing elbows with this divine power on a day-to-day, hour-to-hour, and minute-to-minute basis. The very fact that both we and this special power are locked up "in the Lord" means we are never far away from a fresh surge of superhuman power into our own human spirits. In fact, a new release of God's power within us is as accessible as our very next breath of air!

> A new release of God's power within us is as accessible as our very next breath of air!

It's Yours for the Taking

Several years ago at a large church in the Midwest, I was preaching about this divine flow of power and its accessibility to the believer. At the end of the morning service, I gave an invitation for people who had never been filled with the Holy Spirit, and many people came forward for prayer.

As I approached the altar to pray with those who had come forward, the pastor turned to me and said, "This morning I want you to watch the way we pray for people to be filled with the Holy Spirit. By observing the way it is done in our church, you can flow better with the training our altar workers have received on how to pray for people to receive the infilling of the Spirit."

Complying with the pastor's request, I stepped back to watch as his workers began to pray for people to be filled with the Holy Spirit. One after another, the workers walked behind the people who were kneeling at the altar, patting their backs and saying things like:

- *"You have to pray much harder than you're praying."*

- *"You're not praying loud enough."*

- *"You must cry and plead to receive from God."*

- *"You must tarry here a little longer."*

I was heartbroken as I watched what was happening. These precious, spiritually hungry people had come forward to freely receive from God, but what could have been a beautiful experience had changed into a nightmare. These sincere, incorrectly instructed people began to vehemently beat themselves up spiritually in order to make themselves feel "good enough" to receive from God and be filled with the Spirit.

What a deplorable sight this was to me! To see the infilling of the Holy Spirit reduced to a work of the flesh was disgusting — especially because I knew that the infilling of the Holy Spirit is a work of grace and not of human effort. It was one of the most spiritually obnoxious sights I have ever observed in a church setting.

God knew that He had to make it simple for us to receive His power; otherwise, the majority of us would never receive it. Knowing this about us, God permanently "locked up" His power inside the Person of Jesus Christ, and then He "locked *us* up" in Christ as well! By doing this for us, God placed us in a position to rub elbows with His divine power *continuously*. He graciously fixed it so it would be very difficult for us *not* to freely receive this impartation of superhuman, supernatural strength for the fight.

To experience God's ever-available, ever-accessible power, you must open your heart to it and ask that it be released in your life. By *faith* you must reach out to embrace this special divine power, for because of your position "in the Lord," you are surrounded by it *right now*. At this precise moment, you are immersed in God's supernatural power. *It is yours for the taking!*

> At this precise moment, you are immersed in God's supernatural power. It is yours for the taking!

The only prerequisite to receive this power is that you are "in the Lord." If you are "in Him," as the first chapter of Ephesians speaks of seven times, you are in position — *right now* — to receive a fresh touch of God's strengthening power into your life!

EVIDENCE OF THE HOLY SPIRIT'S POWER

But how can we tell when God's supernatural strength is operating in our lives? Paul answers us in Ephesians 6:10 when he says, "Finally, my brethren, be strong in the Lord, *and in the power of his might.*"

Growing up as a Southern Baptist, I heard many discussions about the Holy Spirit in my home church — discussions about what we believed and what we did *not* believe about the Holy Spirit. As Southern Baptists, we were adamantly opposed to the Pentecostal view that speaking in tongues was *the initial evidence* of the Holy Spirit's empowering.

From our theological point of view, the Pentecostals didn't have a leg to stand on. Although they had many scriptures to prove that speaking in tongues was the evidence of the Spirit's empowering, we believed that we could easily explain away those verses in just a few moments of time.

We believed that speaking in tongues was a phenomenon designed only for the time period referred to in the book of Acts — a special, never-to-be-repeated "transitional period" that lasted only long enough to help the Church get started. According to our view, healing, miracles, and speaking in tongues were given only for this "transitional period" and were never intended to last indefinitely or to be repeated again.

Rather than believe in what we thought were utterly non-intellectual, unintelligible, ecstatic, ridiculous utterances called "tongues," we had our *own evidence* of being empowered by the

Holy Spirit. And just like the Pentecostals, we also had scriptures to back up our theological point of view.

We declared that the *real* evidence of the Holy Spirit's power in a believer's life was the ability to be a "witness" for Jesus Christ. The proof text for this was Acts 1:8, which says, "But ye shall receive power, after that the Holy Ghost is come upon you: and ye shall be *witnesses* unto me both in Jerusalem, and in all Judaea, and in Samaria, and unto the uttermost part of the earth."

So on one hand, the Pentecostals said that *the initial evidence* of the Spirit's indwelling power was the ability to speak in tongues. On the other hand, my former denomination taught that the evidence of the Holy Spirit's power was the ability to be a witness for Jesus Christ.

To be absolutely fair to both Pentecostals and Southern Baptists, I want to stress that, in a measure, they are both correct in their views. Both of these external signs are *evidences* of the Spirit's abiding power in the life of a believer.

Speaking in tongues is definitely the initial evidence of the fresh, infilling presence of the Holy Spirit's power in the life of a believer. The book of Acts reveals our pattern for this truth. God never intended for this book of the Bible to simply relate the events of a "transitional period" that lasted until the Church got her feet on the ground. There is absolutely no scripture for this fictional, manmade, so-called "transitional period." Any honest theologian would admit that. This doctrine (which is embraced by many denominations) was designed to excuse the Church for her powerlessness and for her lack of the supernatural.

However, it is also true that becoming a witness for Jesus Christ is a subsequent, bona fide proof of the Spirit's ongoing, empowering presence. Jesus Himself stated this in Acts 1:8. *This scripture is so clear that no one can dispute the truth that the Holy Spirit's power always produces strong witnesses.*

Yet becoming an effective witness for Jesus is not the *initial* evidence that one has been filled with the Holy Spirit. According to the New Testament pattern recorded in the Book of Acts, the initial evidence is speaking in tongues.

The ability to witness is one of many subsequent evidences that follows after we are initially filled with the Holy Spirit. This same category of subsequent evidences also includes the fruit of the Spirit, the gifts of the Spirit, etc.

KRATOS POWER

But in Ephesians 6:10, Paul gives another very important subsequent evidence of the Spirit's empowering work in our lives! He says, "Finally, my brethren, be strong in the Lord, *and in the power of his might.*"

Let me first remind you that Ephesians 6:10 is a verse about the supernatural power that God has made available for our fight with unseen, demonic powers that come to war against the soul. As we discussed, the word "strong" in Ephesians 6:10 is taken from the word *endunamoo*, which describes *a power designed to infuse a believer with an excessive dose of inward strength.* This particular type of *endunamoo* power is so strong that it can withstand any attack and can successfully oppose any kind of force.

We saw that the supernatural nature of this word can be historically proven, as it was used by early writers from the Greek classical periods to denote special individuals, like Hercules, who had been handpicked by the gods and were supernaturally invested with superhuman strength in order to accomplish a superhuman task.

This is the kind of "strength" that God has made available to *us!*

But now let's see what else Paul has to say about this power. He goes on to say in verse 10, "Finally, my brethren, be strong in the Lord, *and in the power of his might."*

Especially notice the words "power" and "might." These two words are extremely important for you to understand as you progress in your understanding of spiritual warfare and spiritual armor.

The word "power" is taken from the Greek word *kratos*, and it describes what I have come to call *demonstrated power.* In other words, *kratos* power is not a power that you merely adhere to and believe in intellectually. Rather, this *kratos* power is a power that is *demonstrative, eruptive,* and *tangible.* It almost always comes with some type of external, outward manifestation that one can actually see with his or her own eyes. This means that *kratos* power is not a hypothetical power. On the contrary, this power is *very real.*

Ephesians 1:19,20 declares that when God raised Jesus from the dead, He used this very same *kratos* power: "And what is the exceeding greatness of his power to us-ward who believe, according to the working of his mighty power, which he wrought in Christ, when he raised him from the dead...." The *King James* sentence structure is a bit reversed from the original Greek. The Greek says, "...according to the working of *the power of his might....*"

Why is this so significant? Because "the power of his might" is the identical phrase used in Ephesians 6:10 to denote the power that is working behind the scenes to energize us for our combat with unseen, evil powers. Think of that! The kind of power that God used when He raised Jesus from the dead is the very same, exact, identical power that is now at work in us! *We have resurrection power!*

Kratos power refers to the strongest flow of power that exists in the entire universe. In fact, this power is so supreme that in Scripture, it is used only in reference to *God's* power. Man does not possess this kind of power — *unless it has been given to him by God!*

Kratos power is so overwhelming that the mighty Roman soldiers who were guarding Jesus' tomb on resurrection morning fainted and crumbled to the ground beneath the full load of this supernatural force. There they lay — prostrate on the ground, paralyzed, and unable to move — until Jesus' resurrection was complete!

> The kind of power that God used when He raised Jesus from the dead is the very same, exact, identical power that is now at work in us!

Consider how indomitable, overpowering, conquering, and irresistible this *kratos* power was when it flooded the grave where Jesus' dead body lay. The resurrection power of God literally permeated every dead cell and fiber of Jesus' body with divine life — until it became *impossible* for death to hold Him!

Had you been present at Jesus' resurrection, you would have felt the ground trembling as this electrifying force — this overwhelming *kratos* power — entered the tomb where Jesus' body lay. Then you would have watched as this *kratos* power raised Jesus from the dead! This was an *eruptive* power, a *demonstrated* power, an *outwardly visible* power. *It was the strongest kind of power known to God or man!*

And now Paul uses this very word to describe the power that is available for *our* use! In fact, Paul emphatically tells us that if we have had the experience of being filled with the Holy Spirit, this *kratos* power will be *another evidence* of the Spirit's empowering work in our lives.

This is why Paul says, "Finally, my brethren, be strong in the Lord, and in the *kratos....*" The operation of this *kratos* power in a believer's life is evidence that he has been supernaturally empowered by the Spirit of God. Only divinely empowered people possess this *kratos* power.

When the empowering presence of the Holy Spirit is operative in our lives, it releases in us the very same power that physically raised Jesus Christ from the dead. *This kratos power is an eruptive, demonstrative, outwardly visible and manifested kind of power — the kind that we can see and that we will experience.*

This tells us that as soon as this *kratos* power begins to operate in us, it immediately seeks an avenue of release so that it might *demonstrate* itself. In other words, God doesn't give us *kratos* so we can sit idly by and do nothing in life. This power comes to enable us to accomplish some type of *superhuman task*.

Paul knew that, before he could ever begin discussing warfare with unseen forces or the armor of God, he first had to cover the issue of power. Why? Because without this power operating in our spiritual lives, we can't engage in battle with the enemy. We cannot stand against the deeds of darkness in our own strength — *it's an impossibility.* Furthermore, we do not have the strength in ourselves to carry the heavy armor of God we so desperately need in our campaign against the wiles of the devil.

> God doesn't give us *kratos* power so we can sit idly by and do nothing in life. This power comes to enable us to accomplish some type of superhuman task.

Therefore, Paul puts first things first and begins this text on armor by first dealing with the *kratos* power of God.

Without this *kratos* power, we are no match for the adversary and we cannot function in the armor of God. On the other hand, when we have this power at our disposal, the

> When we have this power at our disposal, the devil is no match for us. We are well able to overcome his strategies with the armor God has provided!

devil is no match for *us*. We are *well* able to overcome his strategies with the armor God has provided!

God's Mighty Arm!

Paul continues, "Finally, my brethren, be strong in the Lord, and in the power of *his might*."

The word "might" is taken from the word *ischuos*, and it conveys the picture of *an extremely strong man*, such as a bodybuilder; *a man who is able*; *a man who is mighty*; or *a man with great muscular capabilities*.

Now Paul applies this picture of a strong, muscular man — not to himself, but *to God*! He pictures God as One who is *able*, *mighty*, and *muscular*. So ponder these questions:

- Is there anyone more powerful than God?

- Is there anyone more able than God?

- Is there any force in the universe equal to the muscular ability of God?

With one stroke of His hand, God's mighty arm released so much creative power that the entire universe was flung into being.

With one stroke of His hand, God's mighty arm unloosed so much power that Nimrod and all his wicked cohorts at the Tower of Babel were scattered across the face of the earth.

With one stroke of His hand, God's mighty arm discharged such a powerful force that the civilized world of Noah's day was flooded, and an entire period of civilization was wiped out.

With one stroke of God's mighty arm, such overwhelming power was released that the cities of Sodom and Gomorrah were forever wiped off the face of the earth by fire and brimstone.

With one stroke of God's mighty arm, Egypt's rebellion against God was crushed beyond recognition and the children of Israel were set free.

With one stroke of God's mighty arm, the turbulent, raging Red Sea walls of water collapsed and came tumbling down to swallow up the pursuing chariots of Pharaoh.

With one stroke of God's mighty arm, the wicked powers of the heavenlies were forcibly shoved aside and, although it was physically and medically impossible, Jesus was conceived and miraculously born from a virgin's womb.

With one stroke of God's mighty arm, His power surged into the caverns of hell itself and ripped Jesus out of the pangs of death, stripping principalities and powers naked and making a public display of their embarrassing defeat.

When the mighty arm of God moved on the Day of Pentecost, the Holy Spirit came as a "mighty rushing wind" and filled the Upper Room with His awesome power, supernaturally empowering the disciples to preach the Word while accompanied by signs and wonders.

Today this same mighty arm of God is still working throughout the earth. Where is His powerful, able, mighty muscular ability working today? *In you and me!* Paul's words still apply directly to us when he says, "Finally, my brethren, be strong in the Lord, *and in the power of his might."*

The reason *kratos* power is so powerful and demonstrative (as in the resurrection of Jesus from the dead) is that God's muscles *(ischuos)* are backing it up! Thus, one expositor accurately translates Ephesians 6:10 this way: *"...Be strong in the Lord and in the powerful, outwardly demonstrated ability that works in you as a result of God's great muscular ability."*

All that God is — all the power He possesses and all the energy of His muscular and mighty ability — energizes the *kratos* power that is now at work in believers who have been empowered by the Holy Spirit. And *this* is the power that is at work within you and me!

Questions for Personal Growth or Group Discussion

1. What is the end result of any situation in which we try to take care of our problems using our own strength and natural reasoning?

2. Why are the last three words in Paul's command to "be strong *in the Lord*" so significant for your walk with God?

3. Describe the "transitional period" doctrine that some hold and why that belief hinders a Christian's ability to walk in the supernatural power of God.

4. What are the qualities of *kratos* power that make it different than any other kind of power in the universe?

5. Can you think of a time in your life or in the life of someone you know when the working of God's mighty arm brought deliverance from a strong attack of the enemy?

NOTES:

CHAPTER EIGHT

THE WILES, DEVICES, AND DECEPTION OF THE DEVIL

With God's mighty, supernatural *kratos* power at our disposal, we are now *ready for battle*. We can commence our successful confrontation with unseen demonic spirits that come to wage war against the flesh and the soul!

For this reason, Paul goes on to tell us, "Put on the whole armour of God, that ye may be able to stand against the wiles of the devil" (Ephesians 6:11).

Later we're going to discuss at great length the *wiles, devices,* and *deception* of the devil. But first, let's talk about the phrase "whole armor." That phrase is taken from the Greek word *panoplia,* and it refers to *a Roman soldier who is fully dressed in his armor from head to toe*. Since this is the example Paul puts before us, we must consider the full dress, the *panoplia,* of the Roman soldier.

Because of Paul's many imprisonments, this was an easy illustration for him to use. Standing next to these impressive-looking soldiers during his prison internments, Paul could see the Roman soldier's *loinbelt; huge breastplate; brutal shoes affixed* with spikes; massive, full-length shield; intricate helmet; piercing sword; and long, specially tooled lance that could be thrown a tremendous distance to hit the enemy from afar.

The Roman soldier of New Testament times wore all seven pieces of this armor. These pieces of weaponry, which include both offensive and defensive armor, can still be found in our museums today.

First of all, the Roman soldier wore *a loinbelt*. Although it was the least impressive and most commonplace piece of weaponry that the Roman soldier wore, *it was the central piece of armor that held all the other parts together*. For instance, the loinbelt held the breastplate in place; the shield rested on a clip on one side of the loinbelt; and on the other side was another clip on which the Roman soldier hung his massive sword when it wasn't in use.

This first piece of armor was so ordinary that no soldier would have written home to tell his family about his new loinbelt. Yet the loinbelt was the most important piece of weaponry the Roman soldier owned because of its importance to the other pieces of armor. Without it, the other pieces of weaponry would have fallen off the soldier! (We will cover more on the "loinbelt of truth" in Chapter Ten.)

The Roman soldier also wore a second weapon — *a magnificent and beautiful breastplate*. The breastplate of the Roman soldier was made out of two large sheets of metal. One piece covered the front of the soldier, and the other piece covered his back; then these two sheets of metal were attached at the top of the soldier's shoulders by large brass rings.

Frequently these metal plates were comprised of smaller, scale-like pieces of metal, causing the surface of the breastplate to look very similar to the scales of a fish. Later on, the breastplate was most often referred to as a "coat of mail."

This heavy piece of weaponry began at the bottom of the neck and extended down past the waist to the knees. From the waist to the knees, it took on the resemblance of a skirt. The breastplate was by far the heaviest piece of equipment that the Roman soldier owned. Depending upon the physical stature of the soldier, this piece of equipment could weigh in excess of 40 pounds! In First Samuel 17:5, we are told that Goliath's breastplate weighed "five thousand shekels of brass" — or the equivalent of 125 pounds! (This "breastplate of righteousness" is the topic of Chapter Eleven.)

In addition to this beautiful coat of mail, the Roman soldier also wore a third weapon — *a pair of very dangerous shoes.* These shoes were *not* like the Roman sandals that people wear today, which are merely a flimsy little piece of twine wrapped around the heel and the toe. The shoes that the Roman soldier wore were primarily made of two pieces of metal.

The first piece of the Roman shoe was called a *greave.* This was a piece of bronze or brass that had been wrapped around the soldier's lower legs. Beginning right at the top of the knee, it extended down past the calf of the leg and rested on top of the foot. Because this tube-like piece of metal covered the lower leg of the soldier, the Roman soldier's shoes looked like boots that were made of brass!

In addition, the top, sides, and bottom of the foot were encased in a very thick piece of heavy metal. On the bottom, the Roman soldier's shoes were affixed with extremely dangerous spikes. The spikes on the bottom of a civilian soldier's shoes were approximately one inch long. If, however, the soldier was involved in active combat, the spikes on the bottom of his shoes could be between one and three inches long! These shoes, which Paul amazingly calls "shoes of peace" in Ephesians 6:15, were intended to be "killer shoes." (These "shoes of peace" will be fully dealt with in Chapter Twelve.)

The Roman soldier also carried a fourth important weapon — *a large, oblong shield*. This massive shield was made of multiple layers of animal hide that were tightly woven together and then framed along the edges by a strong piece of metal or wood. (We will cover the "shield of faith" in Chapter Thirteen.)

The fifth weapon that the Roman soldier wore was his *helmet*. This all-important piece of armor, which protected the soldier from receiving a fatal blow to the head, sometimes weighed 15 pounds or more.

Whereas the breastplate was the most beautiful piece of weaponry the Roman soldier possessed, the helmet was the most noticeable. It would have been very difficult to pass by a Roman soldier without noticing his helmet! (We will learn more about this "helmet of salvation" in Chapter Fourteen.)

The sixth weapon of the Roman soldier was his *sword*. Although there were many kinds of swords during that time in history, the sword that the Roman soldier carried was a very heavy, broad, and massive sword specifically designed for jabbing and killing an adversary or foe. (The "sword of the Spirit" will be the subject of Chapter Fifteen.)

Finally, the Roman soldier also carried a seventh weapon — *a specially tooled lance* designed to strike the enemy from a distance.

Most have not recognized the presence of the lance in Ephesians 6:10-18 because it isn't specifically stated. But the lance *must* be present in the text, because we are told to "put on the *whole* armour of God...."

There is no doubt that the lance was a part of the whole armor of the Roman soldier. In order for Paul to carry through on this illustration of the "whole armor of God," it would have been absolutely necessary for him to include the lance in this text.

In the chapters to come, you will see that the lance is indeed a very important part of "the whole armor of God." (The lance will be thoroughly covered in Chapter Sixteen.)

A NEW SET OF CLOTHES

These weapons are clearly taken from Paul's mental picture of a Roman soldier who is dressed in full armor — a soldier who is *dressed to kill*! Having set this example before us, Paul now gives us a powerful word of instruction. He says, "Put on the whole armour of God, that ye may be able to stand against the wiles of the devil" (Ephesians 6:11).

Especially notice that Paul says, *"Put on...."* The phrase "put on" is taken from the Greek word *enduo*. (*Note:* Although *enduo* is similar in appearance to the word *endunamoo*, which we studied in Chapter Seven, these two words are *not* similar in meaning.)

The word *enduo* is frequently used throughout the New Testament. In fact, it is the exact word Luke used when he recorded Jesus saying, "And, behold, I send the promise of my Father upon you: but tarry ye in the city of Jerusalem, until ye be *endued* with power from on high" (Luke 24:49).

The word *enduo* refers to *the act of putting on a new set of clothes.* In light of this, one expositor has properly translated Luke 24:49: "...But tarry ye in the city of Jerusalem until ye be *clothed* with power from on high."

Paul used the word *enduo* throughout his writings to symbolically depict the "putting on" of the new man. In both Ephesians 4:24 and Colossians 3:10, he urges us to "put on the new man." By using the word *enduo* in these two particular passages, Paul tells us we can "put on" the fruit of our new life in Christ in the same way we might put on a brand-new set of clothes.

> We can "put on" the fruit of our new life in Christ in the same way we might put on a brand-new set of clothes.

Now Paul uses the word *enduo* in Ephesians 6:11 in this same way — to denote the act of putting on a new set of clothes. However, this time he uses this word in connection with spiritual armor. He instructs us to "put on the whole armour of God...."

Moreover, Paul uses the *imperative tense* in this text. This means he is not making a suggestion; rather, he is issuing the very strongest kind of command that can be given. In the strongest tone of voice available, Paul is commanding us with great urgency to take a particular kind of immediate action. This action is so important that when Paul speaks to us, he speaks in the *imperative tense* — commanding and ordering us to *be clothed with the whole armor of God*.

We can reject Paul's command — or we can accept it. But if we choose to take his command to heart, we must then learn *how* to put on the spiritual armor God has provided for us.

How Do You Put On the Whole Armor of God?

Paul describes this weaponry as "the whole armour *of God*." Especially notice the phrase "of God." This little phrase is taken from the Greek phrase *tou theo*, and it is written in the *genitive case*.

Simply put, this means our supernatural set of weaponry comes directly *from God*. God Himself is the Source of origin for this armor. Thus, the verse could be accurately translated, "Put on the whole armor *that comes from God*...."

Because this weaponry has its origin in God, it is vital for us to remain in unbroken fellowship with Him in order for us to continually enjoy the benefits of our spiritual armor. If we break fellowship with the Lord, we step away from our all-important

Power Source. But as long as our fellowship with the Lord is unbroken, the Power Source for our spiritual weaponry also remains intact.

> As long as our fellowship with the Lord is unbroken, the Power Source for our spiritual weaponry also remains intact.

I am amazed by people who ignore their spiritual lives and cease to walk in the power of God — and then complain because it seems like all kinds of trouble are breaking loose in their lives! They often look for deep, dark reasons for this trouble that has erupted in their lives — when the explanation for this outbreak of confusion is actually very simple. Spiritual armor has its source in God. So when a believer temporarily ceases to walk in fellowship with and in the power of God, he is choosing to temporarily step away from the Source from which his armor comes!

Just as we draw our life, our new nature, and our spiritual power *from God*, this spiritual armor also comes *from God* as well.

What happens to your spiritual life when you temporarily cease to walk in fellowship with the Lord? In that condition, do you enjoy abundant life as you once did? *Of course not!*

> When a believer temporarily ceases to walk in fellowship with and in the power of God, he is choosing to temporarily step away from the Source from which his armor comes.

While abundant life still belongs to you, this state of stagnation will pull the plug on your spiritual walk, allowing the abundant life you once enjoyed to drain away until you eventually feel empty inside. Why does this happen? *Because abundant life has its source in the Lord!* When you temporarily cease to walk in fellowship with God, you are electing to temporarily walk away from His divine flow of abundant life.

What happens to the power of the Holy Spirit in a believer's life when he develops a "who cares?" attitude about his spiritual development? Does that believer continue to enjoy the operation of God's power in his life? *Certainly not!*

Although the power of God is still available to that believer, his "who cares?" attitude temporarily pulls the plug on his Power Source. Why? *Because this spiritual power has its origin in the Lord!* Thus, when a believer stops walking in fellowship with the Lord, he is choosing to temporarily stop the flow of this divine power into his life.

Furthermore, consider what happens to a believer's ability to walk in his spiritual armor when he temporarily suspends his fellowship with the Lord. Does that believer continue to reap the benefits of his God-given spiritual armor in this state of spiritual suspension? *Of course not!*

Yes, this believer's spiritual armor is still available for him to use and enjoy. But because he has suspended his fellowship with the Lord, he is also opting to temporarily suspend his ability to walk in the armor of God — the very armor God gave to protect and defend him. Why is this? *Because spiritual armor has its origin in the Lord!*

Whenever you put your spiritual life temporarily "on hold," you are opting to lay aside your spiritual armor. And you will only be able to pick up your armor again when you repent and begin to walk in fellowship with the Lord once more.

Many Christians begin each new day by pretending to put on the whole armor of God. As soon as they get out of bed in the morning, the first thing they do is to act as though they are actually putting on each piece of their weaponry.

A person who does this reaches down to his waist and pretends like he is actually wrapping the loinbelt of truth around his body. Then he reaches around his chest as if he is actually placing a breastplate of righteousness across his upper torso. He bends down and acts as if he is putting shoes of peace on his feet. He pretends to put on a helmet of salvation and then reaches over and "picks up" a shield of faith to carry throughout the day. Finally, he simulates the movements of one who is placing a sword in its scabbard at his side.

There is nothing wrong with this daily routine of pretending to put on spiritual armor. In fact, it may help some people focus better on their spiritual walk (especially children). However, this daily simulation of putting on a suit of armor does *not* actually put "the whole armor of God" on anyone.

The armor of God is ours by virtue of our relationship with God!

This is the reason Paul wrote in the genitive case. He wanted us to know that this armor originates *in* God and is freely bestowed upon those who continually draw their life and their existence *from* God.

Your unbroken, ongoing fellowship with God is your absolute guarantee that you are constantly and habitually dressed in the whole armor of God.

Also notice that in Ephesians 6:11, Paul says, "Put on the *whole* armour of God...." God has provided a *complete* set of weaponry for us, not a *partial* one. He has given us the *whole* armor of God.

Remember, the phrase "whole armor" is taken from the word *panoplia* and pictures a Roman soldier who is *fully* dressed in his armor from head to toe. Everything the soldier needed to successfully combat his adversary was at his disposal. Likewise, God has given us *everything* we need to successfully combat opposing spiritual forces! *Nothing is lacking!*

> **Your unbroken, ongoing fellowship with God is your absolute guarantee that you are constantly and habitually dressed in the whole armor of God.**

It is unfortunate that some denominations and Charismatic organizations have majored only on certain parts of the armor of God. Some teach incessantly on the "shield of faith" and the "sword of the Spirit" while neglecting the other pieces of armor God has given believers. Other groups and denominations seem to preach and teach on nothing but the "helmet of salvation" week after week. They have their helmets on — *but otherwise, they are stark naked!*

We are commanded to put on the WHOLE armor of God.

- Thank God for our loinbelt of truth, *but He gave us more than a loinbelt.*

- Thank God for our breastplate of righteousness, *but He gave us more than a breastplate.*

- Thank God for our shoes of peace, *but He gave us more than shoes.*

- Thank God for our shield of faith, *but He gave us more than a shield.*

- Thank God for our helmet of salvation, *but He gave us more than a helmet.*

- Thank God for our sword of the Spirit, *but He gave us more than a sword!*

We have been given the *whole* armor of God — and it is this complete set of spiritual weaponry that Paul commands us to pick up and use continually in the course of our Christian lives!

MAINTAINING A STRATEGIC POSITION OVER THE BATTLEFIELD OF YOUR LIFE AND MIND

As Paul continues in this passage, he tells us *why* we need this armor. He says, "Put on the whole armour of God, *that ye may be able to stand against the wiles of the devil.*"

Especially notice the phrase "...that ye may be able...." The word "able" is derived from the word *dunamis*, and it describes *explosive ability* and *dynamic strength or power*. This Greek phrase could be more accurately translated, "...*that you may have incredible, explosive, dynamic power*...." By using this word *dunamis*, Paul declares that when we are equipped with the whole armor of God, we have explosive and dynamic power at our command!

This *dunamis* power is so strong that it equips us, for the first time in our lives, to confront and pursue the enemy rather than to be pursued by *him*. Because of this *dunamis* power that is at our command when we walk in the whole armor of God, *we* become the aggressors! This is why Paul goes on to say, "...that ye may be able *to stand against*...."

> When we are equipped with the whole armor of God, we have explosive and dynamic power at our command!

The phrase "to stand" is taken from the word *stenai*, and it literally means *to stand*. In this verse, Paul uses the word *stenai* to picture a Roman soldier who is standing upright and tall with his shoulders thrown back and his head lifted high. This is the image of a proud and confident soldier, *not* one who is slumped over in defeat and despondency.

This word *stenai* depicts what we look like in the spirit realm when we are walking in the whole armor of God. This armor puts us in a winning position!

There is no reason for us to live our lives slumped over in defeat. *We are equipped to beat the living daylights out of any foe that would dare assault us.* Hence, we can walk boldly and confidently — with our shoulders thrown back and our heads lifted high — because we are dressed in the whole armor of God!

> There is no reason for us to live our lives slumped over in defeat. We are equipped to beat the living daylights out of any foe that would dare assault us!

There is something else important about this word *stenai* that must be pointed out. This word was used in a military sense, meaning *to maintain a critical and strategic military position over a battlefield.* Why is this so important? Because this meaning of *stenai* implies that we have a responsibility *to stand guard* over the battlefields of our own lives!

If God has called you to fulfill a specific assignment in the Body of Christ, you must *stand guard* and *maintain a critical position* over that assignment until it is completed. The devil doesn't want you to fulfill the call of God on your life, so he will try to attack that divine call and turn it into a battlefield. Therefore, until the job is finished and the battle is won, you must *stand guard* over the will of God for your life. *You must determine that you will not give the enemy an inch.* This is your responsibility!

> Until the job is finished and the battle is won, you must stand guard over the will of God for your life.

Remember — the most important battlefield of your life is your mind!

As stated before in this book, spiritual warfare is primarily a matter of the mind. As long as the mind is held in check and is renewed to right thinking by the Word of God, the majority of spiritual attacks will fail. However, when the mind is left open and unguarded, it becomes the primary battlefield Satan uses to destroy lives, finances, businesses, marriages, emotions, and so on.

This is why one of your most important responsibilities is to *stand guard* over your mind. In doing so, you are actually placing a guard around every other battlefield in your life!

AN EYEBALL-TO-EYEBALL CONFRONTATION!

Notice the next word in this verse! Paul continues, "...that ye may be able to stand *against*...." The word "against" is derived from the word *pros*, and it denotes *a forward position* or *a face-to-face encounter*.

By employing the word *pros* in this verse, Paul is portraying a soldier who is looking his enemy directly in the face — *eyeball to eyeball*! This is a soldier who is standing tall. His shoulders are thrown back, and his head is lifted high. He is so bold, daring, and courageous that he is glaring fearlessly right into the eyes of his adversary. This is the *eye-to-eye confrontation* that the word *pros* undoubtedly depicts!

This clearly demonstrates that, with God's mighty power and His armor on our side, we are more than a match for the enemy. In fact, we are a fearsome and terrible threat to Satan's domain! We should never shudder at the thought of what the devil can do to us, because this spiritual armor puts us in a super-powerful position that makes the devil shudder and tremble at the very thought of what we can do to *him*!

With the armor of God in hand, we are so mighty and powerful in Jesus Christ that the devil and his forces don't have a chance. When we are dressed in this suit of armor, we become mighty spiritual warriors who are *dressed to kill*!

TAKING A STAND AGAINST THE WILES OF THE DEVIL

Why do we need this armor? What are we supposed to "stand against" in this conflict? Paul tells us: "Put on the whole armour of God, that ye may be able to stand against *the wiles of the devil*" (Ephesians 6:11).

But what *are* "the wiles of the devil"?

The word "wiles" is one of three key words you must know and understand when studying the subject of spiritual warfare. The other two words are *devices* and *deception*. It is impossible to have a correct and balanced view of spiritual warfare without having an understanding of these three foundational words.

The word "wiles" is taken from the Greek word *methodos*. It is a compound of the words *meta* and *odos*. The word *meta* is a preposition that simply means *with*. The word *odos* is the Greek word for *a road*. Compounded together, they form the word *methodos*. Literally translated, the Greek word *methodos* means *with a road*.

It is from this word *methodos* that we derive the English word "method." However, the word "method" is not really strong enough to convey the full meaning of *methodos*. This Greek word was carefully selected by the Holy Spirit because it tells us *exactly* how the devil operates and how he comes to attack and assault a believer's mind.

The word "wiles" (*methodos*) is often translated to carry the idea of something that is *cunning, crafty, subtle,* or *full of trickery.* However, the most basic translation of this word is its literal meaning, *with a road.*

By electing to use this word *methodos*, Paul tells us how the devil puts his cunning, crafty, subtle, and tricky deception to work. The word "wiles" clearly reveals that the devil operates *with a road* or *on a road.*

What does this mean?

This means that, contrary to the common belief of most people, the devil does *not* have as many tricks in his bag as he would like us to believe. The word "wiles" (*methodos*) plainly means that the enemy travels on *one road, one lane,* or *one avenue.* In other words, he primarily has only *one trick* in his bag — and he obviously has learned to use that *one trick* very well!

> Contrary to the common belief of most people, the devil does not have as many tricks in his bag as he would like us to believe.

What is that one trick the devil uses against people? Or perhaps we should more correctly ask, "If the devil operates on one single avenue, what is the destination that diabolical road is headed toward?" These questions lead us to the second important word to understand when discussing spiritual warfare: the word *devices*.

THE DEVICES OF THE DEVIL

In Second Corinthians 2:11, Paul gives us a clue as to where this road leads that the devil is traveling on. Paul says, "...We are not ignorant of his [Satan's] *devices*."

The word "devices" is taken from the word *noemata*, which is derived from the word *nous*. The word *nous* is the Greek word for *the mind* or *the intellect*. However, the form *noemata*, as used by Paul in Second Corinthians 2:11, carries the idea of *a deceived mind*. Specifically, this word *noemata* denotes the insidious and malevolent plot of Satan to fill the human mind with *confusion*.

The word "devices" (*noemata*) actually depicts the *insidious plots* and *wicked schemes* of Satan to attack and victimize the human mind. One expositor has even stated that the word "devices" bears the notion of *mind games*. With this in mind, you could translate the verse, "...We are not ignorant of the mind games that Satan tries to pull on us."

Paul used this word "devices" to describe attacks that he had personally resisted, so we know that even he had to deal with the adversary's mental assaults from time to time. Paul knew from experience about the *mind games* the devil tries to pull on people!

It was for this very reason that Paul said, "Casting down *imaginations*, and every high thing that exalteth itself against the knowledge of God, and bringing into captivity *every thought* to the obedience of Christ" (2 Corinthians 10:5).

The devil loves to make a playground out of people's minds! He delights in filling their emotions and senses with illusions that captivate their minds and ultimately destroy them. He is a master when it comes to mind games.

Like Paul, we must make a mental decision to take charge of our minds, "...bringing into captivity *every thought* to the obedience of Christ." We must stop *listening* to ourselves and start *speaking* to ourselves! The devil always tries to manipulate our emotions and physical senses in order to pull a mind game on us. Therefore, we must *speak* to our emotions and senses, dictating to them exactly what to believe!

> We must make a mental decision to take charge of our minds. We must stop listening to ourselves and start speaking to ourselves!

By considering the words "wiles" and "devices," we have now seen two vitally important things that we *must* know about the devil's strategy to attack and victimize the human mind.

First, the word "wiles" (*methodos*) explicitly tells us that the devil travels *with a road* or *on a road*. This road the devil is traveling on is obviously headed somewhere.

Where is that road headed? The word "devices" clearly demonstrates that this road of the devil is headed toward *the mind*.

Whoever controls a person's mind also controls that person's health and emotions. The enemy knows this! Therefore, he seeks to penetrate a person's intellect — a person's mental control center — so he can flood it with deception and falsehood. Once this is accomplished, the devil can then begin to manipulate that person's body and emotions from a position of control.

When Satan succeeds in penetrating and paving a road into a person's mind and emotions, the process of mental and spiritual captivity in that person's life is well under way. What comes next is up to the individual who is under attack. He can abort this devilish process by renewing his mind with the Word and by allowing God's power to do a work within him. But if that person does *not* choose to renew his mind and yield to the work of the Holy Spirit, *it will be only a matter of time before a solid stronghold of deception begins to dominate and manipulate his self-image, his emotional status, and his overall thinking.*

This leads us to the third word we must understand when discussing spiritual warfare: the word *deception.*

THE DECEPTION OF THE DEVIL

Deception occurs when a person believes the lies that the enemy has been telling him. The moment someone begins to accept Satan's lies as truth is the very moment those wicked thoughts and mind games begin to produce the devil's reality in his life.

For instance, the devil may assault your mind by repeatedly telling you that you are a failure. However, as long as you resist those demonic allegations, they will exert absolutely no power in your life.

But what if you begin to give credence to these lies and to mentally perceive them as the actual truth? Those lies will then begin to control you and to dominate your emotions and your thinking. In the end, your faith in those lies will give power to them and will cause them to create a bona fide reality in your life — *and you will become a failure.* This is a manifestation of completed deception.

> The moment someone begins to accept Satan's lies as truth is the very moment those wicked thoughts and mind games begin to produce the devil's reality in his life.

Many marriages fail because of false allegations that the enemy tries to pound into the minds of each spouse. As long as the couple repels these allegations, the devil's lies exert no power in that marriage. However, when one of the spouses begins to pay attention to and dwell on those lies, he or she has taken the first fatal step toward deception.

Take, for instance, the example of a marriage that is in tip-top shape until one of the spouses starts dwelling on unjustified questions and suspicions about the other spouse. This is clearly the work of the enemy to deteriorate the couple's confidence in their marriage.

At first, this spouse absolutely knows that these suspicions are outright lies of the devil. *Indeed,* he or she thinks, *our marriage has never been better!*

But the enemy continues to pound away on this spouse's mind:

- *"Your husband [or wife] isn't pleased with you."*

- *"Your marriage is in trouble."*

- *"This relationship can never last."*

- *"It's too good to be true."*

Sadly, as this dear Christian continues to pay attention to those lying insinuations, the door remains open for the devil to continue pounding away at that person's mind and preying on his or her emotions. After a period of time, the person's mind — battered and weary from worrying — begins to believe those false allegations. That spouse's faith in those lying emotions and suspicions may then empower the lies to become a reality in his or her marriage.

By mentally embracing these false insinuations, this spouse opens the door for the enemy to penetrate his or her mind. Thus, the process of confusion is implemented; mind games are set in motion; and that believer's perception of things becomes twisted and bent. If this seducing, deceiving process is not stopped at this point, it is probably only a matter of time before the weary-minded believer begins to embrace these mental lies as though they were really the truth.

What is the end result of the devil's deception? When believers falsely believe that their marriage is on the rocks, that they will die of a terminal disease, or that they have no hope for the future, they open the door for the enemy to move these lying suggestions from the thought realm into the natural realm, where they become a bona fide reality. *These believers' false perceptions empower the lies, and the devil uses those false beliefs to create HIS reality in the natural realm!*

Perhaps the enemy has constantly bombarded your mind about sickness. Perhaps his lying allegations have repeatedly told you that you are going to contract a terrible disease and die an early death. When these lies first assaulted your mind, you resisted them and refused to believe what you were hearing. Now, however, you have begun to wonder if these thoughts may have some validity.

If you don't *stop* this process, it will only be a matter of time until you truly begin to feel physically sick in your body. *Do not give credence to those lying insinuations!* When you embrace the devil's mind games and perceive them as truth, you give power to them!

> When you embrace the devil's mind games and perceive them as truth, you give power to them!

If you do not take charge of your mind and begin to speak God's truth to yourself to combat the devil's lies, the complete process of deception will continue working in your life. Eventually that process will be complete, and your fears will become reality. *When this occurs, you will be deceived in that area of your life.*

You can see now why these three words — the *wiles, devices,* and *deception* of the devil — are extremely important for us to understand — especially when studying the subject of spiritual warfare.

Let's review: First, the word "wiles" (*methodos*) tells us that the devil operates *with a road*, or primarily with *one avenue* of attack.

Second, the word "devices" (*noemata*) reveals where that avenue is headed: It is headed toward *the mind*. Once that road is paved into a person's mind, the enemy begins to regularly travel in and out of that person's mind and emotions to confuse and scramble his thoughts with wrong thinking, wrong believing, and false perceptions.

Third, "deception" occurs when a person embraces the lie that the devil is telling him. The false perception that this person has embraced empowers that lie to become a bona fide reality in his life. *This is completed deception.*

AN EXAMPLE OF DEMONIC INTIMIDATION

Perhaps the best biblical example of the *wiles, devices, and deceptions* of the devil can be found in the story of David and Goliath.

By studying the true-life story of David and Goliath, you will see all *three* of these negative forces at work.

In First Samuel 17, we see how the devil used Goliath's lying allegations to intimidate and confuse the armies of Israel.

Goliath's outlandish, arrogant, boastful, and proud declarations of the Israelites' demise were so effective that not one soldier from the Hebrew camp was willing to stand up to this aggressor. The Israelite army was rendered functionally paralyzed for 40 days — until a courageous young man named David came along with the power of God to challenge those lies!

> **And the Philistines stood on a mountain on the one side, and Israel stood on a mountain on the other side: and there was a valley between them. And there went out a champion out of the camp of the Philistines, named Goliath, of Gath, WHOSE HEIGHT WAS SIX CUBITS AND A SPAN.**
>
> 1 Samuel 17:3,4

No wonder the Israelites were intimidated by Goliath! The appearance alone of this giant would be intellectually and emotionally overwhelming. Goliath was "six cubits and a span" tall — which is 9 feet 9 inches tall!

> **And he had an helmet of brass upon his head, and he was armed with a coat of mail; and the weight of the coat was five thousand shekels of brass. And he had greaves of brass upon his legs, and a target of brass between his shoulders. And the staff of his spear was like a weaver's beam; and his spear's head weighed six hundred shekels of iron: and one bearing a shield went before him.**
>
> 1 Samuel 17:5-7

Goliath was armed to the max! Notice that the "coat of mail" he wore weighed "five thousand shekels of brass." As I mentioned earlier, 5,000 shekels of brass is *the equivalent of 125 pounds*!

In addition to Goliath's helmet and his breastplate that weighed 125 pounds, he also had greaves of brass and a target (javelin) of brass slung between his shoulders! The staff of his spear was like a weaver's beam — *which means the long staff of his spear weighed at least 17 pounds.* Additionally, the scripture specifically says that the spear's head weighed 600 shekels of iron — *which is the equivalent of 16 pounds.*

One scholar has speculated that the weight of all these pieces of weaponry together — his helmet, breastplate, greaves, brass javelin, spear, and shield — *may have weighed in excess of 700 pounds*!

In every respect imaginable, Goliath was a very frightful sight! How would you feel if you were challenged by a foe who stood 9 feet 9 inches tall and wore more than 700 pounds of weaponry? And if Goliath wore weaponry weighing that much, imagine how much the giant must have weighed himself!

Yet it wasn't Goliath's size or his weaponry that caused the Israelites to shrink back in fear. What did cause the Israelites to fear? *The constant threats and mental bombardment that Goliath hit them with every single day. This mental harassment crippled the Hebrew soldiers so that they lost sight of the awesome ability of God.*

Concerning these continuous threats of Goliath, the Bible says:

> And he stood and cried unto the armies of Israel,
> and said unto them, Why are ye come out to set your
> battle in array? am not I a Philistine, and ye servants
> to Saul? choose you a man for you, and let him come
> down to me. If he be able to fight with me, and to kill
> me, then will we be your servants: but if I prevail
> against him, and kill him, then shall ye be our
> servants, and serve us.
>
> And the Philistine said, I defy the armies of Israel
> this day; give me a man, that we may fight together.
>
> 1 Samuel 17:8-10

These threats of the huge, menacing Goliath were so
emotionally overpowering that the next verse declares, "When
Saul and all Israel heard those words of the Philistine, they were
dismayed, and greatly afraid" (v. 11).

Goliath mentally and emotionally immobilized the armies of
Israel without ever using a sword or
spear! With words alone, he incapac-
itated, disabled, stunned, numbed, and
disarmed the Israelites. The giant's
flagrant and preposterous distortion of
his own greatness was so outrageous
that his words bewitched the listening
Israelite army until they were spellbound under his verbal control.

> Goliath mentally
> and emotionally
> immobilized the
> armies of Israel
> without ever using
> a sword or spear!

In effect, Goliath said to them:

"Who do you think you are to fight with me?"

"Come on, just try to do damage to me, and you'll find out what I'll do to you!"

"What's wrong? Are you afraid to face me and take me on?"

Where do you suppose Goliath learned this kind of foul behavior? From the devil! The devil is a slanderer and an accuser! Today the devil still seeks to incapacitate, disable, stun, numb, and disarm believers the same way he paralyzed the Israelite army through Goliath. The devil's flagrant and preposterous allegations are so outrageous that they often bewitch listening believers until they become spellbound under his control.

This outrageous conduct is still the mental tool the devil uses to assault the minds of believers. He bombards them with threatening thoughts, such as:

- *"You think you're so tough — but I'll show you who the tough guy really is!"*

- *"I'll use this bad situation to beat the life right out of you!"*

- *"I'll strike you down so hard and fast, you won't know what hit you!"*

Lying threats and false accusations are the enemy's attempts to beat a hole through your mind and emotions so you can't think rationally. He comes to pave a road of fear into your mind; then he plays his mind games, trying to fill your mind so full of fear and confusion that you eventually lose the courage you need to step out in faith and obey God's call on your life.

Throwing one slanderous accusation after another at your mind, the devil will do everything he can to slander and belittle you. He will defame, malign, revile, and smear your faith in order to drive you back into the ditch of self-preservation where you never do anything significant for the Kingdom of God.

If you meditate on the devil's threats long enough, you will become "dismayed and greatly afraid," just like the children of Israel who listened to the words of Goliath and became functionally paralyzed by fear for 40 days. You'll find yourself living on the low side of victory — unwilling to take on any new challenges for fear that you might fail, for fear of what others might say, for fear of potential catastrophe, etc.

The devil wants to take you captive and destroy you with the same tools Goliath used against the Israelites. Satan wants to ruin your effectiveness with deceptive suggestions and lying allegations!

THE HARD FACTS OF SPIRITUAL WARFARE

In the midst of all Goliath's lies, the giant did make one statement that was true in verse 9. He said in effect, *"If one of your number is able to fight me and win, we will serve you for the rest of our lives. But if we win, YOU will serve US!"*

These rules of battle that Goliath laid out were the hard facts of warfare during David's day. Whoever won the battle was the champion — whether it was the aggressor or the one who accepted the challenge. Whoever fell in defeat would forever serve the other as a slave. These hard facts of battle are still the rules of spiritual warfare today.

If you conquer all the lying emotions, slanderous accusations, and deceptive suggestions that the devil tries to use in his attempt to neutralize you, you will be able to keep the enemy in a subordinate position for the rest of your life. Once you pull the plug on Satan's intimidating threats and lies, he will no longer be able to hold your mind captive.

If, however, you do *not* learn how to take your thoughts captive, your mind and emotions will be used as tools of Satan to dominate your thought processes for the rest of your life. If you do not take charge of your mind — *learning how to SPEAK God's truth to yourself rather than LISTEN to the enemy's lies* — the devil will continue to use lying emotions and illusions to manipulate, dominate, and control you for the rest of your life.

> Once you pull the plug on Satan's intimidating threats and lies, he will no longer be able to hold your mind captive.

Notice that Goliath said, "*...I defy the armies of Israel this day...*" (v. 10). Today the devil is still breathing out the same kind of blasphemous and terrorizing statements against the people of God, such as:

- *"Just try to walk in divine health!"*
- *"I defy you to believe that your financial situation is going to turn around!"*
- *"I defy you to succeed in the ministry!"*

Although the wicked Philistines never lifted a sword, threw a spear, or budged from their encampment, they conquered the people of God with mental and verbal attacks of intimidation. The Israelites wrongly considered and meditated on Goliath's threats, allowing those threats to flood them with fear. As a result, they were neutralized without a ground war ever taking place!

How often did Goliath come to make these threats? The Word says, "And the Philistine drew near *morning and evening*, and presented himself forty days" (v. 16). Day and night, morning and evening, Goliath came to mentally undo the people of God.

This, of course, is how the enemy still attacks people's minds and emotions. He doesn't strike once and then come back a week later to strike again. Instead, he strikes fast and repeatedly — again and again and again. Morning and evening the devil attacks, intent on his goal of irreparably damaging people's faith and confidence.

THE FLESH COUNTS FOR NOTHING

Let's read on in First Samuel 17 to see what happened next:

> Now David was the son of that Ephrathite of Bethlehemjudah, whose name was Jesse; and he had eight sons.... And David was the youngest: and the three eldest followed Saul. But David went and

returned from Saul to feed his father's sheep at Bethlehem....

And David rose up early in the morning, and left the sheep with a keeper, and took, and went, as Jesse had commanded him [to take food to his brothers]; and he came to the trench....

And as he talked with them [his brothers], behold, there came up the champion, the Philistine of Gath, Goliath by name, out of the armies of the Philistines, and spake according to the same words: and David heard them.

1 Samuel 17:12,14,15,20,23

Notice that verse 23 says, "...And David heard them." This was David's first encounter with the foreboding giant, and something in Goliath's words incited anger in David's soul. What a shock it was for this young shepherd to hear a pagan Philistine insulting the God of Israel and to realize that no one was doing anything about it! In fact, the Israelites weren't just sitting around doing nothing about Goliath. Verse 24 says they actually *ran in terror*: "And all the men of Israel, when they saw the man, *fled* from him, and were sore afraid."

But young David wasn't afraid of this Philistine giant — he was annoyed by Goliath's verbal arrogance!

And David spake to the men that stood by him, saying, What shall be done to that man that killeth the Philistine, and taketh away the reproach from

Israel? for who is this uncircumcised Philistine, that
he should defy the armies of the living God?

1 Samuel 17:26

Immediately David's elder brother took offense at David's
confidence and reprimanded his younger brother for acting too
boldly.

And Eliab his eldest brother heard when he spake
unto the men; and Eliab's anger was kindled against
David, and he said, Why camest thou down hither?
and with whom hast thou left those sheep in the
wilderness? I know thy pride, and the naughtiness of
thine heart; for thou art come down that thou
mightest see the battle.

1 Samuel 17:28

Quite often when young men and women of God step out to
challenge the foe, they are accused of acting too boldly. Their
elder leaders may be correct in pointing out the vast difference
between spiritual boldness and rude arrogance. Nevertheless,
there is a true boldness that the Holy Spirit gives to surrendered
vessels.

David was one such yielded vessel. He was so surrendered to
God's power working through him that a Holy Spirit-inspired
confidence rose up within him. At that point, David simply
could not hold back his righteous anger!

David was stunned by his elder brother's hostile reaction and
the fear that possessed the huge Israelite soldiers surrounding
him. He asked Eliab, "...What have I now done? Is there not a

cause? And he turned from him toward another, and spake after the same manner: and the people answered him again after the former manner" (vv. 29,30).

In essence, David was asking: *"Isn't there a cause here that is worth fighting for? Isn't there one soldier in this camp who is man enough to face this uncircumcised Philistine? Why aren't we fighting?"*

David apparently began to turn from one soldier to the next, asking, *"How about you? Will you fight Goliath?"* It quickly became clear to him that no one had the faith or courage to believe that this vile giant could be killed.

Word of David's confidence and boldness immediately spread through the Israelite camp like wildfire. In the same way, you can be sure that when you make the decision to move in the power of God and to pull strongholds down from your life, *it will make news!* Everyone around you will be talking about your boldness. Some may even try to talk you out of it!

> You can be sure that when you make the decision to move in the power of God and to pull strongholds down from your life, it will make news!

Notice what the Bible says next:

And when the words were heard which David spake, they rehearsed them before Saul: and he sent for him. And David said to Saul, Let no man's heart fail because of him; thy servant will go and fight with this Philistine.

1 Samuel 17:31,32

In David's heart was a willingness to be used of God and a burning desire to see the enemy slain. Saul was so amazed by the young man's supernatural courage that he said to David, "...Thou art not able to go against this Philistine to fight with him: for thou art but a youth, and he a man of war from his youth" (v. 33).

Naturally speaking, David was too young and unskilled in the natural weapons of warfare to do battle with this giant. King Saul knew this. Therefore, looking on things from a fleshly, worldly perspective, Saul knew that David — *naturally speaking* — was no match for Goliath!

However, David had *Heaven's* perspective. He knew that the outward man — the flesh — counted for nothing when it came to moving in the supernatural power of God! So David responded to Saul's doubts with words of faith: "...Thy servant kept his father's sheep, and there came a lion, and a bear, and took a lamb out of the flock: And I went out after him..." (vv. 34,35).

> David had Heaven's perspective. He knew that the outward man — the flesh — counted for nothing when it came to moving in the supernatural power of God!

Goliath wasn't the first enemy David had faced in life — he'd already had eyeball-to-eyeball confrontations with both a lion and a bear! As a shepherd, David had determined that those devourers would *not* steal one thing from him — *not one*. That was the winner's attitude David needed to defeat his enemy every time his enemy struck.

215

We must have this same attitude when the devil comes to manipulate our minds and emotions, to strike family members with disease, to devour our finances, or to internally destroy our church or ministry. Our attitude must be the same as David's attitude. We have to boldly declare to the enemy:

- *"Satan, you cannot have this ministry!"*

- *"Devil, you cannot have our finances!"*

- *"You cannot kill our family members with sickness or disease!"*

- *"You cannot, cannot, CANNOT!"*

If the devil doesn't willingly release that which is ours when we tell him to do so, we will have to respond as David did when the lion and the bear attacked his sheep. David told Saul, "And I went out after him, and smote him, and delivered it out of his mouth: and when he arose against me, I caught him by his beard, and smote him, and slew him. Thy servant slew both the lion and the bear..." (vv. 35,36).

David had already experienced so much of God's power and victory in his life that this Philistine was no threat to him. He had already faced a ferocious lion — *and had experienced God's faithfulness as he was empowered to kill the lion.* David had already faced a bear — *and had experienced God's faithfulness as he was empowered to kill the bear.*

In the same way, we have to "go out after" the devil in the authority Jesus has given us and force him to release whatever he has seized from *us* against our wills!

Moving Beyond the Flesh

As David looked back on his past experiences and reflected on the goodness of God that had already been bestowed on his life, he could now look straight into the face of this conflict with Goliath and declare to King Saul:

> Thy servant slew both the lion and the bear: and this uncircumcised Philistine shall be as one of them, seeing he hath defied the armies of the living God.
>
> David said moreover, The Lord that delivered me out of the paw of the lion, and out of the paw of the bear, he will deliver me out of the hand of this Philistine. And Saul said unto David, Go, and the Lord be with thee.
>
> 1 Samuel 17:36,37

Notice Saul's response to David's desire to be used of God:

> And Saul armed David with his armour, and he put an helmet of brass upon his head; also he armed him with a coat of mail. And David girded his sword upon his armour....
>
> 1 Samuel 17:38,39

David had already killed the lion and the bear without the use of any natural armor or weaponry. However, because of the size of the menacing Philistine giant, Saul thought that David needed more than God's faithfulness!

It was as though Saul was saying to the young man who stood before him, *"David, this fight with Goliath is going to be far more intense than your conflict with the lion and the bear, so let me help you! Let me put my helmet on your head and dress you in my coat of mail. And, here, David — take my sword with you, too, and use it like it's your own!"*

Can you imagine how silly young David must have looked in Saul's massive armor? You can be sure that Saul's intentions were pure. He wanted David to be safe and adequately equipped with armor equal to Goliath's armor. However, Saul's counsel was extremely defective. David had never worn such armor before. Had he gone to battle clothed in the king's heavy armor, he would have been so weighed down that he would have been unable to successfully wage warfare.

This is the reason verse 39 goes on to say, "...And David said unto Saul, I cannot go with these; for I have not proved them. And David put them off him."

Previous to this time, David had defeated his enemies without fleshly weapons. Knowing that he was unaccustomed to these kinds of natural weapons and that they would therefore do him no good, David took off Saul's armor and "...took his staff in his hand, and chose him five smooth stones out of the brook, and put them in a shepherd's bag which he had, even in a scrip; and his sling was in his hand: *and he drew near to the Philistine*" (v. 40).

Notice it says that David "...drew near to the Philistine." David, a young man in his teenage years, charged a giant with

700 pounds of weaponry — with nothing in his hands to kill this giant but a sling and five stones!

According to the natural realm, David was not equipped to fight this kind of foe. But according to the spirit realm, David was dressed in the armor of God and empowered by the power of God. Goliath could not see these spiritual weapons with his physical eyes. Therefore, he had no idea that David was "dressed to kill"!

> And the Philistine came on and drew near unto David; and the man that bare the shield went before him. And when the Philistine looked about, and saw David, he disdained him: for he was but a youth, and ruddy, and of a fair countenance.
>
> And the Philistine said unto David, Am I a dog, that thou comest to me with staves? And the Philistine cursed David by his gods.
>
> 1 Samuel 17:41-43

Goliath was expecting more! He thought the Israelites had finally found a match for him. This is the reason the man who bore his shield went before the giant; this shield-bearer was to protect Goliath from the blows of his challenger. But when Goliath looked around and saw only small, young David, he was *shocked.* Immediately the Philistine giant began to mock both David and his God!

Goliath began to use his tools of mental and verbal harassment, just like the devil does today. Attempting to intimidate David and paralyze him with fear, "...the Philistine said to David, Come to me, and I will give thy flesh unto the fowls of the air, and to the beasts of the field" (v. 44). Just as the entire army of Israel had been functionally immobilized for 40 days by Goliath's outrageous claims, now the Philistine giant was proceeding to use that same strategy again in an attempt *to immobilize and paralyze David with preposterous, bloated boasts and lying allegations*!

> Before the giant's threats had an opportunity to take root in his soul and produce paralyzing fear, David spoke forth his declaration of war against the enemy.

If David had turned his eyes from the Lord and stopped meditating on His faithfulness, he would have begun to consider what Goliath had to say. Soon those threats would have immobilized David, just as they had immobilized the armies of Israel.

But before the giant's threats had an opportunity to take root in his soul and produce paralyzing fear, David spoke forth his declaration of war against the enemy:

> ...Thou comest to me with a sword, and with a spear, and with a shield; but I come to thee in the name of the Lord of hosts, the God of the armies of Israel, whom thou hast defied.
>
> This day will the Lord deliver you into mine hand; and I will smite thee, and take thine head from thee; and I will give the carcases of the host of the Philistines this day unto the fowls of the air, and to

the wild beasts of the earth; that all the earth may know that there is a God in Israel. And all this assembly shall know that the Lord saveth not with sword and spear: for the battle is the Lord's, and He WILL give you into our hands.

1 Samuel 17:45-47

PREVAILING OVER THE PHILISTINES
IN YOUR LIFE

Once David made his declaration of war, he wasted no time. Verse 48 says, "And it came to pass, when the Philistine arose, and came and drew nigh to meet David, *that David hasted....*"

This must have *shocked* Goliath! Most challengers ran away from him, but David "hastened." *In other words, when the moment of conflict finally came and David saw Goliath coming, he picked up his sling and his five stones and RAN toward the giant.* It was as though the young man was saying to himself with relish, "Now the action begins!"

The Word continues: "And David put his hand in his bag, and took thence a stone, and slang it, and smote the Philistine in his forehead, that the stone sunk into his forehead; and he fell upon his face to the earth. *So David prevailed over the Philistine with a sling and with a stone, and smote the Philistine, and slew him...*" (vv. 49,50).

But wait — David wasn't finished yet! While Goliath lay with his face to the ground, stunned by the small pebble that had been hurled from his young opponent's sling, David seized the opportunity to make sure the job was finished!

> ...But there was no sword in the hand of David. Therefore David ran, and stood upon the Philistine, and took his sword, and drew it out of the sheath thereof, and slew him, and cut off his head therewith. And when the Philistines saw their champion was dead, they fled.
>
> 1 Samuel 17:50,51

How about you? Are you tired of the Philistines in *your* life? Are you tired of being mentally harassed and emotionally tormented by the lying insinuations and slanderous accusations of the adversary? How would you like to sling a stone into the head of those accusing thoughts and drop them stunned to the ground — and then cut off their heads so that they can never harass you again?

> Are you tired of being mentally harassed and emotionally tormented by the lying insinuations and slanderous accusations of the adversary?

This is *precisely* why Paul urges us, "Put on the whole armour of God, that ye may be able to stand against the wiles of the devil" (Ephesians 6:11)!

Natural training and education is good, and we all need to receive as much of it as we possibly can. However, we must all eventually discover that natural weapons and natural education will not help us in our fight with unseen, spiritual enemies.

In such moments, we must move beyond the realm of our fleshly means of defense and enter into the realm of spiritual armor. This armor will empower each one of us to successfully "...stand against the wiles of the devil."

THE DEVIL'S MODE OF OPERATION

It would be a great injustice to conclude this chapter without explaining what the name "devil" means. Once you have an understanding of this name, you will know it was the nature of the devil himself that was working through Goliath to intimidate the armies of Israel.

> We must move beyond the realm of our fleshly means of defense and enter into the realm of spiritual armor.

The name "devil" is taken from the Greek word *diabolos* and is a compound of the words *dia* and *ballo*. The word *dia* carries the idea of *penetration*, and the word *ballo* means *to throw something*, such as a ball or a rock.

Literally, the word *diabalos* describes the repetitive action of *hitting something again and again* — until finally the wall or membrane is so worn down that *it can be completely and thoroughly penetrated.*

Thus, the name "devil" (*diabolos*) is not only a proper name for this archenemy of the faith, but it also denotes his mode of operation. *The devil is one who strikes repeatedly, again and again, until he finally breaks down a person's mental resistance. Once that person's mental resistance has been breached, the enemy then strikes with all his fury to penetrate and take captive that person's mind and emotions.*

This is how the enemy works! He will repeatedly try to hit you with lies, suggestions, accusations, and allegations, bombarding you with one slanderous assault after another. In this way, the devil attempts to wear you down — looking for an opportunity to make his move and take you captive in one of your weaker moments.

If the enemy can find you with your guard down, he will then try to pave a road into your mind (*methodos*) so he can confuse your emotions with "mind games" (*noemata*). His goal is to deceive you to the point that you actually begin to believe his threats. If he succeeds, your false perceptions will empower his lies to become a reality in your life.

Now you can better understand the sense of urgency behind Paul's command in Ephesians 6:11. If you're ever going to live free from the enemy's tormenting lies and accusations, it is absolutely imperative that you *"clothe yourself with the whole panoply — the loinbelt, breastplate, shoes and greaves, shield, helmet, sword, and lance — that comes from God, that you may have explosive and dynamic power to stand proud and upright, face to face and eyeball to eyeball, against the roads that the slanderer would try to pave into your mind!"*

QUESTIONS FOR PERSONAL GROWTH OR GROUP DISCUSSION

1. What is the main thing you have to do in order to "put on" the whole armor of God? What changes do you need to make in your daily routine in order to fulfill this requirement?

2. What are specific actions you must take in order to stand guard over the assignment God has given you to fulfill?

3. What is the one method that the devil uses in his strategies against people? How can that knowledge help you stay alert to the specific attacks of the enemy against your own life?

4. What will the end result be in your life if you meditate on the devil's lies and give credence to the mind games he plays on you?

5. Can you think of a specific lie of the enemy that you used to accept as true? What consequences did you experience because you believed that lie, and what changed when you began to embrace the truth?

NOTES:

_____

_____

_____

_____

_____

_____

_____

_____

_____

_____

_____

_____

_____

_____

_____

_____

_____

_____

_____

_____

_____

_____

CHAPTER NINE

WRESTLING WITH
PRINCIPALITIES AND POWERS

*A*s Paul continues in Ephesians chapter 6, he reveals the next key in understanding true spiritual warfare: the identity of whom our battle is against. He says, "For we wrestle not against flesh and blood, but against principalities, against powers, against the rulers of the darkness of this world, against spiritual wickedness in high places" (Ephesians 6:12).

Especially notice how Paul begins this scripture. He says, "For we *wrestle....*" From the very outset of the verse, Paul makes a very strong, pointed, and dramatic statement!

The word "wrestle" is taken from the old Greek word *pale*, and it refers to *struggling, wrestling,* or *hand-to-hand fighting.* However, the word *pale* is also the Greek word from which the Greeks derived their name for the *Palaestra,* a famous house of combat sports.

The Palaestra was a huge building that outwardly looked like a palace. But it was a palace of combat sports, dedicated to the cultivation of athletic skills. Every morning, afternoon, and night, the most committed, determined, and daring athletes of that day could be found there, working out and training in this fabulous building.

Three kinds of athletes primarily worked out at the Palaestra: *boxers*, *wrestlers*, and *pankratists*. These were exceedingly dangerous and barbaric sports. *Why?* To quote from Chapter Seven of my book, *Living in the Combat Zone*:

> First, their boxers were not like ours today. Theirs were *extremely violent* — so violent that they were not permitted to box without wearing helmets. Without the protection of helmets, their heads would have been crushed.

> Few boxers in the ancient world ever lived to retire from their profession. Most of them died in the ring. Of all the sports, the ancients viewed boxing as *the most* hazardous and deadly.

> In fact, these boxers were so brutal and barbaric that they wore gloves *ribbed with steel and spiked with nails*! At times the steel wrapped around their gloves was *serrated*, like a hunting knife, in order to make deep gashes in the skin of an opponent. And as time went on, boxers began using gloves that were heavier and much more damaging.

> If you study the artwork from the time of the early Greeks, it is quite usual to see boxers whose faces, ears, and noses were totally deformed because of these dangerous gloves. You will also frequently see paintings of boxers with blood pouring from

their noses and with deep lacerations on their faces as a result of the serrated metal and spiked nails on the gloves. In addition to this, it was not unusual for a boxer to hit his opponent's face so hard, with his thumb extended toward the eyes, that it knocked the opponent's eye right out of its socket!

Believe it or not, even though this sport was so combative and violent, there were *no rules* — except that a boxer could not clench his opponent's fist. That was the only rule to the game! There were no "rounds" like there are in boxing today. The fight just went on and on and on until one of the two *surrendered* or *died* in the ring....

An inscription from that first century said of boxing: "A boxer's victory is obtained through blood." This was a thoroughly violent sport....

Wrestlers, too, often wrestled to the death. In fact, a favorite tactic in those days was to grab hold of an opponent around the waist from behind, throw him up in the air, and quickly break his backbone in half from behind! In order to make an opponent surrender, it was quite normal to strangle him into submission. Choking was another acceptable practice. Obviously, wrestling was another extremely violent sport.

Wrestlers were tolerant of every imaginable tactic: *breaking fingers, breaking ribs with a waistlock, gouging the face, knocking out the eyes, and so forth.*

Although less injurious than the other combat sports, wrestling was still a bitter struggle to the end…. Wrestling was a bloody, bloody sport….

Then there were *Pankratists*. Pankratists were a combination of all of the above. The word "pankratist" is from two Greek roots, the words *pan* and *kratos*. *Pan* means *all*, and *kratos* is a word for *exhibited power*. The two words together describe *someone with massive amounts of power; power over all; or more power than anyone else.*

This, indeed, was the purpose of *Pankration*. Its competitors were out to prove they could not be beaten and were tougher than anyone else! In order to prove this, they were permitted to kick, punch, bite, gouge, strike, break fingers, break legs, and do any other horrible thing you could imagine…. There was no part of the body that was off limits. They could do anything to any part of their competitor's body, *for there were basically no rules.*

An early inscription says this about *Pankration*: "If you should hear that your son has died, believe it, but if you hear he has been defeated and retired, do not believe it." Why? Because more died in this sport than surrendered or were defeated. Like the other combat sports, it was *extremely violent.*

THE SURVIVAL OF THE FITTEST

Now Paul uses this very illustration to describe our conflict with unseen, demonic powers that have been marshaled against us for our destruction. He says, "For we wrestle not against flesh and blood, but against principalities, against powers, against the rulers of the darkness of this world, against spiritual wickedness in high places" (Ephesians 6:12).

By using the word "wrestle," the old Greek word *pale*, Paul conveys the idea of *a bitter struggle* and *an intense conflict*. In other words, he is describing our warfare with demonic forces as a combat sport similar to those fought in the ancient Palastra!

This means when you are fighting demonic foes, *there are no rules! Anything goes!* All methods of attack are legal, and there is no umpire to cry "foul" when the adversary attempts to break you, choke you, or strangle you.

Whoever fights the hardest and the meanest and whoever lasts the longest is the winner in your confrontation with the enemy. Therefore, you'd better be equipped, alert, and prepared before the fight begins. (For more on how to prepare for this conflict, read all of Chapter Seven in *Living in the Combat Zone*.)

Notice that Paul goes on to say, "For we wrestle *not against flesh and blood*...." At first, this statement of

> Whoever fights the hardest, the meanest, and lasts the longest is the winner in your confrontation with the enemy. Therefore, you'd better be equipped, alert, and prepared before the fight begins.

Paul may seem to be in conflict with what I have been saying in this book. Earlier I stated that the majority of spiritual warfare is with the flesh and the mind.

Is there a conflict between the apostle Paul's statement and what I am saying? *Absolutely not!* Indeed, our real adversaries are an unseen host of wicked spirits that are working behind the scenes. These are the foul forces of darkness that work covertly behind every damnable disaster and moral failure. *However, they can't do anything unless our flesh cooperates with them!* That's why they come to tempt, seduce, deceive, and assault our flesh and our minds.

This is the reason we must deal with the flesh before we attempt to deal with the devil! By living a crucified, sanctified life on a continual basis, we are able to neutralize any attack the enemy would try to wage against our flesh. Why is this? *Because dead men and women do not have the capacity to respond!* You can kick dead people; spit at dead people; curse at dead people; or try to tempt, deceive, and seduce dead people — but no matter *what* you do, they do not respond!

> By living a crucified, sanctified life on a continual basis, we are able to neutralize any attack the enemy would try to wage against our flesh.

Likewise, the majority of demonic attacks against us will never produce anything of serious consequence if we are living a crucified life and reckoning ourselves to be "dead to sin" on a daily basis (Romans 6:6,7,11).

PRINCIPALITIES AND POWERS

Who are these evil forces that are constantly working behind the scenes to seduce, deceive, control, and manipulate the flesh and the mind? Paul answers that question as he continues: "For we wrestle not against flesh and blood, *but against principalities, against powers, against the rulers of the darkness of this world, against spiritual wickedness in high places.*"

Paul tells us that there are four classifications of demon spirits:

1. Principalities

2. Powers

3. Rulers of the darkness of this world

4. Spiritual wickedness in high places

Before we deal with each of these individually, something else must first be noted. Notice that Paul mentions the word "against" in Ephesians 6:12 *four times* in connection with the devil! Why is this important? Because grammatically, he could have used the word "against" once in reference to all four levels of demonic spirits. But rather than do this, Paul chose to repeat the word "against" again and again four different times!

When a truth is repeated in Scripture like this, it is always for the sake of *emphasis.* For instance, in John chapters 14, 15, and 16, Jesus refers to the Holy Spirit as "the Comforter" four different times. This clearly means that the Lord Jesus Christ is trying to drive a very important truth into our hearts about the Holy Spirit.

Likewise, in those same chapters of John, Jesus refers to the Holy Spirit as "the Spirit of Truth" three different times. Once again, Jesus repeats Himself for the sake of *emphasizing a very important truth.*

We also see in the Bible that, whenever God calls out to notable biblical characters, He always calls them by name not once, but two or three times. For instance, when God called Moses, He said, "...Moses, Moses..." (Exodus 3:4). When God called Saul of Tarsus, He said, "...Saul, Saul..." (Acts 9:4). And Samuel was so important to the plan of God that God called him by name not once, not twice, but *three* times. In the middle of the night, God called out, *"Samuel...Samuel...Samuel..."* (*see* 1 Samuel 3:4-8).

So when God is dealing with truth that is of paramount importance, or when God calls out to an extremely important biblical character, He always repeats Himself. This, of course, leads us back to Ephesians 6:12, where the Holy Spirit repeats the word "against" *four times* within the context of *one verse!* This means the Holy Spirit is telling us something *very, very important.*

The word "against" that is used four times in this verse is taken from the Greek word *pros.* The word *pros* always depicts *a forward position* or *a face-to-face encounter.* In fact, this very word is used in John 1:1 to describe the preincarnate relationship between the Father and Jesus. It says, "In the beginning was the Word, and the Word was *with* God...."

The word "with" in this verse is taken from the word *pros.* A more accurate rendering of John 1:1 would be *"in the beginning was the Word* [Jesus], *and the Word* [Jesus] *was face to face with God...."*

This word *pros* clearly reveals the *intimacy* and *close relationship* that exists between the Members of the Godhead. It gives us a picture of the Father and Jesus in a relationship so *close* and *intimate* that the Father can almost feel the Son's breath on His face! Now this same word of intimacy, this word that is used to denote a face-to-face relationship between the Father and the Son, is used to describe a face-to-face encounter with unseen, demonic spirits that have come to assault us.

This means that at some point in our Christian experience, we *will* come into *direct contact* with evil forces. Ephesians 6:12 could thus be translated: *"We wrestle not against flesh and blood, but face to face with principalities, eyeball to eyeball with powers, head-on with rulers of the darkness of this world, and shoulder to shoulder with spiritual wickedness in high places."*

> At some point in our Christian experience, we will come into direct contact with evil forces.

THE DEVIL'S RANK-AND-FILE FORCES

All serious scholars agree that the language of Ephesians 6:12 is military in nature. It seems evident that Paul received a revelation of how Satan's kingdom has been aligned militarily.

At the very top of Satan's dark domain, there is a group of demon spirits that Paul calls "principalities." The word "principality" is taken from the word *archas*, an old word that is used symbolically to denote *ancient, ancient times*. Furthermore, it is also used to depict *individuals who hold the highest and loftiest positions of rank and authority*.

By using the word *archas*, Paul emphatically tells us that at the very top of Satan's domain is a group of demon spirits who have held their lofty positions of power and authority ever since ancient times — probably ever since the fall of Lucifer.

Then Paul goes on to mention "powers" as those evil forces that are second in command in Satan's dark dominion.

The word "powers" is taken from the word *exousia*, and it denotes *delegated authority*. This tells us that there is a lower-ranking group of demon spirits who have received *delegated authority* from Satan to do whatever they want to do, wherever they desire to do it. Thus, the demon spirits in this second group use their delegated authority to carry out all manner of evil and wickedness.

Next, Paul mentions "the rulers of the darkness of this world." What an amazing word this is! It is taken from the word *kosmokrateros* and is a compound of the words *kosmos* and *kratos*. The word *kosmos* denotes *order* or *arrangement*, and the word *kratos* has to do with *raw power*.

When these two words are compounded together into the word *kosmokrateros*, the new word depicts *raw power that has been harnessed and put into some kind of order*.

This word was technically used by the ancient Greeks to describe certain aspects of the military. The military was filled with young men who had a lot of natural ability — *raw power*, if you will. In order for that raw power to be effective, it had to be harnessed and organized (*kosmos*).

Thus, young soldiers with abounding energy were taught to be submitted, disciplined, ordered, and perfectly arranged. *This is the picture of rank and file.* In the end, all of those men, with all of that raw ability, were turned into a massive force.

Now Paul uses this same idea in Ephesians 6:12. By using the phrase "rulers of the darkness of this world," Paul tells us that the devil deals with his dark legions of demon spirits as if they were military troops. Satan organizes his demon spirits in rank and file, gives them orders and assignments, and then sends them out like troops who are committed to kill.

It is a spiritual reality that we have more authority than the devil; we have more power than the devil; and we have the Greater One living within us. As I pondered these truths one day, I asked the Lord, "If we have more authority, if we have more power, and if we have the Greater One living inside us, why does it seem that the Church is full of so much defeat?"

I will never forget what the Holy Spirit whispered to my heart. He said, *"The reason the Church is experiencing so much defeat is that the devil has something the Church does not have!"*

I quickly asked, "Lord, what is that?"

It was then that the Lord quickened Ephesians 6:12 to my understanding. The word *kosmokrateros* came alive in my heart, and then I understood!

The word *kosmokrateros* ("rulers of the darkness of this world") is a military term that has to do with *discipline, organization,* and *commitment.* The devil is so serious about doing damage to humanity that he deals with demon spirits as though they are *troops!* He puts them in rank and file and organizes them to the hilt. *Meanwhile, the average Spirit-filled believer often doesn't stay in one church for more than one year at a time!*

Yes, we do have more authority than the devil has; we do have more power than the devil has; and we do have the Greater One living in us. The Church of Jesus Christ is loaded with heaps and heaps of raw power. *But at this particular time, that power is disconnected and disjointed by a Body that lacks discipline, organization, and commitment!*

> As Christians, we have no power shortage, nor are we short of God-given authority. We simply have a great lack of discipline, organization, and commitment.

As Christians, we have no power shortage, nor are we short of God-given authority. We simply have a great lack of discipline, organization, and commitment. In order to change this, we must buckle down in the local church and begin to view ourselves as the troops of the Lord! *Once we match the discipline, organization, and commitment that the enemy possesses in his camp, we will begin to move into the awesome demonstration of God's power!*

Finally, Paul mentions "spiritual wickedness in high places." The word "wickedness" is taken from the word *poneros* and is used to depict *something that is bad, vile, malevolent, vicious, impious, or malignant.*

It is significant that Paul saves this Greek word until the end of this verse. By doing this, he is revealing to us the ultimate aim of Satan's dark domain: These demon spirits are sent forth from the spirit realm to afflict humanity in all manner of *bad, vile, malevolent, vicious, impious, and malignant ways.*

REVEALING NAMES, SYMBOLS, AND TYPES OF THE DEVIL IN THE BIBLE

Virtually all reputable scholars of the Church, past *and* present, agree that we have an adversary who hates the Gospel, detests the presence of the Church, and works around the clock to discredit the message of Jesus Christ.

The devil's entrance into the life of a believer is allowed primarily through that believer's negligence. He slips in through an uncommitted, unrenewed area of the mind — *a loophole* — and then begins to wage warfare against the mind and flesh of that individual.

> The devil's entrance into the life of a believer is allowed primarily through that believer's negligence.

Rather than hide from this foe, we must turn our eyes to the Scriptures to see what *God* has to say about him. There are many names, symbols, and types for the devil throughout the Old and New Testaments, each revealing a different facet of the devil's twisted, perverted nature and his mode of operation.

Our enemy is known as:

- *Abaddon* (Revelation 9:11)

- *Accuser* (Revelation 12:10)

- *Adversary* (1 Peter 5:8)

- *Angel of light* (2 Corinthians 11:14)

- *Apollyon* (Revelation 9:11)

- *Beelzebub* (Matthew 10:25; 12:24)

- *Belial* (2 Corinthians 6:15)

- *Devil* (Ephesians 6:11; 1 Peter 5:8; Revelation 12:9)

- *Dragon* (Revelation 12:9)

- *Evil one* (Matthew 6:13)

- *Murderer* (John 8:44)

- *Prince of this world* (John 12:31)

- *Prince of demons* (Matthew 9:34 *NIV*)

- *Prince of the power of the air* (Ephesians 2:2)

- *Roaring lion* (1 Peter 5:8)

- *Satan* (Luke 10:18)

- *Serpent* (Revelation 12:9)

ROMAN ARMOR
OF THE
FIRST AND SECOND
CENTURIES

ROMAN CAESARS AND EMPERORS

Augustus
27 B.C. - A.D. 14

Tiberius
A.D. 14-37

Caligula
A.D. 37-41

Claudius
A.D. 41-54

Nero
A.D. 54-68

Galba
A.D. 68-69

The Roman soldier wore seven primary pieces of weaponry. He had a huge helmet that was an elaborate, ornate, and decorative piece. It was intricate and interesting to look upon.

The breastplate began at the top of the soldier's neck and extended down to his waist and below his hips. It was often made of two pieces of metal that were attached at the top of the shoulders by brass rings. It could be fashioned of metal mesh or small pieces of metal that were woven together to make it look like the scales of a fish.

The loinbelt was the central piece of weaponry. When not in active combat, the shield and sword rested on the loinbelt.

A shield used in battle was a long, door-shaped weapon intended to protect the soldier during a skirmish. The sword was two-edged and used for stabbing an enemy at close range.

The Roman soldier's shoes were also deadly weapons. On the bottom were nails that gave the soldier a solid footing and crushed an enemy underfoot. The Roman soldier also wore greaves that protected his legs from cuts, bruises, and wounds so he could keep marching regardless of the terrain where he was forced to fight.

The Roman soldier also carried a lance that was used for striking an enemy from a distance.

[LEFT] An artist's depiction of a Roman soldier taken from the altar of Donitius Ahenobarbus. Notice the helmet, breastplate, loinbelt, shield, sword, and lance. This is the typical dress of a Roman soldier, exactly the image that Paul had in his mind when he wrote Ephesians chapter 6.

Otho	Vitellius	Vespasian	Titus	Domitian	Nerva
A.D. 69	A.D. 69	A.D. 69-79	A.D. 79-81	A.D. 81-96	A.D. 96-98

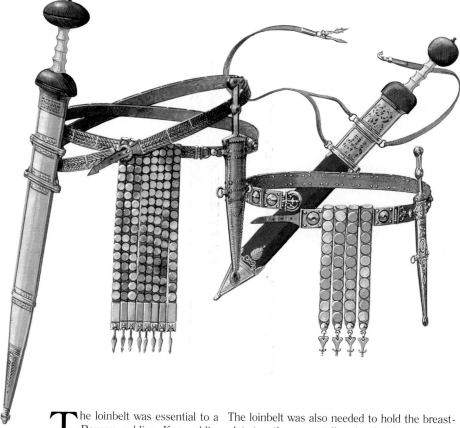

The loinbelt was essential to a Roman soldier. If a soldier attempted to conduct warfare without this part of his armor, it would have spelled disaster, for many other pieces of weap-onry were connected to the loinbelt.

The Roman soldier's oblong shield rested on a clip that was attached to the side of the loinbelt.

The two-edged sword dangled at the side of the Roman soldier in a sheath that was attached to the loinbelt, which made the loinbelt vital to his security.

The loinbelt was also needed to hold the breast-plate together, especially in battle. The two pieces of metal that formed the breastplate were held together at the waist by the loinbelt. If a soldier had attempted to conduct warfare without a loinbelt, he would have come undone in the midst of battle.

. . . .

[ABOVE] An artist's rendering of actual loinbelts that were used by Roman soldiers during the first century. This is precisely the picture Paul had in mind when he wrote about the loinbelt in Ephesians 6:14.

ROMAN CAESARS AND EMPERORS

Trajan
A.D. 98-117

Hadrian
A.D. 117-138

Aelius
A.D. 136-138

Antoninus Pius
A.D. 138-161

Marcus Aurelius
A.D. 161-180

Lucius Verus
A.D. 161-169

Several kinds of breastplates were worn by the Roman soldier. One kind was beautiful (as pictured to the left), but not made for war. It was a highly decorative piece of weaponry that was primarily used in parades or military ceremonies.

When fighting, the Roman soldier needed a breastplate that would completely protect him against all manner of assault (as pictured below). Therefore, the Roman soldier needed a breastplate that allowed maximum mobility and durability. He also required a breastplate that was so tightly woven together, it would successfully hold up under the pressure of battle and of daily wear and tear.

[BELOW] This breastplate is an example of the type of breastplate that was most often used by the Roman army in the second half of the first century — the time period when the apostle Paul wrote about spiritual weapons in Ephesians 6:10-18.

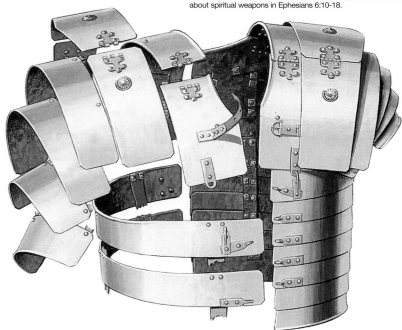

Commodus	Pertinax	Didius Julianus	Pescennius Niger	Clodius Albinus	Septimius Severus
A.D. 177-192	A.D. 193	A.D. 193	A.D. 193-194	A.D. 195-197	A.D. 193-211

The breastplate of the Roman soldier was the most beautiful, shiniest, most glamorous piece of weaponry that the Roman soldier possessed.

The first thing an onlooker noticed when viewing a Roman soldier was not his loinbelt, shoes, sword, or helmet, as intricate and important as these pieces of armor were. The first thing an onlooker noticed was the soldier's breastplate. The breastplate began at top of the neck and covered the soldier nearly all the way to his knees. It was composed of two different flanks of metal. One flank went down the front, and the other went down the back. The two flanks were held together at the top by metal rings or by right inner weaving of metal rings that were not visible to the eye but were crucial for holding the breastplate together as one piece. Quite often, the metal flanks were comprised of smaller pieces of metal that were tightly woven together.

The breastplate was the heaviest piece of weap-onry that the Roman soldier wore. At times it weighed in excess of 40 pounds, and some breastplates were reported to weigh 75 pounds or more.

The breastplate of the Roman soldier was made of highly polished metal or brass and was beautiful to look at. When the Roman army marched in the afternoon sun and the sunlight reflected off the soldiers' breastplates, it would create a blinding effect for their enemies.

The breastplate protected the vital organs of the body, giving the Roman soldier a sense of protection from enemy attacks. As long as his breastplate was securely in place, the soldier could march forward confidently into battle with no fear of being struck in one of his vital organs.

[RIGHT] A Roman soldier from the second half of the first century — the time when the apostle Paul wrote about

ROMAN CAESARS AND EMPERORS

Caracalla
A.D. 198-217

Geta
A.D. 209-212

Macrinus
A.D. 217-218

Diadumenian
A.D. 218

Elagabalus
A.D. 218-222

Severus Alexander
A.D. 222-235

T he shoes of the Roman soldiers were made of a mixture of leather and metal. Often the top of the shoe was fashioned of very durable leather or even metal. The sides were held together by multiple pieces of durable leather. On the bottom, the shoes were affixed with extremely dangerous nails that were intended to hold the soldier in place and that were also used to kick, wound, and even kill an opponent.

[BOTTOM] Below are illustrations of the shoes worn by Roman soldiers. Notice the nails affixed to the bottom of the shoes that were intended to hold the soldier in place. These shoes were weapons the Roman soldier could use to give an enemy a deadly wound.

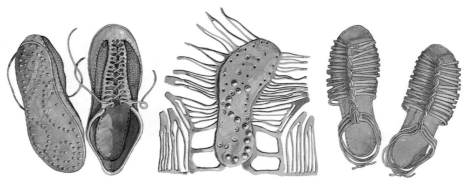

ROMAN CAESARS AND EMPERORS

Maximinus I
A.D. 235-238

Gordian I Africanus
A.D. 238

Gordian II Africanus
A.D. 238

Balbinus
A.D. 238

Pupienus
A.D. 238

Gordian III
A.D. 238-244

The greave of the Roman soldier was a piece of beautifully tooled metal that began at the top of the knee, extending past the lower leg to rest on the upper portion of the foot. This was a vital piece of weaponry for the Roman soldier because a lacerated, bruised, or broken leg could mean death. Roman soldiers therefore wore these metal greaves to be certain that their lower legs were protected at all times as they walked through extremely dangerous terrain or faced the assaults of the enemy.

[RIGHT] An example of a Roman centurion from the first century. Notice the greaves of metal on his lower legs.

[BOTTOM] An illustration of greaves worn by Roman soldiers from the first century when the apostle Paul wrote about spiritual weapons. This protective metal gave the Roman soldier the assurance that his legs would not be damaged during battle or on long marches.

ROMAN CAESARS AND EMPERORS

Philip I	Philip II	Trajan Decius	Herennius Etruscus	Hostilian	Trebonianus Gallus
A.D. 244-249	A.D. 247-249	A.D. 249-251	A.D. 251	A.D. 251	A.D. 251-253

The Roman soldier owned two kinds of shields — a small, round decorative shield used primarily for public parades or ceremonies and an oblong shield that was long in length and wide in width. The Greek word *theron* — usually the word for *a door* — was used to describe this latter shield because it was shaped long and wide like a door. This was just the opposite of the smaller decorative shields used in parades, which were totally inadequate for protecting a soldier in battle. The *theron* shield used in battle completely covered the Roman soldier.

In the majority of cases, the Roman soldier's shield was composed of multiple layers of thick leather that were firmly laid on top of a foundation of wood. Usually six layers of animal hide were specially tanned and then woven together so tightly that the shield became nearly as strong as steel. One layer of leather is tough, but six layers of tightly woven leather made the Roman soldier's shield extremely durable, exceptionally strong, and nearly impenetrable.

Although these six layers of animal hide made the soldier's shield strong and durable, the shield could become stiff and breakable over a period of time if he didn't take care of it properly. Therefore, the Roman soldier had to know how to maintain his shield in top-notch condition. Every morning one of his first tasks was to attend to his shield — applying oil and then rubbing it deep into the leather to keep it soft, supple, and durable in the middle of a fight. Failing to properly maintain one's shield was an invitation for a fatal blow.

[LEFT] A depiction of a Roman soldier from the middle of the first century. There is no doubt that this is the type of shield the apostle Paul had in mind when he wrote about the shield of faith in Ephesians 6:16.

ROMAN CAESARS AND EMPERORS

Volusian	Aemilian	Uranius Antoninus	Valerian I	Gallienus	Valerian II
A.D. 251-253	A.D. 253	A.D. 253-254	A.D. 253-260	A.D. 253-268	A.D. 253-255

[ABOVE] Roman legionaries forming a *testudo*, or tortoise shield roof, used when approaching walls.

When Roman soldiers marched forward in battle, they often locked their shields together to form a nearly indivisible and unconquerable unit. This act of locking shield to shield enabled the Roman forces to move forward like a tank without suffering many losses.

Because the shield was composed of multiple layers of animal hide, it required daily maintenance in order to keep it soft, supple, and pliable. When the Roman soldier awakened, he reached first for his shield and then for a small vial of oil. After saturating a piece of cloth with oil, he would begin to rub the heavy ointment into the leather portion of the shield. Without this daily application of oil, the shield would harden and crack when put under pressure and eventually fall to pieces. Therefore, if a Roman soldier wanted to live a long life, it was imperative for him to take that vial of oil and apply it to his shield every day of his military life.

Before going into battle, a Roman soldier would also dip his shield into water, saturating it with water until it was soaked. Thus, if his shield was struck by the flaming arrows of the enemy, the water-soaked shield would not catch fire and would extinguish the flames.

[RIGHT] This is exactly the type of shield used by Roman soldiers during the first century. Most often the outer rim was made of metal that clamped down on the leather and fixed it to the wooden base. This shield was wide and long like the door of a house.

ROMAN CAESARS AND EMPERORS

Saloninus	Macrianus	Quietus	Regalianus	Postumus	Laelianus
A.D. 259	A.D. 260-261	A.D. 260-261	A.D. 260	A.D. 259-268	A.D. 268

The helmet of the Roman soldier was very ornate, intricate, and often beautiful. Rather than a simple piece of metal that had been formed to fit the soldier's head, it was frequently highly decorative with all kinds of etchings and engravings.

As if these etchings and engravings were not enough, a huge plume of feathers or colored horsehair often stood straight up from the top of the helmet. If the helmet was to be used in a public parade or ceremony, this brightly colored plume of feathers or horsehair could be long enough to drape down the soldier's back.

The helmet was made of metal, usually bronze, and equipped with pieces of metal to protect the cheeks and jaws. Because it was extremely heavy, its interior was lined with sponge in order to soften the weight of the helmet on the soldier's head.

[LEFT] A depiction of a Roman soldier's helmet. This helmet dates to the second century and is fashioned of bronze and metal in the style of helmets worn by soldiers in the middle part of the first century.

The word "helmet" is from the Greek word *perikephalaia*. The word *peri* means *around*, and the word *kephalaia* is the Greek word for *the head*. When compounded together, the new word describes *something that is tightly fixed around the head in order to protect it.*

The opponent of a Roman soldier carried a battle-axe that was intended to take the heads off their enemies. If a Roman soldier entered battle without a helmet, it was nearly certain that he would lose his head. Therefore, the Roman soldier's helmet was essential in order to protect his head in battle.

As beautiful and noticeable as the helmet was, it was much more than a fabulous piece of weaponry. It was one of the most important defenses the Roman soldier had in battle.

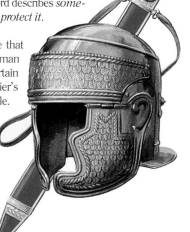

[RIGHT] An illustration depicting a cavalry helmet from the first century. This was the most common kind of helmet used by the Roman army of Paul's time.

ROMAN CAESARS AND EMPERORS

Marius
A.D. 268

Victorinus
A.D. 268-270

Tetricus I
A.D. 270-273

Tetricus II
A.D. 270-273

Claudius II Gothicus
A.D. 268-270

Quintillus
A.D. 270

Gallic: iron;
mid-1st century

Holland: silvered bronze;
early 1st century

Gallic: bronze;
1st century

Italy: bronze;
mid-1st century

Germany: bronze;
early 1st century

Holland: iron;
late 1st century

Italy: bronze;
mid-1st century

Germany: iron
and bronze;
late 1st century

Germany: iron and bronze;
mid-1st century

Alsace: bronze;
mid-1st century

Romania: iron;
late 1st century

Israel: iron
and bronze;
early
2nd century

This page illustrates various samples of helmets that were worn by Roman soldiers in different parts of the Roman Empire during the first and second century A.D.

Although stationed in different locations in this far-flung empire, the helmets remained basically the same in construction and style. The helmet was an essential piece of weaponry, primarily designed to protect the head from an enemy's assaults.

No soldier would deliberately go into battle without a helmet, since such an action would most likely result in sustaining a death blow.

ROMAN CAESARS AND EMPERORS

Aurelian	Vabalathus	Tacitus	Florianus	Probus
A.D. 270-275	A.D. 271-272	A.D. 275-276	A.D. 276	A.D. 276-282

[ABOVE] A relief of Roman soldiers from the tomb of Prefect Tiberius Flavius Miccalus.

There were actually five different kinds of swords used by Roman soldiers at the time that Paul wrote about the "sword of the Spirit" in Ephesians 6:17.

The first sword used by the Roman soldier was called *the gladius sword*. It was an extremely heavy, broad-shouldered sword with a long blade. Of all the swords, the gladius was the most aesthetically beautiful; however, because of its weight, it was also the most cumbersome and awkward to use.

This particular sword was a two-handed sword, which meant it required two hands to use it due to its immense weight. It was also sharpened only on one side.

The second sword was shorter and narrower. It was approximately 17 inches long and about 2 1/2 inches in width. Hence, it was lighter than the other swords. This sword grew in popularity throughout the empire because it was so much easier to carry and swing.

ROMAN CAESARS AND EMPERORS

Carus
A.D. 282-283

Numerian
A.D. 283-284

Carinus
A.D. 283-285

Julian of Pannonia
A.D. 284-285

Carausius
A.D. 287-293

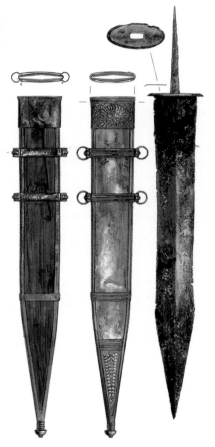

The *third sword* used by the Roman army was even shorter than the second sword. In fact, it was so short that it looked more like a dagger than a sword. This dagger-like sword was carried in a small, hidden scabbard beneath the soldier's outer coat. It was used to inflict a mortal wound into the heart of an enemy or an aggressor.

The *fourth sword* Roman soldiers used was a long and very slender sword. This sword was primarily used by the cavalry, as opposed to the more durable swords that were carried by the infantry. Additionally, this long, slender sword was also used in a sport that was similar to modern-day fencing. However, no soldier would have wanted to enter into combat with this kind of sword.

The *fifth sword* was the type of sword that Paul had in mind when he wrote about spiritual armor in the sixth chapter of Ephesians. In that verse he used the word *machaira* to denote the "sword of the Spirit." This refers to a brutal weapon that was approximately 19 inches long and razor-sharp on both sides of the blade. Because both sides of this sword were razor-sharp, it was more dangerous than the other swords. At times, the very tip of the sword turned upward, causing the point of the blade to be extremely sharp and deadly.

This two-edged blade inflicted a wound far worse than the other swords. Before the Roman soldier withdrew this particular sword from the gut of his enemy, he held it very tightly with both hands and gave it a wrenching twist inside the man's stomach, often withdrawing the opponent's entrails as he pulled the sword from his body.

Of all the swords available, this was the most dangerous sword of all. Although the other swords were deadly, this one was *a terror to the imagination*! This sword was not only intended to kill, but to completely rip an opponent's insides to shreds. *It was a weapon of murder*!

[ABOVE and BELOW] A depiction of Roman soldiers' swords and scabbards, as used at the time when Paul wrote about spiritual weaponry in Ephesians 6:17. The sword of the Roman soldier was designed to kill, not to merely injure an enemy.

ROMAN CAESARS AND EMPERORS

Allectus
A.D. 293-296

Domitius Domitianus
A.D. 296-297

Maximianus
Three Reigns

Maximianus
First Reign: A.D. 286-305
Second Reign: A.D. 306-308
Third Reign: A.D. 310

Constantius I
A.D. 305-306

Although the lance is not specifically mentioned by name in Ephesians 6, the lance *has* to be in this text; otherwise, we do not have the whole armor of God. However, the lance *is* included in the set of spiritual equipment and can be found in Ephesians 6:18, where Paul writes, "Praying always with all prayer and supplication in the Spirit...." I call this *the lance of prayer and supplication.*

The lances used by the Roman army varied in size, shape, and length. Over the course of many centuries, these various lances were modified substantially. The Roman soldier used all kinds of lances. The old Greek lance used during Homer's time was normally made of ash wood and was about six to seven feet long, having a solid iron lance-head at the end. Like the lance itself, the iron head of the lance varied in form. Often it resembled a leaf, a bulrush, a sharp barb, or simply a jagged point.

Some lances were small; others were long. The smaller, shorter lances were used for gouging or thrusting an enemy up close, whereas the longer lances were used for hurling at an enemy at a distance. Most Roman soldiers carried both lances, short and long. With the aid of the shorter lance, they could thrust through the body of their adversary from close range. With the longer lance, they would strike their adversary with a deadly blow from afar. After successfully hitting an enemy with this longer lance, the Roman soldier would draw his sword and run to finish off the enemy while he lay wounded on the ground.

There were short lances, long lances, narrow lances, wide lances, pointed lances, jagged lances, multiple-blade lances, and so on. The Roman army used a lance called the *pilum.* These *pilum* lances were used when an opposing force came to attack the Romans' encampment. Rather than wait for the enemy to come upon them and initiate the fight, thus taking many losses, the Romans hurled this extremely heavy lance through the air toward their foes. By doing this, they could strike enemy soldiers to the ground before they were able to penetrate the Roman encampment.

[RIGHT] The *pilum* in New Testament times was six feet long, with the iron lance-head at the top of the lance and the iron shaft at the bottom both measuring approximately three feet in length.

EMPEROR CONSTANTINE

As Constantine wrestled for control of the Roman Empire, in a vision he saw a cross and heard a voice proclaim, "IN HOC SIGNO VINCES" or "In this sign conquer." Assuming power, Constantine promulgated the Edict of Milan, which made Christianity a permissible religion.

[ABOVE] The artist's rendition shows a group of Roman soldiers walking together. Notice their shields, helmets, loinbelts, lances, and other pieces of armor. The Roman army was the mightiest military force the world had ever seen. As believers, we are equipped with spiritual weaponry that is much mightier than natural weapons. God intends for us to use these spiritual weapons to set captives free and to take territory for the Kingdom of God.

Roman soldiers were trained killers and the finest weapons of war that existed during the first century. Just as they were equipped with natural armor, Paul teaches that God has equipped us with spiritual armor that puts us in a position to vanquish every spiritual foe.

The exact weight of all this armor on an average Roman soldier varied according to the physical stature of the soldier. But regardless of the size of the soldier, all Roman soldiers carried a very heavy amount of armor.

During Paul's many imprisonments, he was chained and held captive by such Roman soldiers. In this environment, the Holy Spirit began to speak to Paul about spiritual weaponry. There at Paul's side was a perfectly dressed and fully armed soldier who had been trained in the skill of warfare. This soldier was literally "dressed to kill." Hour by hour, day after day, and week after week during Paul's incarceration, he lived side by side with these heavily dressed, trained killers. As Paul sat in this environment and looked at the fully armed soldier at his side, the Holy Spirit began to speak to him, developing his understanding of spiritual weaponry.

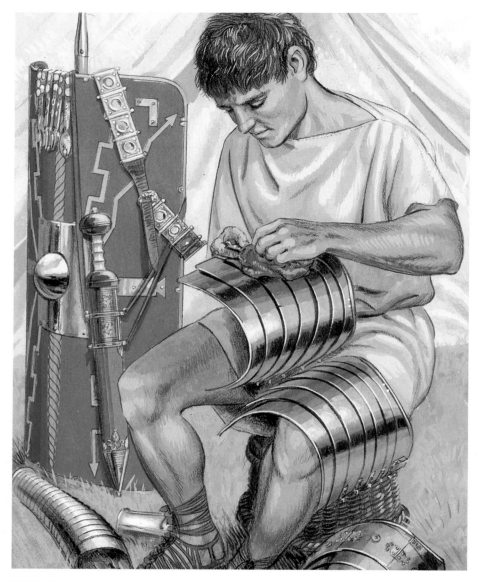

[ABOVE] A Roman soldier cleaning and lubricating his equipment. A part of a soldier's daily routine was the proper care and maintenance of his weaponry. Likewise, we must continually ensure that *our* spiritual equipment is in top-notch condition.

The apostle Paul told us, "Wherefore take unto you the whole armour of God..." (Ephesians 6:13). The words "take unto you" are from the Greek word *analabete*. The word *ana* means *to repeat an action*; *to do something again*; or *to do it like you once did it*. The word *labete* means *to receive* or *to take*. When these words are compounded together, the word *analabete* portrays a soldier who is not wearing his armor as he once did, but who now needs to reach down, pick up his armor, put it on, and use it as he previously did in his life.

This clearly means it is your responsibility to make certain that you are dressed in the whole armor of God. If you are not walking in spiritual weaponry as you once did, you can make the choice today to reach down, pick up your spiritual armor from the place where you left it, put it back on, and walk again in the power of God. The choice is yours — but you can do it today.

These names, symbols, and types of Satan can be divided into four categories:

1. Satan's destructive bent

2. Satan's perverted nature

3. Satan's desire to control

4. Satan, the mind manipulator

SATAN'S DESTRUCTIVE BENT

Of the 17 names, symbols, and types given above, two are devoted to Satan's insatiable desire to *destroy*.

The names *Abaddon* and *Apollyon* are used to describe the devil in Revelation 9:11. The name *Abaddon* is the Hebrew equivalent of the Greek name *Apollyon*. Both of these names mean *destroyer*.

In reference to Satan, Revelation 9:11 says, "And they had a king over them, which is the angel of the bottomless pit, whose name in the Hebrew tongue is *Abaddon*, but in the Greek tongue hath his name *Apollyon*."

> Demon spirits, over which Satan rules as a king, possess the same destructive nature as their master. They also operate according to the instructions Satan gives them as he sends them forth to destroy.

You can be certain that demon spirits, over which Satan rules as a king, possess the same destructive nature as their master. They also operate according to the instructions Satan gives them as he sends them forth to *destroy*.

SATAN'S PERVERTED NATURE

Of the titles given in the list above, five of them have to do with the devil's twisted, perverted nature. Those five are found in the following names, symbols, and types: "Beelzebub," "Belial," "dragon," "evil one," and "murderer."

BEELZEBUB

The name "Beelzebub" was initially used by the Philistines of the Old Testament to describe the god of Ekron. It literally meant *lord of the flies* (2 Kings 1:2-6). Originally it was spelled "Baalzebub." As time progressed, the Jews altered *Baalzebub* to *Beelzebub*, which added an even dimmer idea to this particular name of the devil. This new name "Beelzebub" now meant *lord of the dunghill* or *lord of the manure*.

Two powerful and important images of Satan are presented in these two names. First, he is presented as "Baalzebub," the *lord of the flies*. This is clearly the picture of Satan masquerading himself as the lord of demon spirits. Obviously, the Philistines looked upon demon spirits in the same way one would look upon nasty, dirty *flies* that bite, torment, and irritate.

Secondly, he is presented as "Beelzebub," the *lord of the dunghill*. By adding a twist to this particular name of Satan, the Jews revealed a very important characteristic of the devil. Just like nasty, dirty flies, both the devil and his evil spirits are attracted to "dunghills," or environments where rotting, stinking carnality pervades. This is the environment where Satan thrives best.

BELIAL

The name "Belial," which is of Greek origination, means *worthless*. This name is always used in connection with *filthiness* and *wickedness*. Whenever it is used, either in the Old Testament or the New Testament, it is used to depict *extremely evil men*. For instance, First Samuel 2:12 tells us that Eli's sons were "sons of *Belial*."

What an example Eli's sons were of this word "Belial"! They were fornicators and thieves, full of idolatry and rebellion. These terrible traits were ingrained into their character to such an extent that God's judgment came upon them, and they were removed from the scene in one day's time. Because First Samuel 2:12 calls them "sons of *Belial*," we know they obtained this horrid behavior from Satan, who is himself the origination of the name "Belial."

DRAGON

The word "dragon" is also used in Revelation 12:9 to depict the devil. It says, "And the great dragon was cast out, that old serpent, called the Devil, and Satan, which deceiveth the whole world: he was cast out into the earth, and his angels were cast out with him."

It is clear from this verse that the terms "dragon" and "serpent" are used interchangeably in reference to Satan's twisted, demented, and perverted nature. By employing both of these pictures, the Bible presents the devil as a deadly, poisonous, ready-to-strike-and-kill creature.

EVIL ONE

The next biblical example of the devil can be found in what is traditionally called "The Lord's Prayer." In Matthew 6:13, the Lord Jesus prayed, "And lead us not into temptation, but deliver us from evil...." The Greek language more accurately reads, *"...but deliver us from the evil one."*

From this usage, we know that Jesus looked on the devil as the "evil one." No one was more familiar with Satan than Jesus; hence, it is important to us that Jesus, knowing the devil so well, would label him thus.

MURDERER

It was also the Lord Jesus who told us that Satan is a "murderer." In John 8:44, Jesus told the scribes and Pharisees, "Ye are of your father the devil, and the lusts of your father ye will do. He was a murderer from the beginning, and abode not in the truth, because there is no truth in him...."

The murderous nature of Satan was first manifested in Genesis 4:8, when he inspired Cain to slay his brother Abel. It was also Satan's murderous nature that inspired Herod to kill all the babies in Bethlehem-Ephrata. We continue to see the devil's murderous nature in the deaths of millions of early Christian martyrs and still today wherever murderous injustice prevails on the earth. *Murder is a part of Satan's demented nature.*

SATAN'S DESIRE TO CONTROL

Satan's strong desire to *control* the spirit realm, the world, and every human government and human institution in this world system is evidenced by the fact that the Bible calls him "the prince of this world," "the prince of demons," and "the prince of the power of the air."

PRINCE OF THIS WORLD

By calling Satan "the prince of this world," even Jesus recognized his temporal control over certain things in this earthly sphere.

> **By calling Satan "the prince of this world," even Jesus recognized his temporal control over certain things in this earthly sphere.**

You might remember that Satan himself personally offered Jesus the "kingdoms of this world" during Jesus' 40 days and nights of testing in the wilderness. Jesus was confronted by this "prince of the world" during those 40 days and resisted the devil's power until His adversary fled. Jesus spoke from personal experience when he referred to this temporal claim of Satan.

PRINCE OF DEMONS

In Matthew 9:34, Satan is also called "the prince of demons." The word "prince" is taken from the Greek word *archontas* and refers to *one who holds the first place* or *one who holds the highest seat of power.*

The title "prince of demons" most assuredly reveals that Satan holds the highest-ranking seat among a host of diabolical spirits. The word "prince" denotes that there is rank and file and some form of organization to Satan's system of governing his kingdom. We have already seen this in Ephesians 6:12.

PRINCE OF THE POWER OF THE AIR

The apostle Paul called Satan "the prince of the power of the air" (Ephesians 2:2). Again, the word "prince" is taken from the Greek word *archontas*, meaning *one who holds the highest seat of power.*

This is in complete agreement with Ephesians 6:12, which states that under Satan's control, there are varying degrees of spiritually wicked power: principalities, powers, rulers of the darkness of this world, and spiritual wickedness in high places.

SATAN, THE MIND MANIPULATOR

Finally, we come to the last and largest category of the names, symbols, and types of Satan in the Bible. In this last category, we discover that Satan truly is *the master of mind games.*

Let's look at five names, symbols, and types of our enemy that specifically have to do with his ability to twist, deceive, and lie to people's minds. He is called the "adversary," "roaring lion," "angel of light," "devil," and "Satan."

ADVERSARY

The name "adversary" is extremely important as we attempt to understand the devil's mode of operation. It is taken from the Greek word *antidikos*, which is a compound of the Greek words *anti* and *dikos*.

The word *anti* simply means *against*. However, in the older and more classical Greek language, it was used to denote *the mental condition of a man or woman who was on the edge of insanity*. This, in fact, was a terribly dangerous person who would do someone great harm if he or she was not restrained. Therefore, the word *anti* is quite a nasty word.

The second part of the word "adversary" is taken from the Greek word *dikos*. *Dikos* is the root of the Greek word meaning *righteousness*. It refers to *justice, rightness, fairness,* and *righteousness*.

When the two words are compounded together, they portray *one who is adamantly opposed to righteousness*. Because the word *anti* carries the idea of *hostility*, this tells us that the devil is one who *is hostile toward righteousness* or who *desires to destroy righteousness and obliterate it*.

This means that the devil is not just passively opposed to the presence of righteousness or righteous people. *He is actively*

> The devil is not just passively opposed to the presence of righteousness or righteous people. He is actively pursuing them and doing all within his power to wipe them out!

pursuing them and doing all within his power to wipe them out! He *hates* righteousness!

In one way or another, Satan mentally tries to devour us with present temptations or with past memories. He does all of this in order to assault our sense of righteousness. His ultimate goal is that we would eventually be left high and dry with no confidence before God, devil, or man.

This is precisely why Peter said, "Be sober, be vigilant; because your adversary the devil, as a roaring lion, walketh about, seeking whom he may devour" (1 Peter 5:8).

ROARING LION

This leads us to the next title of Satan. Peter says he is like unto "a roaring lion." What awe and fear the mighty roar of a lion strikes in the heart of frail man!

However, in the case of the devil, his roar is more fearsome than his bite.

Colossians 2:15 victoriously declares, "And having spoiled principalities and powers, he [Jesus] made a shew of them openly, triumphing over them in it."

By means of the Cross and the resurrection, Jesus Christ stripped these demonic powers bare of the authority they once possessed. Jesus' victory over them was so thorough that He even "made a shew of them openly." (For a more detailed description of this phrase, *see* Chapter Nine of *Living in the Combat Zone*).

> By means of the Cross and the resurrection, Jesus Christ stripped these demonic powers bare of the authority they once possessed.

However, this has not stopped the devil from trying to *sound* dreadful. Through his continuous hassling of our thoughts, his insinuations about failure, his concoction of unrealistic fears in our souls, and his constant onslaught against our minds, Satan tries to beat us down into defeat. This constant "roaring" in our souls is just another attempt of the adversary to wear us down, wear us out, and then swallow us up in self-pity.

> The enemy is looking for those who are weak in faith, ignorant of the Word of God, isolated unto themselves, and not mature enough to stand in the face of his constant, hassling allegations.

Notice that the object of the adversary is to seek those "whom he may devour" (1 Peter 5:8). The word "seek" implies that not everyone will fall prey to these tactics.

Satan is not seeking just *anyone* to devour; he is seeking those whom he *may* devour. *In other words, the enemy is looking for those who are weak in faith, ignorant of the Word of God, isolated unto themselves, and not mature enough to stand in the face of his constant, hassling allegations.*

These are the individuals this "roaring lion" is seeking after, and his object is to *devour* them. The word "devour" comes from the Greek word *katapino*, and literally means *to swallow up completely*.

ANGEL OF LIGHT

Satan is also called an "angel of light." In dealing with the problem of false prophets, false teachers, false apostles, and deceivers who were trying to worm their way into the Corinthian Church, Paul says in Second Corinthians 11:14, "And no marvel; for Satan himself is transformed into an angel of light."

This is another clear picture of this master mind-manipulator. Satan disguises himself to be something that he really is not! Again, this kind of attack normally comes against a person's mind. The portrayal of Satan as an "angel of light" is a vivid example of his deceptive power to twist people's thinking.

THE DEVIL

Of course, Satan is also called "the devil." In fact, the New Testament refers to him as such more than 40 times!

The name "devil" is taken from the Greek word *diabolos*. It is a compound of the words *dia* and *balos*. *Dia* means *through* and carries with it the idea of *penetration*. The word *balos* is taken from the word *ballo*, which means *I throw*, as in throwing a ball or a rock. When the two words are compounded, the new word depicts *the act of repeatedly throwing a ball or rock against something until it penetrates that barrier and breaks through to the other side.*

Therefore, in the name "devil," we are not only given the proper name of this archenemy but also his mode of operation. His name means that he is *one who continually strikes and strikes and strikes again — beating against the walls of people's minds over and over again — until, finally, he breaks through and penetrates their thought processes.*

SATAN

This enemy of both God and man is called *Satan*, which is taken from the Hebrew word *shatana* and means *to hate and to accuse*. It is used more than 50 times in the Old and New Testament, and it also carries with it the ideas of *slander and false accusation*.

A PREREQUISITE TO SPIRITUAL WARFARE

It was because of this archenemy that Paul wrote to the Ephesian church and urged them to "put on the whole armour of God..." (Ephesians 6:11).

However, keep in mind what Paul told the Ephesian believers to do before he ever told them to put on the whole armor of God! Paul urged:

- Put away lying (4:25).

- Speak truth with your neighbor (4:25).

- Be angry, and sin not; don't let the sun go down on your wrath (4:26).

- Give no place to the devil (4:27).

- Let him who stole steal no more (4:28).

- Let no corrupt communication proceed out of your mouth (4:29).

- Grieve not the Holy Spirit (4:30).

- Let all bitterness, wrath, anger, clamor, evil speaking, and malice be put away from you (4:31).

We must not forget that a consecrated life is a prerequisite to real spiritual warfare. If these areas of our lives are left unattended, uncommitted, and unsurrendered, we have left gaping loopholes through which Satan is able to continue to exert his hellish schemes in our lives.

> Our lack of commitment and the secret places of our lives that have never been fully surrendered will stop us dead in our tracks whenever we try to deal with the devil's attacks.

Screaming, yelling, screeching, stomping, and shouting at the devil will not accomplish one single thing if we have deliberately, or simply by negligence, allowed "the loins of our minds" to go unchecked and ungirded. Our lack of commitment and the secret places of our lives that have never been fully surrendered will stop us dead in our tracks whenever we try to deal with the devil's attacks.

On the other hand, when we choose to live holy and surrendered lives — carefully guarding our minds and equipping ourselves with the whole armor of God — we become AWESOME weapons in the hands of an Almighty God!

QUESTIONS FOR PERSONAL GROWTH OR GROUP DISCUSSION

1. What is the number-one way to neutralize any attack the devil might wage against your flesh?

2. What three characteristics of the devil's kingdom are qualities that the Body of Christ needs as well? How does the lack of these qualities within the Church give an advantage to the enemy?

3. How does the enemy gain entrance into a believer's life? What steps can you take to make sure you never allow the devil to gain access into *your* life?

4. What tactics does the devil use to assault your sense of righteousness? What is the end goal he is trying to achieve, and how can you keep him from succeeding?

5. What does the devil look for as he seeks someone whom he may "devour"? What characteristics must a believer possess before the enemy can gain that kind of access into his life?

NOTES:

CHAPTER TEN

THE LOINBELT OF TRUTH

*G*od has not left us naked before the enemy; He has provided us with spiritual weaponry that has the ability to counterattack and defeat any scheme that the devil would try to use against us. God knows that in order for us to successfully fight the unseen powers that have been marshaled against us, we must have His special supernatural power that He has provided for this fight.

> God has not left us naked before the enemy.

We have seen that in Ephesians 6:10-18, Paul deals with key elements of spiritual warfare that we need to know and appropriate in our personal lives. In this chapter, we will begin to examine the specific pieces of armor that God has given to the Church.

In Ephesians 6:14-18, Paul says this:

> **Stand therefore, having your loins girt about with truth, and having on the breastplate of righteousness; and your feet shod with the preparation of the gospel of peace; above all, taking the shield of faith,**

wherewith ye shall be able to quench all the fiery darts of the wicked.

And take the helmet of salvation, and the sword of the Spirit, which is the word of God: praying always with all prayer and supplication in the Spirit....

As stated before, Ephesians 6 is not the first time Paul lists spiritual armor in Scripture. In the book of First Thessalonians, the oldest book of the New Testament, Paul also gives a shorter list of spiritual armor.

In First Thessalonians 5:8, Paul says, "But let us, who are of the day, be sober, putting on the breastplate of faith and love; and for an helmet, the hope of salvation."

This earlier version is clearly a very limited view of spiritual armor compared to the list we find in Ephesians 6. Paul's earlier view was so undeveloped that he referred to the breastplate as one of "faith" and "love." The only other weapon he mentioned in this earlier text, besides the breastplate, was the helmet of salvation.

PAUL'S EXPANDED VERSION OF SPIRITUAL ARMOR

In First Thessalonians, Paul's list of armor is brief. But in Ephesians, he gives an exhaustive list of spiritual weaponry. What happened between these two texts?

Through the years, the Holy Spirit began speaking to Paul, just as He speaks to us. As Paul began to meditate on the small amount of knowledge he had of spiritual armor, the Holy Spirit began to open up this subject for him with fresh revelation. As the years went by, this process continued until the Holy Spirit had fully developed Paul's knowledge of spiritual armor.

Thus, by the time Paul writes Ephesians 6, he no longer has an incomplete view of spiritual weaponry. Now he can see the whole picture — the Holy Spirit's full revelation of the armor God has provided for the believer. With that complete revelation in mind, Paul now begins to write about the full armor of God.

Notice how Paul begins this text in Ephesians 6:14. He says, "*Stand therefore....*" The Greek word for "stand" is that word *stenai*, meaning *to stand upright*. It is the image of *one who is so confident that he is standing with his head held high and his shoulders thrown back.* Paul obviously has the picture of a Roman soldier in mind — the kind of soldier who is very proud to be a soldier.

This is precisely the picture the Holy Spirit is painting for us in this verse. When you have donned the full armor of God, you have every reason to stand up straight and be confident in God!

> When you have donned the full armor of God, you have every reason to stand up straight and be confident in God!

Notice the next statement: "Stand therefore, *having your loins girt about with truth....*" Now we come to the first piece of weaponry that Paul lists in this expanded version of spiritual armor: *the Roman loinbelt.*

FOR REVIEW

On the top of his head, the Roman soldier wore a huge *helmet*. It was a very elaborate, ornate, decorative piece of weaponry, intricate in all its parts and interesting to look at. That's one reason the Holy Spirit calls our salvation a "helmet of salvation," for our salvation is the most elaborate, ornamental, intricate thing God has ever done for us!

In addition to this, the Roman soldier wore *a breastplate* that began at the top of his neck and extended down to his hips, going past his hips as a skirt down to his knees. The breastplate was made of two pieces of bronze or brass. One sheet of metal covered the soldier's front, and the other covered his back. These sheets of metal were attached by solid brass rings on the top and sides. The surface of the breastplate looked like the scales of a fish, and it was often referred to as a "coat of mail."

As if this weren't enough, the Roman soldier wore *greaves* on his legs and dangerously spiked *shoes* on his feet.

It is important to note that the Roman soldier was completely covered by his armor. He had a helmet on his head, a breastplate on his upper torso and midsection, and he was covered with metal from the top of his knees to the bottom of his legs.

> **It is important to note that the Roman soldier was completely covered by his armor.**

The soldier's greaves were very decorative and beautiful. They were made of a piece of metal, normally bronze or brass, that was wrapped around the shin or calf of the leg and extended from the knee to the foot. A heavy piece of metal covered the top of the foot, and strong straps of hide covered the sides. On the bottom of the foot were spikes one to three inches long.

Notice how much metal this man was carrying! He was dressed in a metal helmet; his breastplate was metal; his greaves and shoes were metal; and attached to his loinbelt was a little ring where he could clip his shield, which was also partially made of metal.

In addition to all of this weaponry, the Roman soldier also carried a lance or spear that rested along the ridge of his back and sat in a specially designed pouch attached to the loinbelt.

The Most Important Weapon

Now let's take some time to look at each piece of our spiritual armor more in depth. Paul begins his description of the armor of God by saying, "Stand therefore, *having your loins girt about with truth*...."

I initially thought the loinbelt must have been a beautiful weapon, like the others listed in this text. But the loinbelt was the least attractive, the least noticeable, and the most boring piece of armor that the Roman soldier wore!

When a Roman soldier was wearing his beautiful breastplate of brass, who would notice his belt? If you were to describe a man's clothing, would you begin with his belt? You can hardly even see it. You would probably start out by describing his jacket; then you'd move on to his shirt, his necktie, and even his shoes. But you wouldn't begin with his belt, would you?

Your belt seems to be an insignificant little thing — until you take it off! Then you discover how important that belt really is! Take it off, and your pants might start falling down. And as your pants fall down, your shirt can come untucked. And if you've lost your pants and your shirt has come untucked, you look like a mess!

It's easy to fall apart when you don't have your belt on. You'll spend most of your time trying to keep your pants pulled up. You won't feel very confident, and you certainly won't want to make any fast moves!

That is precisely what the loinbelt did for the Roman soldier — it held all the pieces of his armor together. He might be wearing all his great weaponry, but if his loinbelt was not in place, everything would fall apart. *Thus, it was said that the loinbelt was the most vital part of all the weaponry the Roman soldier wore.*

For example, the Roman soldier's shield was attached to the loinbelt. If he had no loinbelt, he had no resting place for that massive shield. If he had no loinbelt, he had no place to hang his sword. If there was no loinbelt, there was nothing for his lance to rest upon. If he didn't have a loinbelt, there was nothing to keep his breastplate from flapping in the wind. *The loinbelt held it all together!*

The soldier's armor would have literally fallen apart, piece by piece, if he hadn't had the loinbelt fixed in its place around his waist. That's why the loinbelt was so vital to the Roman soldier.

Without it, he had absolutely no confidence in fighting. With it, he was assured that all the pieces of his equipment would stay in place so he could move quickly and fight with great fury.

Thus, Paul says, "Stand therefore, *having your loins girt about with truth...*" (Ephesians 6:14).

A VISIBLE PIECE OF ARMOR

The majority of your spiritual armor is invisible. For instance, you can't physically see the breastplate of righteousness. You can't physically see your shoes of peace, your shield of faith, your helmet of salvation, your sword of the Spirit, or your lance of intercession. These are *invisible weapons*.

But you *can* see one weapon. In fact, there is only one spiritual weapon that is visible to the sight — the loinbelt of truth.

The loinbelt of truth is the written Word of God! This is the only spiritual weapon that has taken on a physical, natural form and has passed tangibly from the spirit realm into our hands! *It is the most important piece of weaponry that we possess.*

> There is only one spiritual weapon that is visible to the sight — the loinbelt of truth.

If you saw a Roman soldier, would you begin describing his outfit with his belt? No, you would probably say, "Oh, look at that helmet! Look at those shoes and that breastplate! My, look at that shield, that sword, and that lance! Oh, I almost forgot — he's wearing a belt too."

This, however, was not the Holy Spirit's approach when He inspired Paul to write about our spiritual armor. He went straight to the middle of the soldier and began describing the armor of God by mentioning the soldier's belt.

> When you ignore the Word of God and cease to apply it to your life on a daily basis, you have willfully chosen to let your entire spiritual life come apart at the seams!

God is making a point here: He's saying that the piece of armor that is in the middle of the man is the most important weapon *to* the man. If you take off that weapon, the man will fall apart.

Likewise, when you ignore the Word of God and cease to apply it to your life on a daily basis, you have willfully chosen to let your entire spiritual life come apart at the seams!

THE DIFFERENCE BETWEEN *LOGOS* AND *RHEMA*

It is important to point out that there are two kinds of words from God. There is the *logos*, which is the written Word of God, and there is the *rhema*, which is a fresh, specially quickened and revealed word from God.

It is sensible to recognize that you will not always receive a *rhema* every time you would like to receive one. But you can always receive from the *logos* — the written Word, the Bible. *When all else fails, your Bible will still be within an arm's reach!*

This may not sound as exciting as receiving a supernatural word from the Lord. But keep in mind that Paul likens the Word of God to a Roman soldier's loinbelt. The loinbelt wasn't pretty; it looked rather drab and was extremely commonplace. Every soldier had one of those "old things"!

This is the way some people view the Bible. They have so many Bibles around their house that they have lost their appreciation for it. They toss it aside with the attitude, *I'm not going to study this anymore. I've studied and studied it, and now I'm tired of it. There isn't anything else for me to get out of it.*

But if you lay aside your Bible (your "loinbelt of truth"), in time you'll begin to lose your sense of righteousness. Lay aside that loinbelt of truth, and you will slowly begin to lose your sense of peace. Lay aside that loinbelt of truth, and you will feel the joy of your salvation begin to deplete. If you toss that loinbelt of truth out of your life, you will begin very quickly to lose your ability to believe God and to walk in faith.

You absolutely *cannot* function as a believer without the Word of God having an active and central role in your life. You may run on a little steam from the past for a while, but you won't run very far.

If you remove the loinbelt — the Word of God — it will only be a matter of time until you begin to fall to pieces spiritually. Demonic assaults will break through that invisible barrier that used to protect you, and chaos will take over in your life.

THE ONLY WAY TO SUCCEED SPIRITUALLY

God has allowed me to minister in thousands of church services over the years. As we have traveled, we have made several observations.

Some ministers have tried to build their churches on praise and worship. Praise and worship are wonderful, but a person cannot build a church on this alone. *Praise and worship are not the loinbelt!*

Others have tried to build churches on social gatherings. Times of fun and fellowship are good and needed in the local church, but a person cannot build a church on the foundation of social gatherings. *Social gatherings and church fellowships are NOT the loinbelt!*

Others have attempted to build their church entirely on prayer. Of course, prayer is vital. We have desperately needed a new emphasis on prayer in our day, *but prayer is not the loinbelt!* Only the loinbelt will hold everything together for us, both as individual believers and as the corporate Body of Christ.

The Bible is the only piece of spiritual armor that is tangible to hold and visible to the eye. It was so important for us to have the Word of God in our possession that God permitted this divine Word to pass from the spirit realm into our world so we could hold it in our hands. *This is the most important piece of armor God has given us.* Think about it: *We can actually "hold" this weapon!*

Paul declares that this "loinbelt of truth" is so powerful and crucial, it can take the average individual and cause him or her to be "...perfect, throughly furnished unto all good works" (2 Timothy 3:17).

What is *your* aim? Do you want to succeed spiritually? Do you want to defeat the Philistines that continually come against your life? Do you want to be spiritually equipped?

If you want to walk through life clothed in your spiritual armor, you must begin by taking up the Word of God and permanently affixing it to your life. You have to give it a central place and a dominant role, allowing it to be the "loinbelt" that holds the rest of your weaponry together. The Bible must be the governor, the law, the ruler, and "the final say-so" in your life.

The written Word has the power to "...throughly *furnish* you unto all good works." The word "furnish" is taken from the Greek word *exartidzo*, which means *to completely outfit* or *to fully supply*. It was used to depict wagons or ships that were completely outfitted with gear.

> The Bible must be the governor, the law, the ruler, and "the final say-so" in your life.

By using this word, Paul tells us that the inspired Word of God will equip us with the "gear" we need in order to walk in the power of God and to maintain our victorious position over the devil.

HOW TO WALK IN RIGHTEOUSNESS

When you affix the loinbelt of truth onto the center of your life and faithfully ensure that it stays in place, everything else comes together. For instance, do you want to learn how to enjoy your God-given righteousness?

The writer of Hebrews says, "For when for the time ye ought to be teachers, ye have need that one teach you again which be the first principles of the oracles of God; and are become such as have need of milk, and not of strong meat. *For every one that useth milk is unskilful in the word of righteousness: for he is a babe*" (Hebrews 5:12,13).

According to this verse, you deliberately choose *not* to develop your understanding of righteousness when you ignore the Word of God. On the other hand, you can reverse this by spending time in the Word of God — meditating on it, praying over it, and studying it. As you do, you will discover that a wonderful, prevailing sense of righteousness will become a part of your thought life!

> For Christians who neglect the Word of God, it is only a matter of time before they feel very condemned in nearly every area of their lives.

For Christians who neglect the Word of God, it is only a matter of time before they feel very condemned in nearly every area of their lives. Although declared righteous by God when they were first saved, these Christians are not conscious of their God-given righteousness because they haven't made the Word a priority in their lives.

So if you want to enjoy walking through life clothed with the breastplate of righteousness, you must first put on the loinbelt of truth by making the written Word of God the top priority in your life. The Word will furnish you with righteousness.

How To Walk in Peace

Would you like to experience more peace in your life? Paul tells you how to make this a reality when he says, "And let the peace of God rule in your hearts..." (Colossians 3:15).

Naturally speaking, very few Christians experience this "ruling" peace of God in their hearts. Because of their hectic schedules and the rushed pace of this modern era, the vast majority of believers experience inner turmoil, frustration, and an entire host of flip-flop emotions.

But you can't depend on emotions to lead and guide you because emotions can deceive you. *This is why you must allow the peace of God to rule in your heart.*

The word "rule," as used in this verse, is taken from the word *brabeuo*. It was used to picture *an umpire* or *one who called the shots at a public game*. This umpire was the governor of the game, the one who decided the winner! So by employing this word, Paul is actually saying, *"Let the peace of God be the umpire that calls the shots in your life...."*

How do you come to this place where peace is that prevalent in your life? How do you come to the place where your mind, emotions, fears, and frustrations cease to control you?

Paul tells you in the next verse: "Let the word of Christ dwell in you richly in all wisdom; teaching and admonishing one another in psalms and hymns and spiritual songs..." (Colossians 3:16).

Especially notice the command, *"Let the word of Christ dwell in you richly...."* There are two key words in this phrase: the words "dwell" and "richly."

The word "dwell" is taken from the word *enoikeo*, which is the Greek word meaning *to take up residence*. It is the idea of *settling into a house* or *making oneself feel at home*.

The word "richly" is from the word *plousios*. It carries the idea of *extreme extravagance* and *luxurious living*.

Therefore, when Paul says, "Let the word of Christ dwell in you richly...," he is actually saying, *"Let the word of Christ take up residence in your life and come to feel completely at home in you. Give it the warmest, most extravagant and luxurious reception that is possible...."*

What happens when you give the Word of God this kind of priority in your life? *The peace of God will begin to rule, umpire, and call the shots in your daily life.*

How To Walk in Strong Faith

How do you walk in strong, believing faith? How does the "shield of faith" become a daily reality in your life? In Romans

10:17, Paul gives you the answer: "So then faith cometh by hearing, and hearing by the word of God."

Do you want to walk in faith? Then get in God's Word and stay there. Give it the most important place of priority in your life! Only the Word of God can produce consistent, ongoing faith.

> Do you want to walk in faith on a daily basis? Then get in God's Word and stay there.

I hope you can now understand why the Holy Spirit began this text on spiritual armor with the loinbelt. *If you do not have the loinbelt of truth firmly positioned in your life, you will not be able to experientially walk in the other pieces of weaponry God has given you.*

THE HELMET AND THE SWORD

Now we come to the "helmet of salvation"! The word "salvation" is taken from the root *sodzo*, which conveys the ideas of *deliverance, safety, preservation, soundness of mind*, and *healing*.

How would you like to habitually walk in your Christ-purchased deliverance, safety, soundness of mind, and healing? Would you like that? Then you must put on your helmet!

In First Thessalonians 5:8, you are told that *salvation* is a "helmet." Then in Ephesians 6:17, you are told to *"take* the helmet of salvation." So what is the connection between the concepts of salvation and the mind? How do you put on the helmet of salvation?

Paul told Timothy, "And that from a child thou hast known the holy scriptures, *which are able to make thee wise unto salvation...*" (2 Timothy 3:15). The power of God's Word has a way of making us mentally alert and wise unto salvation. As we give our minds to the Word of God, the Word itself begins to build a measure of deliverance, safety, preservation, soundness of mind, and healing into our lives on every level.

> As we give our minds to the Word of God, the Word itself begins to build a measure of deliverance, safety, preservation, soundness of mind, and healing into our lives on every level.

This tells you that *Scripture puts a helmet on your head*! As you renew your mind to the Word of God, the truth contained in that Word becomes your spiritual helmet.

In addition to your wearing salvation as a helmet, Ephesians 6 also informs you that you have a mighty and powerful sword called "the sword of the Spirit." Would you like to wield this "sword of the Spirit" in your life on a more consistent basis? How can it be developed? *Where can you find this sword?*

Where did the Roman soldier find his sword when he needed it? It was hanging in its scabbard along his side, attached to a clip that hung from his *loinbelt*! Therefore, he had to keep that loinbelt on in order to keep his sword nearby!

What does the loinbelt represent in Ephesians 6? *The written Word of God.* Therefore, this tells us that most of the time the "word from the Lord" we need will come directly out of the Bible — just as the Roman soldier's sword came right out of a scabbard that hung on his loinbelt. *The loinbelt and the sword were connected.*

Today many Christians pray, "Lord, I need *a word*! God, I need for You to speak to me in some special way! I am facing this crisis, and I need *a word* from You about it, Lord!" These people spend all their time hoping to have a dream or a vision from God or trying to find someone who will prophesy their answer to them. When they go to church, they are always hoping that someone will give them a special answer that will direct them in the way they should go.

I praise God for dreams, visions, prophecy, words of knowledge, and words of wisdom. However, there is something more *dependable* than a word of knowledge, a word of wisdom, or a message in prophecy. As Peter said, "We have also *a more sure word* of prophecy..." (2 Peter 1:19).

So do you need a special *word* from the Lord? Do you need a *rhema*, a "sword of the Spirit"? This is how you get it: Make it a priority to read and study the Word of God, and your *rhema* will most likely be quickened to you as you walk in the Word.

As the writer of Hebrews said, "For the word of God is quick, and powerful, and sharper than any twoedged sword, piercing even to the dividing asunder of soul and spirit, and of the joints and marrow, and is a discerner of the thoughts and intents of the heart" (Hebrews 4:12). When you walk in the

Word of God, you are in position for the Word to pierce "...even to the dividing asunder of soul and spirit, and of the joints and marrow..." and to discern the thoughts and intents of your heart.

What happens if you choose to ignore the loinbelt — the Word of God — and to try your luck with another approach? Many saints have tried this. They've foolishly taken off their loinbelt and put down the Bible. Their attitude is, *I've tried the Bible, and I'm weary of it. I can walk in power and authority without maintaining time in the Word of God.*

By thinking this way, a person unsnaps his loinbelt and puts it down. He can walk like that for a while, but soon things begin to come loose. Soon he hears something jiggling — then, lo and behold, his breastplate falls right off his body! His sword drops to the ground! His lance tumbles to the floor!

> **Never forget: The written Word of God supports everything else in your walk with God!**

What happened? That person took off his loinbelt; hence, he had nothing to hold his spiritual life together. Now without protection, he has put himself in a dangerous position where the enemy can come to strike him with afflictions and troubles.

Never forget: *The written Word of God supports everything else in your walk with God!*

WINNING OR LOSING IS *YOUR* CHOICE

I want you to understand that if you are not walking daily in the power of God's Word, neither are you walking in your God-given suit of spiritual armor. Without the Word of God operational in your life, you have no support for other pieces of spiritual weaponry. For you, there is no fight. Your battle is over before it ever begins. You have forfeited your victory by rejecting the most important piece of weaponry of all: the Word of God.

> Without the Word of God operational in your life, your battle is over before it ever begins.

That Word holds your sense of righteousness in place — and you *need* your sense of righteousness. That Word holds your peace in place — and you *need* your peace, for peace is a major weapon, both defensive and offensive. And without your helmet of salvation to protect your mind, your mind will begin swimming with unbelief and doubt when the enemy comes to swing his battle ax to rob you of deliverance, soundness of mind, and healing.

Some people sit in a closet in the dark, hoping to get a *rhema* from God. But they would be more likely to receive their *rhema* word if they turned on the light, picked up their Bible, and began to meditate on God's Word. One of those verses could suddenly leap right off the page and become a mighty sword in their hand and in their mouth!

THE REPRODUCTIVE ABILITY OF GOD

Notice, too, that the loinbelt covered the Roman soldier's loins. Why did the soldier have his loins protected so heavily? *Because he wanted to preserve his ability to reproduce.*

Because the loinbelt is representative of the Word of God and the loinbelt was historically a protection to the reproductive abilities of a man, this tells us something else very significant. *It plainly shows us that our ability to produce for God is directly tied to our relationship with the Word of God.*

You become sterile spiritually if you don't have God's Word actively operating in your life. You do nothing; you produce nothing; you demonstrate no anointing or healing power. *When you get out of the Word of God, you are reduced to a state of spiritual barrenness.*

> When you get out of the Word of God, you are reduced to a state of spiritual barrenness.

Even God creates, produces, and reproduces by His Word. Hebrews 11:3 says, "Through faith we understand that the worlds were framed by the word of God...."

God produced the worlds through His Word!

Do you know what happened to you when you were saved? First John 3:9 says, "Whosoever is born of God doth not commit sin; for his *seed* remaineth in him: and he cannot sin, because he is born of God."

The word "seed" is taken from the Greek word *spermata*. It is where we derive the word "sperm."

Here we have a picture of the new birth! Just as a woman becomes pregnant by a man's seed and conceives a child in her womb, the apostle John says that when we are born again, God injects his own divine "seed" into our human spirits. Once that seed is placed into us, *that divine seed then immediately begins to produce the life and character of Jesus within us.*

This divine "seed" (*spermata*) is the reason we cannot go on living the way we once did before we met the Lord. The life, character, nature, and attributes of God are in that "seed," similar to the way a father's eye color, hair color, and temperament is in *his* seed. Once the nature of God is planted into us, that divine life forever breaks the power of canceled sin — *and the life of God begins to rule and reign in our lives*!

What does the "seed" of God look like? What *is* the "seed" of God? Peter tells us: "Being born again, not of corruptible seed, but of incorruptible, *by the word of God,* which liveth and abideth forever" (1 Peter 1:23).

> Everything God produces, He produces through the instrumentation of His Word.

God made the worlds with the Word of God, and He recreated you with His divine "seed." Everything God produces, He produces through the instrumentation of His Word.

The Major Mistake Believers Make

It could be that you have recently been asking the Lord, "Why is my life in such a mess?" Or you may have been asking, "Where did my peace go? Where is the victory I used to experience?"

I believe the Lord is asking you some questions in return. He is asking you, "Where is that loinbelt I gave you? Why haven't you been in My Word? Who took off your belt?"

So my solemn advice to you is this: If you are going to go into spiritual combat, don't go into this kind of fight without your loinbelt. If you do, it will only take one hit from the enemy, and all your armor is going to come tumbling off!

Other believers make the mistake of thinking, *I know I ought to spend some time in the Word today, but I really don't have the time. I'll wait until the next time I go to church. Our pastor is such a good teacher! I'll just wait until then. I know he'll feed me well.*

Finally, the long-awaited church service comes. Then these Christians go home, and the next day they realize that they ought to spend some time in the Word. But now they say, "Well, I'll just wait until the next church service. That last service was so good! I know the next one will be even better."

Let me ask you this question: Do you still ask your mother to dress you? What would your mother think if you asked her, "Mother, would you please dress me today?" She would say, "What do you mean? You actually want me to put your clothes on you? You're not a baby anymore. Go dress yourself!"

But that is exactly what many believers do! When they come to church on Sunday or to midweek service, knowing they haven't been in the Word all week long, they are saying, "Preacher, would you please dress me in my armor? Would you put my belt on me?"

Understand this: *The teaching of the Word from the pulpit should only confirm what you have already heard God say personally to you through His Word during the week.*

> The teaching of the Word from the pulpit should only confirm what you have already heard God say personally to you through His Word during the week.

Your pastor's preaching is not to be the *only* Word you receive. It's intended by the Holy Spirit to pull the belt that is *already* on you a little tighter.

When individuals in the Body of Christ get in the Word of God for themselves every day and go to church to listen to the teaching of the Word that comes forth, their actions pull their belt tighter. Their righteousness fits even better. Their sense of peace is locked on even more securely.

When believers get these two elements of Bible study flowing together in their lives, the Body of Christ *really* gets dressed!

Now we can see more clearly why the Holy Spirit started with the belt when He described our weaponry in Ephesians 6. He wanted to emphasize the absolute importance of the loinbelt of truth. That's why, through Paul, the Holy Spirit said, "Stand therefore, *having your loins girt about with truth....*"

THE PSALMIST WHO UNDERSTOOD
THE CENTRALITY OF THE WORD

When you read Psalm 119, you can clearly hear the psalmist's deep love for God's Word:

> Blessed are the undefiled in the way, who walk in *the law of the Lord*. Blessed are they that keep *his testimonies*, and that seek him with the whole heart. They also do no iniquity: they walk in his ways.

> Thou hast commanded us to keep *thy precepts* diligently. O that my ways were directed to keep *thy statutes*! Then shall I not be ashamed, when I have respect unto all *thy commandments....* I will keep *thy statutes....*

> Wherewithal shall a young man cleanse his way? by taking heed thereto according to *thy word*. With my whole heart have I sought thee: O let me not wander from *thy commandments*.

> *Thy word* have I hid in my heart, that I might not sin against thee. Blessed art thou, O Lord: teach me *thy statutes*.

> With my lips have I declared all *the judgments of thy mouth*. I have rejoiced in the way of *thy*

testimonies, as much as in all riches. I will meditate in *thy precepts*, and have respect unto thy ways.

I will delight myself in *thy statutes*: I will not forget *thy word*. Deal bountifully with thy servant, that I may live, and keep *thy word*.

Open thou mine eyes, that I may behold wondrous things out of *thy law*. I am a stranger in the earth: hide not *thy commandments* from me.

Psalm 119:1-19

It is obvious that the Word was central to this psalmist. Do you see how much he loved and needed the "loinbelt of truth" in his life? This man said, "I *have* to have God's Word! I meditate on it. I don't run away from it. Lord, please don't hide it from me. Reveal it to me. I promise You that I will walk in it. I will think on it. I will keep it."

THE KEY TO VICTORY AND SUCCESS

This psalmist understood that God's Word was the key to complete victory and complete success in life. In verses 20-24, he pleads:

My soul breaketh for the longing that it hath unto *thy judgments* at all times. Thou has rebuked the proud that are cursed, which do err from *thy commandments*.

Remove from me reproach and contempt; for I have kept *thy testimonies*. Princes also did sit and speak against me: but thy servant did meditate in *thy statutes*.

Thy testimonies are also my delight and my counsellors.

When you get into spiritual conflict, you can know that evil forces — like those who opposed this man — will rise up against you. But the Word says that as you meditate on God's statutes, He will remove their reproach and contempt. In other words, the "loinbelt of truth" will equip you to remove those foul forces and prevent them from causing harm in your life.

In verses 57-59, the psalmist says:

Thou art my portion, O Lord: I have said that I will keep *thy words*. I intreated thy favour with my whole heart: be merciful unto me according to *thy word*. I thought on my ways, and turned my feet unto *thy testimonies*.

The writer of this psalm is saying, "Lord, Your Word is going to be first and foremost in my life!" He continues in verses 60-63:

I made haste, and delayed not to keep *thy commandments*. The bands of the wicked have robbed me: but I have not forgotten *thy law*.

At midnight I will rise to give thanks unto thee because of *thy righteous judgments*. I am a companion of all them that fear thee, and of them that keep *thy precepts*.

THE WORD'S BEST ADVICE

Here in verse 63 is the best advice you will ever get in your entire life! The psalmist says, "I am a companion of all them that fear thee, and of them that keep thy precepts."

My advice to you, and the Word's advice to you, is that your companions be people who walk in the Word. *You need people around you who understand the centrality of the Word as much as you do.*

This psalmist is saying, "My companions love your Word as much as I love it." *It is so crucial that you are careful to choose your friends wisely.* Walk with people who walk with the Lord and in His Word as seriously as you do.

> You need people around you who understand the centrality of the Word as much as you do.

In verses 129 and 130, the psalmist goes on to say:

> *Thy testimonies* are wonderful: therefore doth my soul keep them. The entrance of *thy words* giveth light; it giveth understanding unto the simple.

Once again, this writer is proclaiming, "Lord, your Word is central in my life!" In verses 131-134, he continues:

I opened my mouth, and panted: for I longed for *thy commandments*. Look thou upon me, and be merciful unto me, as thou usest to do unto those that love thy name.

Order my steps in *thy word*: and let not any iniquity have dominion over me. Deliver me from the oppression of man: so will I keep *thy precepts*.

Notice how much the psalmist needs the Word: He is actually *panting* after it! He is saying that because he keeps God's precepts, he knows that God will deliver him. Then in verses 135 and 136, he says this:

Make thy face to shine upon thy servant; and teach me *thy statutes*. Rivers of waters run down mine eyes, because they keep not *thy law*.

This man is saying, "I am so grieved because I see people who don't listen to your Word, and it is destroying them. They don't keep your law, and they are being killed. They are being ruined. Iniquity and sin are overtaking them!"

Why did the psalmist say this? Because he knew that keeping the Word of God central in our lives saves us from destruction. Then in verses 153-157, he goes on to say:

Consider mine affliction, and deliver me: for I do not forget *thy law*. Plead my cause, and deliver me: quicken me according to *thy word*. Salvation is far from the wicked: for they seek not *thy statutes*.

> Great are thy tender mercies, O Lord: quicken me according to *thy judgments*. Many are my persecutors and mine enemies; yet do I not decline from *thy testimonies*.

In other words, people who aren't seeking the Word of God do not experience the blessings of their salvation (v. 155). It is almost as though the psalmist is saying, "In spite of those who . refuse to seek Your truth, I take refuge in Your Word."

In verses 158-160, the psalmist continues:

> I beheld the transgressors, and was grieved; because they kept not *thy word*.

> Consider how I love *thy precepts*: quicken me, O Lord, according to thy lovingkindness. *Thy word* is true from the beginning: and every one of *thy righteous judgments* endureth for ever.

The writer is saying, "I will not err from the Word of God. It is always right. It is central in my life. It delivers me, preserves me, and keeps me." Throughout Psalm 119, the psalmist's theme is the centrality of the Word of God in his life. There is no doubt about it — this person had on the "loinbelt of truth"!

Many believers quote Revelation 12:11, which says, "And they overcame him [the devil] by the blood of the Lamb, and by the word of their testimony...." But what "word of our testimony" is it talking about? The Word of God. That is the *only* testimony we have!

THE WAY TO WIN

Again, Ephesians 6:14 starts out, "Stand therefore, having your loins girt about with truth...." When you put on the loinbelt of the Word and determine to make it a priority in your life, you are well on the way to winning your battles in life!

> When you put on the loinbelt of the Word and determine to make it a priority in your life, you are well on the way to winning your battles in life!

After you put on the Word of God, you may not *feel* righteous at first. But just keep walking in the Word, and a deep sense of righteousness will spring up in your life!

You also may not feel any peace at first. But the Bible promises, "Thou wilt keep him in perfect peace, whose mind is stayed on thee..." (Isaiah 26:3). How do you keep your mind stayed on the Lord? By walking in the Word and allowing the Word of Christ to dwell in you richly. Then the peace of God *will* rule in your heart!

Do you say you need a sword — a special *rhema* word from the Lord? Well, the Word of God is quick, active, and operative, sharper than any two-edged sword.

Do you say you need a shield of faith? Romans 10:17 says, "Faith cometh by hearing, and hearing by the word of God." Get in the Word of God. Hear the Word of God. Meditate on the Word of God. It will put a shield into your hand!

If you intend to challenge the assaults of the adversary against your body, mind, family, friends, money, or business, my solemn advice to you from God's Word is this: *Pick up that loinbelt and put it on, because without it, you are in serious trouble!*

But when you have your loinbelt of truth firmly fixed in your spiritual life, you are well positioned to put on all the other pieces of weaponry. With the loinbelt of truth securely in place, you can know that nothing will come loose or fall off. Now you can move swiftly, furiously, and victoriously against every onslaught of the enemy!

QUESTIONS FOR PERSONAL GROWTH OR GROUP DISCUSSION

1. Why is the loinbelt the central piece of spiritual armor that holds every other aspect of your spiritual walk together?

2. What would happen to your sense of righteousness if you stopped feeding on the written Word of God?

3. How do you come to a place in your walk with God where peace rules as umpire over your thoughts and emotions in every situation? As you examine your own spiritual walk, can you honestly say that you are steadily progressing toward that goal?

4. What must you do to prepare yourself to receive a specific word from the Lord for a given situation?

5. As you take an honest look at your own life, can you see areas that are beginning to fall apart at the seams because you have neglected the Word of God? What practical changes can you make to restore divine order to those particular areas of your life?

NOTES:

_____

_____

_____

_____

_____

_____

_____

_____

_____

_____

_____

_____

_____

_____

_____

_____

_____

_____

_____

_____

_____

_____

CHAPTER ELEVEN

THE BREASTPLATE OF RIGHTEOUSNESS

As Paul continues in Ephesians 6, he reveals to us the next piece of our spiritual weaponry. He says, "Stand therefore, having your loins girt about with truth, and having on *the breastplate of righteousness*" (Ephesians 6:14).

Righteousness is a weapon — it is our breastplate! You may ask, "How could righteousness be a weapon? Why would Paul call it a breastplate? In what way does it serve us as armor?"

We know that righteousness is part of our spiritual arsenal because Paul calls it a weapon in this sixth chapter of Ephesians. He mentions it in the same context with the "loinbelt of truth," the "shield of faith," the "helmet of salvation," the "sword of the Spirit," and the "lance" of intercession. In Second Corinthians 6:7, Paul again refers to righteousness as a weapon. It reads, "By the word of truth, by the power of God, by *the armour of righteousness*...." Here righteousness is plainly called "armor." Another reference where righteousness is called armor is Isaiah 59:17, where it says, "For he put on *righteousness as a breastplate*...."

In order to understand *why* Paul calls righteousness a breastplate in his list of spiritual armor, you must first understand what Paul had in mind as he thought of the Roman soldier's breastplate.

The breastplate was the shiniest, most beautiful, and most glamorous piece of weaponry that the Roman soldier possessed. When people walked up to a Roman soldier, they certainly didn't notice his loinbelt first. They didn't even notice his shoes or his sword. And as conspicuous as the soldier's helmet was, the piece of armor that immediately caught the attention of onlookers was not his helmet, but his large, shiny, gorgeous breastplate.

The first thing a person would notice when looking at a Roman soldier was his beautiful breastplate. The breastplate began at the top of his neck and went all the way down to the knees. It was composed of two different pieces of metal. One piece of metal went down the front, and the other went down the back. These two pieces of metal were held together by solid brass rings on top of the shoulders. Quite often these larger sheets of metal that covered the front and the back of the man were comprised of smaller, scale-like pieces of metal, similar to the scales of a fish.

This was the heaviest piece of weaponry that the Roman soldier wore. At times, it weighed in excess of 40 pounds. And, remember, Goliath's breastplate weighed approximately *125* pounds!

THE BEAUTY OF THE BREASTPLATE

The breastplate was extremely elaborate and beautiful. It was made either of bronze or brass — usually brass. And the more Roman soldiers wore their breastplates as they walked and marched, something incredible would begin to happen.

When you rub two shiny pieces of metal against each other for a long time, they begin to add a luster to each other. These pieces of metal may have started out shiny, but this new luster makes them shine even brighter.

This is exactly what happened when the Roman soldier walked around with his breastplate on. Those smaller, scale-like pieces of metal would rub against each other, thus causing each piece to develop a beautiful luster. In addition, brass is a golden color that shines and sparkles when it is out in the sun, especially if it is a fine piece of brass. Therefore, when the fully armed soldier went outside on a sunny day, the rays of the sun would reflect off his breastplate and create a dazzling spectacle.

Thus, we see that the beauty of the Roman soldier's breastplate was enhanced by his using it and walking around clothed in it. Had the breastplate been stored in a dark room and never used, it would have been beautiful simply because it was made out of brass. But as the soldier used his breastplate and walked around wearing it, the breastplate became more and more beautiful with time.

Have you ever been driving in your car when suddenly the sun glinted off an outside piece of metal, hitting your eyes with such a glare that you could hardly see the road? If so, you can imagine what it would have been like to walk past a Roman soldier clothed in his brass breastplate with all that added shine and luster! When a Roman soldier walked out into the afternoon sunlight, he must have looked like a rainbow, casting beams wherever he went!

What do you suppose it was like when an entire legion of Roman soldiers walked out into the sunshine? The entire mountainside or valley where they were marching would begin to shine as they moved forward in their bright and gleaming breastplates!

> Your righteousness is not only a defensive weapon to protect you from the blows of the enemy, but it is also an offensive weapon to assist you as you assault the enemy and take back lost territory!

Now apply these characteristics of the Roman breastplate to your righteousness. The more you wear your breastplate of righteousness, walking through life fully conscious of your righteousness in Christ, the more brightly you will shine as a light in a dark world of sin. And as you walk with your breastplate firmly in place, you will learn that your righteousness is not only *a defensive weapon* to protect you from the blows of the enemy, but it is also an *offensive weapon* to assist you as you assault the enemy and take back lost territory!

SOMEONE WANTS TO HURT YOU

If you were not engaged in battle, you wouldn't need to wear this kind of weaponry. But you do need to wear this kind of weaponry because someone out there wants to hurt you *very* badly!

In Ephesians 6:11, we saw that when we have on "the whole armour of God," we are able "to stand against the wiles of the devil." The devil wants to assault us. He wants to tell us that we are *not* righteous and that we are of no value to God or to man. This is why the Holy Spirit tells us that we have righteousness as a "breastplate" to protect us.

Remember, the word "devil" is taken from the Greek word *diabolos*, which describes *one who strikes again and again and again until, finally, he penetrates the mind with slanderous accusations.* Because the devil desires to penetrate and immobilize a person's mind and emotions, he especially delights in finding believers who do not know they are righteous. They are easy prey!

The devil sneers as he whispers to your mind, *"You're the worst believer who has ever lived. Do you think God is going to do anything with you? God can't use you, you stupid thing!"*

If you don't have your "breastplate of righteousness" firmly fixed in place, those slanderous accusations will most likely penetrate your mind and emotions. If that happens, the devil will then be able to deal an effective blow that injures your spiritual walk immensely.

> Because the devil desires to penetrate and immobilize a person's mind and emotions, he especially delights in finding believers who do not know they are righteous. They are easy prey!

Christians who don't know they have been made righteous in Christ tend to habitually walk in condemnation. Why? Because the devil never misses a chance to insert a condemning thought in their minds. People who don't know they have been made righteous also continually walk in guilt for the same reason. The enemy loves to bombard them with lying accusations that penetrate their minds and make them feel like failures.

On the other hand, when you know that God has made you righteous — when you have your breastplate of righteousness fixed firmly in place — it doesn't matter how many arrows the enemy shoots against you because not one arrow will penetrate. No word of condemnation, no false allegation, and no guilty thought will penetrate your heart or lodge in your mind when you are walking in your breastplate of righteousness.

> No word of condemnation, no false allegation, and no guilty thought will penetrate your heart or lodge in your mind when you are walking in your breastplate of righteousness.

Unfortunately, it seems like about 90 percent of the Body of Christ is walking in condemnation, with their shoulders slumped over and their heads hanging low. The enemy has victimized many to the point that they can no longer pray with confidence. He has convinced others that they will never be *good enough* to be used by God. Yet the Word plainly tells believers in verse 14 of our text to *"stand — throw back your shoulders, hold your head up high, and walk tall and confidently, as all proud and victorious soldiers do!"*

When you understand that God has freely imparted righteousness to you and that this God-given righteousness now serves you as a gorgeous breastplate, it will affect your attitude quite positively and profoundly. You will discover that your level of confidence rises dramatically because an attitude of righteousness imparts both confidence and tremendous authority.

With that confidence in operation, you will move out to do all kinds of exploits for God. Sometimes you will become so bold and confident in your God-given righteousness that those who don't know you may not understand. They might take your newfound boldness the wrong way and accuse you of being egocentric or arrogant. They won't understand that you are just a Christian who has recently learned you are "the righteousness of God in Him [Christ]" (2 Corinthians 5:21).

You have learned that God has clothed you in a gorgeous, beautiful, bright, shining piece of armor called "the breastplate of righteousness." You have just discovered that you don't have to take the devil's lying threats anymore because you are *dressed to kill*"!

THE CORRECT ATTITUDE FOR WARFARE

When Roman soldiers went out to fight, their commanding officer told them: "It would be better for you to die on the battlefield than to come back here and tell us that the enemy won, so don't return to our encampment until the enemy has been annihilated. Make sure that you come home a winner, or don't come home at all."

You can be sure that those kinds of statements affected the attitude of those soldiers! They immediately began to mentally gear themselves up for the fight. They went into weeks and months of preparation. They did everything they could to prepare their minds and attitudes.

You see, your mental attitude has everything to do with how well you perform in the midst of a fight. If you are mentally and emotionally defeated *before* you go into a fight, you should not go into battle. Why? Because your negative attitude has already determined the outcome of that battle! You *will* be defeated. But by developing an attitude of righteousness in your life and learning how to view yourself through the work of the Cross, you will receive a divine impartation of confidence and boldness that will always put you on the winning side of victory!

> Your mental attitude has everything to do with how well you perform in the midst of a fight.

You must become mentally prepared. This is why the apostle Peter said, "Wherefore *gird up the loins of your mind*, be sober, and hope to the end..." (1 Peter 1:13).

This is the picture of a Greek runner. In order to run faster and better, he takes hold of his tunic and tucks it up underneath his belt. By doing this, he "girds up" his tunic, freeing his legs from getting caught in it when he runs.

Likewise, Peter commands us to gather up all the loose ends of our minds — to pull them up, tuck them under our belts, figuratively speaking, and then run our race free of encumbrances. In other words, if we are to successfully run our spiritual race and fight this fight of faith, *we must prepare ourselves both emotionally and intellectually.*

However, in order to do this vital work of emotional and mental preparation, *you must know that you are righteous in Christ.* This knowledge will positively affect your attitude as it prepares your heart and your mind for battle. And once you have your breastplate of righteousness firmly fixed in place, you will be able to fight any foe and face any enemy!

It is of the highest importance that you make this knowledge a key part of your mental make-up, for even when you are thoroughly convinced of your rightstanding with God, the devil will still attempt to tell you that you are *not* righteous. That's why you have to know that you *know* that God has made you righteous in Christ!

SCRIPTURES ON RIGHTEOUSNESS

In order to establish the fact of your God-given righteousness, let's quickly look at several verses on this subject.

In Second Corinthians 5:21, Paul says, "For he hath made him [Jesus] to be sin for us, who knew no sin; that we might be made the righteousness of God in him."

You are righteous! When you begin to meditate on this truth and it really begins to penetrate your mind and your thinking, your attitude *will* change. You will develop a righteousness consciousness. You will no longer say that you *want* to be righteous; instead, you will realize that you *are* righteous. It is this insight that will give you a new sense of assurance and confidence to run your race and defeat the enemy at every turn.

Another important scripture about righteousness is found in Romans 3:21,22. These verses say, "But now the righteousness of God without the law is manifested, being witnessed by the law and the prophets; *even the righteousness of God which is by faith of Jesus Christ unto all and upon all them that believe....*"

According to these verses, a God-given righteousness rightfully belongs "...unto all and upon all them that believe...."

> When a believer finally grabs hold of the truth that God has graciously imparted righteousness to him, that knowledge changes him.

What stronger statement can be made to prove that all believers are dressed in righteousness?

In Romans 5:17, Paul says, "For if by one man's [Adam's] offence death reigned by one; *much more they which receive abundance of grace and of the gift of righteousness shall reign in life by one, Jesus Christ.*"

This verse is saying that when a believer finally grabs hold of the truth that God has graciously imparted righteousness to him, that knowledge *changes* him. He no longer views himself as a little, unimportant, defeated believer. He is so affected in his attitude that he begins to move with assurance from a life of chronic defeat to a life of reigning in life like a king!

You may ask, "If all believers have been made righteous and are supposed to reign in life like kings, why do so many believers live defeated lives?" Because their minds have not been renewed by the Word of God to this correct thinking! They *think* they are unworthy and of no value, and they *behave* as though they are unworthy and of no value. Because they *think* they are unrighteous, they go through life acting as if they *are* unrighteous.

On the other hand, when you receive the revelation that you are righteous, you throw back your shoulders and confidently face the situations of life with the attitude, "Look at me! I've got a breastplate of righteousness fixed to my life! I am the righteousness of God in Christ Jesus!"

There is no doubt about it — when this knowledge gets planted deep in your heart, it CHANGES you!

A New Source of Confidence

As stated earlier, when you begin to walk in your breastplate of righteousness, that new sense of righteousness will impart an incredible confidence to your spiritual life.

In First John 5:13 and 14, the apostle John says, "These things have I written unto you that believe on the name of the Son of God; that ye may know that ye have eternal life, and that ye may believe on the name of the Son of God. *And this is the confidence...."*

The word "confidence" is taken from the Greek word *parresia* and has been translated in other places as *boldness* or *openness*. This word portrays the picture of a person who is exceptionally *open* and *bold* in how he approaches situations — so open and bold that he almost appears to be arrogant.

John continues to say, "And this is the confidence [*Greek: great boldness*] that we have in him, that, if we ask any thing according to his will, he heareth us: and if we know that he hear us, whatsoever we ask, we know that we have the petitions that we desired of him" (1 John 5:14,15).

An attitude of righteousness will profoundly affect your prayer life! If you do not know that you have rightstanding with God, you cannot pray with confidence. If you're not aware that you have been given righteousness as a breastplate, you won't be able to do *anything* with confidence.

> An attitude of righteousness will profoundly affect your prayer life!

Many Christians pray defeated prayers because they don't know they are righteous. In fact, you can tell when someone isn't walking in their "breastplate of righteousness" by listening to the way that person prays. His or her prayers are filled with defeat.

On the other hand, when believers walk in their "breastplate of righteousness," they pray with power and authority. They know that because of that breastplate, they can come directly into the presence of God and pray with great boldness.

POWERLESS RELIGION VS.
POWERFUL RELIGION

In Acts 3, Peter and John were going to the Temple at the hour of prayer when suddenly they saw a man who had been crippled for many years.

> **Now Peter and John went up together into the temple at the hour of prayer, being the ninth hour, and a certain man lame from his mother's womb was carried, whom they laid daily at the gate of the temple which is called Beautiful, to ask alms of them that entered into the temple.**
>
> Acts 3:1,2

Notice that this man was being laid daily at the gate of the temple called *"Beautiful."* "Beautiful" was not the real name of this gate; it was an expression to describe what this gate looked like. It was an absolutely gorgeous area of the temple, so it was called the *"beautiful gate"* by the people. It was decorated with all kinds of wonderful, ornate columns and other lavish architectural details.

Yet as beautiful as this gate of the temple was, this man had never found healing there. That gate was situated before a place of worship with beautiful, formal buildings — a place where absolute quietness was required for fear of being "irreverent" or "irreligious." But with all the formality and piety of this place, the needs of this one man had never been met. This is a picture of what religion has to offer — a form of godliness, but no power.

The Bible goes on to tell us what the crippled man did when he saw Peter and John. It says, "Who seeing Peter and John about to go into the temple asked an alms. And Peter, fastening his eyes upon him with John, said, Look on us" (Acts 3:3,4).

The Bible says that Peter fastened his eyes upon him. The word "upon" is taken from the Greek word *eis*, which means *into*. So when the Bible says Peter fixed his eyes *upon* the man, it is actually telling us that Peter walked up to this poor cripple and stared straight *into* his eyes. Once he had the man's complete attention, Peter declared, "Look at me!"

Why did Peter say this? *Because he knew he had something life-changing to offer this crippled man.*

Once you realize that you have been given a breastplate of righteousness, you will walk through life wanting to tell *everyone* to look at you. Like Peter, you will know that you have something to offer people that they need! Thus, the knowledge of your righteousness affects the way you deal with people.

The next verses say, "And he gave heed unto them, expecting to receive something of them. Then Peter said, Silver and gold have I none; but *such* as I have give I thee..." (Acts 3:5,6).

To translate this word "such" is a very poor translation indeed. It should have been translated, "...but *who* I have give I thee...." Peter wasn't giving that man a "such"; he was giving that man a "*who*" — Jesus Christ! Peter and John then released the power of God into that lame man's body, and the man was healed!

Peter and John could move in such confidence because they knew they were righteous. Righteousness will affect you in the same way. It will change your attitude about yourself and about people and situations around you. *When you have been positively influenced by an understanding of righteousness, it gives you the assurance you need to step out and boldly do the work of God.*

So before you run out to engage in warfare with the enemy, make sure you possess this kind of assurance. The enemy will try to slander and accuse you. He will try to tell you that you are a good-for-nothing. He will try to convince you that God won't use you and that no one will listen to you.

> **When you have been positively influenced by an understanding of righteousness, it gives you the assurance you need to step out and boldly do the work of God.**

That's why it is so vital for you to know that God has given you a breastplate of righteousness. *And when you walk through life wearing that breastplate, everything changes for the better.*

RIGHTEOUSNESS: A DEFENSIVE WEAPON

Righteousness serves as a *defensive* weapon. In regard to this aspect of righteousness, Isaiah says, "I will greatly rejoice in the Lord, my soul shall be joyful in my God; for he hath clothed me with the garments of salvation, *he hath covered me with the robe of righteousness...*" (Isaiah 61:10).

Notice that this robe covers and protects you from head to foot. By using this expression, Isaiah tells you that righteousness will act as a defense for you.

In Isaiah 51:7 and 8, Isaiah announces: "Hearken unto me, *ye that know righteousness,* the people in whose heart is my law; fear ye not the reproach of men, neither be ye afraid of their revilings. For the moth shall eat them up like a garment, and the worm shall eat like wool: *but my righteousness shall be for ever, and my salvation from generation to generation.*"

When you are dressed in righteousness, you do not have to fear what man or the devil can do to you. Your righteousness will protect and sustain you, while your enemies are eaten like a moth eats a garment or like a worm eats wool. God's gift of righteousness in your life, however, is permanent; it will last from generation to generation and forever!

When you walk in righteousness, you wear a weapon of defense against the enemy's slanderous accusations and insidious strategies.

> When you walk in righteousness, you wear a weapon of defense against the enemy's slanderous accusations and insidious strategies.

The righteous are never permanently affected by afflictions. Psalm 37:17 says, "For the arms of the wicked shall be broken: but *the Lord upholdeth the righteous.*"

The righteous always outlast any attack that comes against them. The enemy may come to remove the influence of the righteous, but Proverbs 10:30 declares, "The righteous shall *never* be removed...."

How important is it for you to walk in your righteousness? It's absolutely crucial if you don't want to be "removed"! You must have your breastplate of righteousness firmly fixed in place when you begin your confrontation with the adversary, or he will do everything within his power to *remove* your victory and *eliminate* your godly influence in other people's lives!

Righteousness: An Offensive Weapon

The breastplate that the Roman soldier wore was beautiful to look at and effectively protected the soldier from attack. But the breastplate did something else that was very important as well.

Keep in mind that the breastplate of the Roman soldier was made of especially bright and shining golden brass. When that soldier threw back his shoulders and the afternoon sunshine hit that metal, it cast a blinding glare into the eyes of all who were watching.

The brilliance of the soldier's breastplate blinded the eyes of his opponent so thoroughly that the opponent could not see to fight. When the breastplate was used in this way, it served as an *offensive* weapon.

Similarly, when you truly begin to walk in righteousness, all you have to do is walk into a dark situation, and that darkness will begin to flee from you. Evil forces always flee from righteousness because they cannot endure the brilliant light that righteousness reflects into their eyes!

Righteousness will equip you not only in a spiritual way, but it will affect you in the *natural* realm as well. *Righteousness will make you noticeable.* When you are dressed in righteousness, you are actually dressed in the Lord Jesus Christ. You are as brilliant and powerful as Jesus Himself when you are wearing this breastplate! With your breastplate of righteousness fixed firmly in place, God's glory radiates from your life to all those around you.

> With your breastplate of righteousness fixed firmly in place, God's glory radiates from your life to all those around you.

Every Roman soldier owned a beautiful breastplate of brass. However, if that breastplate was going to be useful to the soldier, he had to put it on. As stated already, the more he walked in that breastplate, the more beautiful it became as the individual smaller pieces of scale-like metal began to add a luster to each other.

This is exactly what happens when you begin to walk in your righteousness. As you do, you will experience what the Roman soldier experienced — your breastplate will begin to get more and more beautiful over time.

So throw back your shoulders and be bold! You are the righteousness of God in Christ Jesus! You have on a breastplate of righteousness. Keep walking; keep marching; keep moving forward — and don't let the enemy talk you out of enjoying the benefits of your rightstanding with God!

As you walk in your "breastplate of righteousness," a righteousness consciousness will begin to develop, overtaking your false emotions of unworthiness and condemnation. *And with every step you take in righteousness, you will become more and more gorgeous to the eyes of God — and more and more blinding to the eyes of the enemy!*

QUESTIONS FOR PERSONAL GROWTH
OR GROUP DISCUSSION

1. Why is a believer who lacks understanding of his righteousness such easy prey for the enemy?

2. In what ways does the breastplate of righteousness work as an offensive weapon to destroy the enemy's attacks against you?

3. Have you ever entered a challenging situation with the mental attitude of someone who had already lost the battle? Compare the outcome of that particular situation with a time when you did it right — engaging the enemy with the bold confidence of someone who understands righteousness!

4. Consider your present prayer life. Do you pray with boldness and confidence, or are your prayers weak and hesitant? Do you see a need to meditate more on what it means to be righteous in God's eyes?

5. How might a greater understanding of your righteousness in Christ affect the way you go about your daily affairs and how you relate to other people?

NOTES:

_____

_____

_____

_____

_____

_____

_____

_____

_____

_____

_____

_____

_____

_____

_____

_____

_____

_____

_____

_____

_____

_____

_____

CHAPTER TWELVE

SHOES OF PEACE

*I*n the sixth chapter of Ephesians, Paul continues expounding on the whole armor of God. He says, "And your feet shod with the preparation of the gospel of peace" (Ephesians 6:15).

The Roman soldier's shoes were not ordinary shoes. In the first place, they were made out of bronze or brass — usually brass — and the shoes were primarily composed of two parts: 1) the *greave*, and 2) the *shoe* itself. These shoes were exceptionally dangerous to any foe.

The *greave* was a tube-like piece of bronze or brass that began at the top of the knee and extended down past the lower leg, finally resting on the upper portion of the foot. It was made from a warped sheet of beautifully tooled metal that had been specifically formed to fit around the calf of the Roman soldier's leg. As stated earlier, this tube-like piece of metal caused the Roman soldier's shoes to look like boots that were made of brass.

The *shoe* itself was made of two pieces of metal. On the top and bottom, the foot was covered with fine pieces of brass. The sides of the shoe were held together by multiple pieces of durable leather. On the bottom, these shoes were equipped with *extremely dangerous spikes* that were *one or more inches long.* If a soldier was involved in active combat, his spikes could have been close to *three* inches long. *Believe me, these were killer shoes!*

Paul had these very shoes in mind when he said, "And having your feet shod with the preparation of the gospel of peace" (v. 15). When you realize what these shoes looked like and how dangerous those sharpened spikes could be, you begin to understand why it is so amazing that Paul would use this illustration to describe "peace"!

According to Paul, "peace" is an awesome weapon, both *defensive* and *offensive.* Peace not only *protects* you, but it also provides you with a brutal weapon to wield against the enemy when he attacks. If you use the weapon of peace correctly, it will keep spiritual foes where they belong — *under your feet!* One good kick, and the enemy's strategies against you will be crushed!

> Peace not only protects you, but it also provides you with a brutal weapon to wield against the enemy when he attacks.

Notice that Paul says, "And having your feet *shod....*" The word "shod" is derived from the word *hupodeomai.* This is a compound of the words *hupo* and *deo.* The word *hupo* means *under,* and *deo* means *to bind.* Taken together as one word (*hupodeomaz*), this word conveys the idea of *binding something very tightly on the bottom of one's feet.*

Therefore, this is not the picture of a loosely fitting shoe. This is the picture of a shoe that has been tied onto the bottom of the foot *extremely tightly*.

Now Paul uses this same word to tell us that we must firmly tie *peace* around our lives. If we only give peace a loosely fitting position in our lives, the affairs of life will easily knock our peace out of place. Hence, we must position peace *firmly* in place, "binding" it around our minds and our emotions in the same way that Roman soldiers made sure to "bind" their shoes very tightly onto their feet.

When peace has this firm grip in our lives, we are then ready for action! Thus, Paul continues, "Having your feet shod with *the preparation...*." The word "preparation" comes from the word *etoimasin* and carries the idea of *readiness* or *preparation*.

However, the word *etoimasin*, when used in connection with Roman soldiers, portrayed men of war who had their shoes tied on very tightly and hence had a *firm footing*. With the assurance that their shoes were going to stay in place, they were ready to march out onto the battlefield and confront the enemy.

Therefore, the word "preparation" (*etoimasin*) conveys the idea of *solidity, firmness*, or *a solid foundation*. Because Paul has carefully chosen this word to denote the action of peace in our lives, he is clearly telling us that when peace is foundational in our lives, we have a *firm footing*.

Peace gives us a foundation so secure that we can step out in confident faith without being moved by what we see or what we hear. This aggressive peace also puts us in a position to look

> Peace gives us a foundation so secure that we can step out in confident faith without being moved by what we see or what we hear.

directly into the face of the adversary or a challenge without fear or intimidation.

Paul continues, "And having your feet shod with the preparation of the gospel of *peace*...." The word "peace" is taken from the Greek word *eirene*, an old word that conveys the idea of *a peace that prevails* or *a conquering peace*. When used in salutations, as Paul uses it in his epistles, the word means *blessings and prosperity in every area of one's life*.

By using this word, Paul declares that when an individual receives the truth of the Gospel message into his or her heart, that truth brings blessings and prosperity along with it. In fact, the word "peace" (*eirene*) implies that this conquering force will be so strong and effective, all the chaos formerly experienced by that individual will be replaced with a *peace that prevails* in every area of his or her life.

If this supernatural peace is being disturbed in your life and chaos is attempting to regain its former place, you need to recognize that you are *under seige*.

However, the presence of chaos and the absence of peace does not *necessarily* mean that the enemy has attacked you. It may be a signpost that you have violated some principle of Scripture or that you have disobeyed the will of God for your life. So before you run out to fight the devil off your back, look in the mirror! The devil is not always the source of your problems. Be honest with yourself and with God. Examine your life to see if *you* caused this lack of peace in your life.

Before you shift blame for a personal failure in your life to someone else, or before you claim that the devil is after your peace, take a moment to examine *yourself*. See if *you* left a gaping hole open somewhere along the way that gave rise to your current dilemma.

> Before you run out to fight the devil off your back, look in the mirror! The devil is not always the source of your problems.

God's perfect plan is that this prevailing and conquering peace will dominate your life. When this kind of peace is firmly fixed in your mind and emotions, there is little the devil can do to move you! This peace gives you a firm footing. Regardless of how hard the enemy or the daily affairs of life hit you, *this prevailing and conquering peace will hold you in place*!

TWO KINDS OF PEACE

There are two different kinds of peace that a believer can experience. First, there is *peace with God*. Peace with God is what a person experiences when he or she first comes to the Lord for salvation. Once repentance is complete and the hostility of the old man is gone, a new peace with God comes into being.

As Paul said, "And, having made peace through the blood of his cross...you, that were sometimes alienated and enemies in your mind by wicked works, yet now hath he reconciled" (Colossians 1:20,21).

Peace with God is a spiritual condition that belongs to all believers. It is the condition that comes into being when the barrier between God and man dissolves and the alienated mind comes into harmony with God. This, of course, is what genuine conversion is all about.

In addition to the peace with God that is the birthright of all believers, there is also the *peace of God*. It is possible to have peace *with* God without experientially knowing the peace *of* God, for they are two very different things.

Many people are at peace *with* God by virtue of their conversion experience, but they are *not* walking in the peace *of* God. Instead of being dominated by this prevailing, conquering peace that surpasses natural understanding, these people walk in constant fretfulness, anxiety, worry, and all kinds of other turmoil.

This is the reason that peace has been given to us as a weapon. The *peace of God* is *a protective peace.* It protects you from fretfulness, anxiety, worry, and everything else that the devil might try to use to disturb your enjoyment of abundant life.

DOMINATING PEACE

Although we have covered this once already, let me repeat it again for the sake of emphasis. Paul says, "And let the peace of God rule in your hearts..." (Colossians 3:15). In this verse, Paul commands us to let "the peace of God *rule* in your hearts...." The word "rule" is a key to understanding this overcoming, conquering, and dominating supernatural *peace of God.*

The word "rule" is taken from the Greek word *brabeuo.* This word was used to portray *the umpire or referee who judged the athletic games in the ancient world.* Why did Paul use this word to illustrate the peace of God ruling in our hearts?

By choosing to use this illustration, Paul tells us that there is a place whereby the peace of God — instead of fretfulness, anxiety and worry — can begin to call the shots and make all the decisions in your life. You could translate the verse:

- *"Let the peace of God call the shots in your life...."*

- *"Let the peace of God umpire your life and your actions...."*

- *"Let the peace of God referee your emotions and your decisions...."*

The devil takes advantage of unrenewed areas of your mind, attempting to turn them into emotional roller coasters that constantly have you feeling *up* one day and *down* the next. Furthermore, even if there *weren't* a personal devil to attack you, the ever-changing affairs of life alone would be enough to keep you continually tossed to and fro in your mind and emotions.

This is why we *must* learn to let the peace of God "rule" in our hearts — especially in these difficult days in which we live!

When this supernatural peace rules in your heart — umpiring your life and serving as a referee to your emotions and your decisions — the devil cannot gain the foothold in your life he desires to have. *Satan can't play games with your emotions or your mind when they are being governed by peace!*

> Satan can't play games with your emotions or your mind when they are being governed by peace!

Do you see why Paul included *peace* in this section of Scripture about spiritual weaponry? When you are walking in the peace of God, the enemy's assaults lose their power to harm you. Such onslaughts are simply not effective against you when you're walking in the overwhelming, conquering, and prevailing peace of God!

PEACE: A DEFENSIVE WEAPON

To see further why Paul used the illustration of a Roman soldier's shoes to depict "peace," we must carefully consider how the soldier's shoe was made and what this dangerously spiked shoe did for the soldier.

The *greave* began at the top of the knee and extended down past the lower leg, all the way to the upper portion of the foot. Why do you suppose the upper portion of the Roman soldier's footwear covered the entire lower half of his legs? And why was this greave made of solid bronze or brass?

This particular piece of armor was very important! After all, it was the greave that protected the soldier's legs from being bruised, lacerated, or broken in battle.

A bruised, lacerated or broken leg could quickly spell disaster for a soldier. A bruised leg meant he would probably be impaired in his fighting and in his ability to swiftly respond to an attack. A lacerated leg meant he could potentially lose large amounts of blood and become too weakened to fight. A broken leg meant he could not stand to defend himself. And in this humbled position, it was far easier for a soldier's enemy to take his head off his shoulders!

Because of these potential dangers, the Roman soldier had to be certain that his legs were protected. A damaged leg most assuredly meant that the struggle would be more intense and, potentially, fatal.

Furthermore, commanding officers gave orders that required Roman soldiers to carry out difficult missions. At times, these dangerous missions required the soldiers to walk through *rocky places* and to scale *difficult barriers.*

Without protective guards on their lower legs, the soldiers' legs would have been severely wounded and bruised as they made their way past rough, sharp rocks. However, because these soldiers had greaves of brass tightly bound around their legs, they could walk through the rockiest and roughest of places without getting one scrape or bruise! Their *greaves* protected the soldiers from danger and gave them the assurance they needed to proceed in the mission that had been given to them.

Likewise, God may give *you* an assignment in life that leads you through some challenging places. If you do not have the protective peace of God at work in your life, it is highly probable that you will be mentally and emotionally bruised and battered by rocky relationships and rough situations.

On the other hand, when the peace of God is ruling in your heart, mind, and emotions, you can forge your way through the rockiest of situations and never get one scrape or bruise. Therefore, it is God's peace that enables you to successfully fulfill any mission He gives you in this life!

Not only did Roman soldiers walk through rocky places, they were called to walk through *thorny places* as well. If you have ever been forced to walk through a large thorn patch, you know how wicked those thorns can be! If you get caught in them, they can tear your legs to pieces!

But Roman soldiers rarely got a scratch. Their legs didn't bleed, their legs were never scuffed, and their legs were never seriously damaged by these fearsome thorns. *Their legs were completely covered and carefully protected by their greaves of brass that had been wrapped around their legs to protect them from getting injured.*

Similarly, if you make it past the rocky places in your life and are headed toward victory, the enemy may try to abort your victory by forcing you through a thorn patch. Your thorn patch may be a difficult financial situation, a bad marriage, a sick body, or a challenge against your ministry or place of employment.

But when the *peace of God* is working in your life, you will also make it through those sticky situations, just as you successfully made it through the rocky places. The prevailing, conquering peace of God will rule to such an extent that you can walk through those thorny places in life without receiving one poisonous prick to your mind and emotions!

There was another reason Roman soldiers wore these greaves of brass. A favorite tactic of the enemy was to dash up to his opponent and kick him so hard in the shin that it broke his leg. Once the soldier had fallen to the ground where he could not defend himself, the enemy would draw his sword and decapitate him.

The Roman soldiers' greaves of brass protected them from these kinds of assaults. It would have been very difficult, if not entirely impossible, for an opponent to kick a greave *so* hard that it would break the soldier's leg. Those brass greaves were specifically designed to guard the soldier's legs against such attacks. As long as Roman soldiers walked with their greaves firmly in place, they could be assured that no enemy would ever be able to break their legs and then take their heads off their shoulders.

These brass greaves enabled the soldier to walk through the rockiest of places *and never get hurt*. The greaves enabled the soldier to walk through wicked thorn patches *and never get scratched*. And because of these protective greaves, the enemy could kick repeatedly at the Roman soldier's shins, and *his legs would never be broken*.

HOW PEACE PROTECTS YOU

Do you see why Paul viewed peace as a weapon of defense? When you are walking in the peace of God, that peace protects you from cuts, scrapes, bruises, and hurts. It is like a protective greave, shielding your mind and your emotions from wounds and fears that could impair your life of faith.

With the peace of God operative in your life, you can walk through the rockiest and most difficult situations imaginable and never get bruised, cut, or seriously injured.

> With the peace of God operative in your life, you can walk through the rockiest and most difficult situations imaginable and never get bruised, cut, or seriously injured.

When the peace of God is ruling in your life, you can walk through those thorny situations that the enemy devises to destroy you, your family, your business, or your church family. During those times, you will wake up and realize, "I'm going through some extremely difficult times, *and I've never had more joy*! Why haven't I been more bothered by all this trouble? Why haven't I been bruised by this situation? *I seem to have total peace!*"

As long as you walk in the peace of God, that supernatural peace will continue to give you the protection you need. You can walk through horribly sticky situations and never get pricked when you are walking in this divine peace!

You may have known people who, naturally speaking, were going through very difficult times in their personal lives and yet continued to display joy in their lives and on their countenance. You may have wondered, *How are they making it through this time in their lives without losing their minds? How do they do it?*

There is only one answer: *the peace of God*. When you are walking in the peace of God, you often don't even realize how difficult your predicament is! You may not even be aware that the enemy is trying to fatally wound you (even though everyone else around you is aware of it!) when you are insulated by God's supernatural peace.

> When you are walking in the peace of God, you often don't even realize how difficult your predicament is!

How is it possible to go through all of these potential dangers without noticing it or without getting hurt? Because the *peace of God*, like a Roman soldier's *greave*, is protecting you so completely that you can carry on in life undisturbed by these events.

PROTECTION FROM THE DEVIL'S ATTACKS

You must know this one thing: The devil will try to kick you in the shins and cause you to fall flat on your face in your spiritual walk. I *guarantee* it!

Try to believe God for a healing — and see if the devil just sits back and watches without giving you a run for your money! Satan doesn't *want* you to be healed. So to keep you from receiving your healing, he will try all kinds of tricks to get you to doubt and to focus in on your symptoms instead of God's promises.

Try to believe God for prosperity — and see if the devil just sits back and passively watches as the blessings of God begin to freely pour into your life. No! The devil doesn't *want* you to have God's best! When you begin to grow and move into an increase of material blessings, the enemy will come against you as hard as he possibly can. He will try to lambaste you and beat you down into defeat. You might say that he will try to kick you in the shins, break your legs, and then take off your head!

What will protect you from that kind of a "kick in the shins"? What will protect your mind and emotions from that kind of onslaught? *The peace of God* is the weapon that will defend you and keep you safe in the midst of such trying circumstances.

> This supernatural peace pulls the plug on the devil's effectiveness. If he can't disturb your peace, he can't disturb *you*!

This supernatural peace pulls the plug on the devil's effectiveness. If he can't disturb your peace, he can't disturb *you*! He may try, but that peace will paralyze his efforts. He has no power to successfully attack you in such cases because you are immersed in the *peace of God*. This peace is one of the most important pieces of spiritual weaponry you possess!

You may be thinking, *My life is falling to pieces! At the present moment, I can feel each and every one of the devil's kicks — and they HURT! And in the past when I walked through those rocky and thorny ordeals, I got all kinds of cuts, scrapes, and bruises that still bother me. To this very moment, every wound I received during those difficult times still inflicts my mind and emotions.*

If this is really the case in your life, then you need to be clothed with the *peace of God*. It will protect you and carry you through times that are difficult and hard to bear.

So stay alert to this truth: As you grow in your walk with God, spiritual confrontations *will* come to challenge your new growth. Therefore, you must walk in the prevailing and conquering peace of God; otherwise, the enemy will throw you into a state of mental and emotional irrationality that will destroy your effectiveness for the Kingdom of God.

How To Set a Guard Around Your Heart

Along this same line of thought, Paul said, "And the peace of God, which passeth all understanding, shall *keep* your hearts and minds..." (Philippians 4:7).

The word "keep" is taken from the word *tereo*, and it means *to keep*, *to guard*, *to protect*, or *to garrison*. It is the picture of a band of Roman soldiers who are *standing watch* over something that needs protection.

By using this word, Paul tells us that the peace of God will keep and guard your heart and mind! Peace will surround your heart and mind, just as a band of Roman soldiers surrounded important dignitaries and places of special importance to guard them from possible harm.

Just as these soldiers kept outside nuisances from attacking important people or from breaking into special places, so peace keeps fretfulness, anxiety, worry, and all the other wiles of the devil from breaking into your life. When God's peace is active in your life, it surpasses all natural understanding in its ability to protect, guard, keep, and defend you from the enemy's attacks.

> When God's peace is active in your life, it surpasses all natural understanding in its ability to protect, guard, keep, and defend you from the enemy's attacks.

As Isaiah 26:3 says, "Thou wilt keep him [i.e., *will garrison him like a soldier, protecting, guarding, and defending him*"] in perfect peace, whose mind is stayed on thee...."

SPIKES FOR STANDING FIRMLY

Have you ever felt the devil trying to drive you back from the will of God for your life?

Has God ever spoken to you and told you to stand on a certain Bible promise — only to hear the devil telling you that it will never come to pass and that you will fail? Have you ever been mentally assaulted by the enemy in this way?

Maybe you are believing that God will work a miracle in your life, and the devil is trying to pull down your faith and keep you from moving into your land of blessing. If this describes your situation, you need to make doubly sure you've put on your shoes of peace, because *when you have peace on the bottom of your feet, a herd of elephants couldn't move you or knock you down!*

On the bottom of a Roman soldier's shoes were extremely dangerous spikes that were one to three inches in length. They served the soldier in two very important ways.

First, these spikes helped to hold the soldier's footing in place. When a soldier had three-inch spikes on the bottom of his feet and those spikes were firmly planted into the earth, that soldier became very difficult to knock over or to move!

God gives us supernatural peace to firmly plant our feet in the ground. His peace enables us to say, "Regardless of what I see or what I hear, *I'm not moving!* I don't care how hard it becomes, the peace of God keeps me here, and I'm not moving until the work of God in this area of my life is finished."

> God's peace enables us to say, "Regardless of what I see or what I hear, I'm not moving!

In other words, the peace of God gives you a firm footing! The devil may attack and attack, but when you have the peace of God functioning in your life, you will never be moved. *That peace will hold you in place!*

A person who has the peace of God actively functioning in his or her life is like a tall palm tree that is blown viciously by the winds of a hurricane. The fierce winds may bend the tree over, but when the storm passes, that palm tree pops right back up to its former position. Although the storm was severe, the roots of that tree held it in place.

In Ephesians 6:14, the Holy Spirit through Paul said, *"Stand therefore...."* In First Corinthians 16:13, Paul urges us, *"Watch ye, stand fast in the faith...."* Then in Second Corinthians 1:24, Paul says, *"...For by faith ye stand."*

Have you ever tried to stand in faith? Have you ever tried to stand for a miracle? Have you ever tried to stand for a financial situation to turn around? Or have you ever tried to stand in faith for a relationship to be healed? There is a whole lot more to "standing" than first meets the eye!

It's interesting to note that the majority of verses in the New Testament that have to do with *standing* also have to do with *faith*. When you stand in faith, the enemy will try to eliminate your faith, knowing that the elimination of faith will bring you to defeat. The enemy doesn't *want* you to maintain your stance of faith!

What will keep you in place as you seek to stand in faith? What will enable you to maintain your ground when vicious winds of opposition come your way? *The supernatural peace of*

God. Just as the roots of a tree hold the tree in place when strong winds come against it, God's peace, firmly fixed to the bottom of your feet, will hold *you* in your stance of faith as well.

Perhaps you have a relative who is terminally ill, and the medical doctor has said he or she only has a short time to live. Friends tell you to "accept it" and work through the emotions of losing a

> **What will enable you to maintain your ground when vicious winds of opposition come your way? The supernatural peace of God.**

loved one. The devil whispers into your ear and tells you that your relative will not recover.

At that particular moment — *when you are deciding whether or not to stand in faith* — every possible opportunity will come to move you from that place of belief in God. But you must plant your feet firmly into the soil of His Word and declare, "I don't care what the medical reports say or what the devil tries to whisper to me — God is going to move in my relative's life, and I'm not moving until He does! I am going to maintain this stance of faith!"

Only the peace of God will keep you in that place of confidence. Why? Because every other statement you hear will try to persuade you to back away from the promise of God's Word!

Perhaps you're facing a financial crisis. Maybe you've been believing God for a miracle to turn your situation around, and the devil has been saying to your mind:

"You're going to go bankrupt. You're going to lose your witness in the community. The whole town is going to talk about you. God isn't going to come through with this miracle you've been praying and believing to receive. I know you sowed offerings into the church, but you should have held on to that money. Now you really need it! If you hadn't given that money to the Lord, you wouldn't be in this mess right now!"

When the devil comes to accuse your mind and emotions like this, what is going to keep you in the middle of God's will? What is going to hold you in that place of faith? What is going to enable you to keep standing in faith on the Word? *The peace of God!*

HOW TO HAVE IMMOVABLE FAITH

When the peace of God is operative in your life, it puts spikes on the bottom of your feet that hold you in place. *The supernatural peace of God makes you immovable.*

The reason so many believers do not receive from God is that they don't walk in the *peace of God.* The first time they get hit with a challenge or the first time the devil hits them with a slanderous thought, they give in to their emotions and throw in the towel.

These believers' doubt-filled words and actions tell the devil, "Okay, you can have the ground I was trying to take by faith. You can have it. That's right, Devil, my relative will never be healed. That's right, Devil, I am going to go bankrupt. I'll just give up right now. I guess you're right; I shouldn't have obeyed the Word of God and given my tithes and offerings to the Lord."

You just need to understand this fact: The devil will always try to convince you that you have financial problems because you gave money to the Lord. Satan will always remind you of that ten dollars you gave — as if that ten dollars would have been enough to change your financial situation!

There will be plenty of opportunities for you to hear the adversary's slanderous accusations during the course of your Christian life. Therefore, you must learn how to plant your feet firmly into the soil of God's Word and then by faith to stay right where you are — unmoved and unhindered by the devil's threats and lies.

Peace is a divine weapon that will insulate you from these vicious attacks. The peace of God will keep you when Satan tries to shove doubt into your mind. The peace of God will guard your heart and mind, even when Satan is doing everything he can think of to make you lose your mind. *The peace of God is a KEEPING peace!*

PEACE: AN OFFENSIVE WEAPON

Up to this point, we have primarily dealt with the *defensive* nature of peace, and we have seen that peace is *protective*. Now we will see that peace is also an *offensive* piece of weaponry.

In Romans 16:20, Paul said, "And the God of peace shall bruise Satan under your feet shortly...."

Notice first the word "bruise." It is taken from the Greek word *suntribo*, and it was historically used to denote *the act of smashing and utterly crushing grapes into wine*. Have you ever accidentally stepped on a grape and felt it squish out from under your heel or toes? It's rather messy, isn't it? This is precisely the idea of the word "bruise."

The word "bruise" (*suntribo*) was also used to denote *the act of snapping, breaking, and crushing bones*. In fact, this is the picture of breaking bones so terribly that they can never be mended or healed. *These are bones that have been utterly smashed and crushed beyond recognition.*

With this in mind, Roman 16:20 teaches us that Satan's only rightful position is under our feet, completely subdued. In fact, the devil has been so subdued that, figuratively speaking, he has been squished like smashed grapes and his bones have been broken and crushed to pieces!

> Satan's only rightful position is under our feet, completely subdued.

It is important to point out that this "smashing" and "crushing" of Satan is done in cooperation with God. Alone, you are no match for this archenemy. Remember, he is a fallen angel. Even in his fallen state, he has retained much of his original intelligence. He is very smart, cunning, and crafty, and he is also extremely strong.

This is the reason that Paul says, "And *the God of peace* shall bruise Satan *under your feet....*" In other words, this is a joint partnership between you and God Himself. By yourself, you could never keep Satan subdued. But with God as your Partner, the devil has no chance of ever slipping out from under your heel!

Jesus completely destroyed Satan's power over you through His death and resurrection. Satan was utterly smashed, crushed, and bruised by Jesus' victorious resurrection from the dead. Now your God-given mission is to reinforce the victory already won and to demonstrate just how miserably defeated Satan already is!

> Your God-given mission is to reinforce the victory already won and to demonstrate just how miserably defeated Satan already is!

The enemy may try to lord himself over you, and he may attempt to exert his foul influence in your life. However, most of his attacks are merely empty threats and illusions he uses to feed fear into your mind. If Satan can get you to believe his hellish tales, your faith will dwindle, your strong stance will waver, and he will truly begin to take a temporal position over you that does not belong to him. *But the only place that rightfully belongs to the devil is the small space of ground that is right underneath your feet!*

The victory is already yours! Your healing, your miracle, your financial blessing — all of these are already yours! Jesus accomplished a total, complete, and perfect work on the Cross of Calvary and in His resurrection from the dead!

IT'S TIME TO DO SOME WALKING!

Let me remind you of something extremely important. In Joshua 1, God *freely* gave the children of Israel the Promised Land. However, in order for them to possess and enjoy this privilege, they had to go in and put their feet on the ground that God had *freely* given them. God told Joshua, "Every place that the sole of your foot shall tread upon, that have I given unto you..." (Joshua 1:3).

Yet the land God had promised His people was infested with giants and opposition. In order to possess God's promise to them, the Israelites had to do some walking and fighting. They had to fight for the kingdom of Ai, the city of Jericho, and so on. These enemy infestations were not going to easily give up their ownership and surrender to the people of God. Yet in time, the kingdom of Ai was destroyed, the walls of Jericho collapsed, and the people of God prevailed *because God was on their side*!

It may be that there are areas of sin in your life that seem to linger and defeat you. There may be habits that have held you for a long, long time or personal struggles that seem impossible to overcome. But at the Cross of Jesus Christ, every single one of those hindrances was resolved. Their power over your life was utterly shattered.

Now it is time for you to do some walking! Just like the Israelites of old, freedom is yours. Now *you* must go in and *possess the land*!

If the devil is foolish enough to think he can stand in your way, just remember — God is right there with you! This is a joint partnership between you and God! Therefore, march straight ahead and claim what is yours. And if the devil refuses to move, take this as an opportunity to "smash him like grapes" and "crush him" beyond recognition. *This is your chance to demonstrate Satan's defeat!*

> **Just like the Israelites of old, freedom is yours. Now you must go in and possess the land!**

With "the God of peace" on your side, you're a whole lot bigger than the devil! So throw back your shoulders, hold your head up high, and dig your heels down as deep as you can. Don't listen to Satan's hellish accusations and threats. Rather, when he whispers his lies to your mind and emotions, *wiggle your heel down even deeper into the dirt to remind him that he isn't coming out from underneath your feet*!

WHAT DOES 'SHORTLY' MEAN?

Paul goes on to say, "And the God of peace shall bruise Satan under your feet *shortly....*"

Notice that Paul ends this powerful statement with the word "shortly." This word is taken from the Greek word *tachos* and depicts the picture of *a large group of Roman soldiers marching down a street.* The word "shortly" describes *how* they marched.

These ancient men of war were taught to take very *hard, short, heavy steps* when they marched in formation. Therefore, when a large group of Roman soldiers came marching through town, their noise could be heard everywhere as they stomped and pounded the cobblestone and marble pavement in the streets.

The clapping of the soldiers' shoes upon that pavement served as a warning to the community. You see, these were Roman soldiers. They were very proud, and were taught that they were to stop for no one! If a little old woman fell on the ground in front of them, that was her problem, not theirs! She should have known better than to get in front of Roman soldiers.

In such events, they were instructed to keep marching, marching, marching — all the while stomping, pounding, and clapping their heavy feet and spikes upon the pavement. Imagine what that poor old woman would have looked like after an entire group of stomping, pounding feet with spikes on the bottom of them had walked over her!

Now Paul uses this same illustration to portray our victorious position in Jesus Christ. By using the word "shortly," which depicts *the stomping and pounding and the short, heavy steps* that Roman soldiers took, Paul is giving us an extremely graphic picture!

If the devil wants to stand in front of you and try to oppose you and the work of God in your life, then don't stop and ask him to move! *Just keep marching!* Keep stomping and pounding as you move forward to obey the plan of God for your life — and as you move forward in faith, *do as much damage to the enemy as you possibly can*!

Make Paul's words in Romans 16:20 *your* statement of faith: "The God of peace shall bruise Satan under *my* feet shortly!" There is no doubt about it! *The peace of God is an awesome and powerful weapon!*

QUESTIONS FOR PERSONAL GROWTH OR GROUP DISCUSSION

1. In what way does peace give you a firm footing when you encounter precarious and rocky situations in life?

2. What is the first step to take when you recognize that you are under siege and that chaos is attempting to override peace in your life?

3. Explain how it is possible for you to be at peace *with* God and still fail to walk in the peace *of* God.

4. When your mind and emotions are being governed by peace, how will peace help you respond to a sudden onslaught of difficult circumstances?

5. Think back to how you have responded to difficult situations in the past. What can you do to make sure you respond in peace the next time you face a sudden challenge?

NOTES:

_____

_____

_____

_____

_____

_____

_____

_____

_____

_____

_____

_____

_____

_____

_____

_____

_____

_____

_____

_____

_____

_____

CHAPTER THIRTEEN

THE SHIELD OF FAITH

*A*fter mentioning the weapon of peace, Paul immediately proceeds to our next piece of spiritual armor — the "shield of faith." He says, "Above all, taking the shield of faith, wherewith ye shall be able to quench all the fiery darts of the wicked" (Ephesians 6:16).

As we begin this discussion on the shield of faith, it is imperative once again to point out that the shield and the loinbelt were inseparably linked to each other. The massive shield of the Roman soldier rested on a small clip attached to his loinbelt when it was not in use.

As we have already seen in Chapter Ten, the loinbelt is representative of the written Word of God, the Bible. Attached to this "loinbelt of truth" is the shield, which is representative of *faith*. The conclusion is simple but extremely important to understand: *Your faith is attached to the Word of God!*

If you fail to give the Word of God a place of top priority in your life, it is only a matter of time before your faith will begin to dwindle and wane — because the presence or absence of faith is determined by the presence or absence of God's Word. Faith and the Word of God are *inseparable*.

> The presence or absence of faith is determined by the presence or absence of God's Word. Faith and the Word of God are inseparable.

This is why Paul said, "So then faith cometh by hearing, and hearing by the Word of God" (Romans 10:17). Faith and the Word of God are so uniquely tied together that where there is no Word, there is no faith. In the same way, if faith is absent in a person's life, you will find that the Word of God is absent as well.

As we discussed earlier, Paul began this text on spiritual armor by listing the loinbelt of truth first. Paul looked at a Roman soldier wearing a big helmet on his head, a bright and shining breastplate, brass greaves, a specially tooled lance, a two-edged sword, and a large, oblong shield. Yet after viewing all of these more impressive pieces of armor, Paul began his description by pointing to the *loinbelt* wrapped around the man's waist!

Why did Paul do this? Because the Holy Spirit wanted to tell us something very important: *The Word of God is central and foremost to everything else that we have in God.*

Your ability to walk in the knowledge that you are righteous in Christ hinges entirely upon the centrality of God's Word in your life. Get out of the Word, and it is only a matter of time before you will begin to lose that wonderful sense of righteousness.

Your ability to walk in peace is decided by whether or not you are giving God's Word a place of preeminence in your life. When the Word of God has that foremost position, the peace of God is then released to call the shots and to guard your heart and mind. But if you get out of the Word, it is only a matter of time before that abiding sense of peace will be replaced by the anxious cares of this life.

Likewise, your ability to walk in strong faith is also determined by the presence or absence of God's Word in your life. Again, Paul said, "Faith cometh by hearing, and hearing by the Word of God" (Romans 10:17). *Faith is a result of the impartation of God's Word into the human heart.* Thus, if the Word of God does not have an important place in your schedule, it will be impossible for you to grow in faith.

The practical outworking of your salvation is greatly affected by the renewing of your mind with the Word of God. Although born again and destined for Heaven, you will not be able to enjoy the benefits of your salvation now — *in this life* — unless you permit the power of God's Word to continually work to transform your mind.

> **If the Word of God does not have an important place in your schedule, it will be impossible for you to grow in faith.**

Furthermore, there will be no sword of the Spirit at your disposal if the loinbelt of truth has no place in your life. The sword of the Roman soldier rested in a scabbard that hung from the loinbelt. This is another picture of the necessity of the written Word of God in our lives. That *rhema* word you desperately need will probably come directly from the Bible as the Holy Spirit quickens a verse to your heart.

Thank God for those special moments when the Spirit speaks a word to your heart! When such words from the Lord come to your heart, what joy they bring! But you shouldn't base your Christian life entirely on these *rhema* words from God. You may not always receive a personal "word from the Lord," but you will always have the dependable, ever-present Word of God — the loinbelt of truth — to build your life upon and to give you direction.

This piece of spiritual armor is always available and accessible to you. You can even touch this one! And if you have this most important weapon in hand, in time you will have everything else you need to live a victorious Christian life.

THE SHIELD OF FAITH

Now let's move on to discuss the shield of faith, the next weapon in our spiritual arsenal. Again, Ephesians 6:16 says, "Above all, taking the shield of faith, wherewith ye shall be able to quench all the fiery darts of the wicked."

Roman soldiers owned two kinds of shields. They used one in public parades and ceremonies and the other in battle.

The first shield was denoted by the Greek word *aspis*. This *aspis* shield was *a small, round shield that was primarily a decorative piece of equipment to be used in public ceremonies and parades.*

This particular shield was absolutely gorgeous! It was decorated with all kinds of intricate etchings, engravings, and markings on the front. In addition, the front middle portion of this small shield often depicted an artist's rendition of a previous victorious military campaign. This *aspis* shield was beautiful, but it was too small to be used in an actual military confrontation.

The second kind of shield used by the Roman soldier was the one to which Paul makes reference in Ephesians 6:16 when he speaks of the shield of faith. This particular word for "shield" is taken from the Greek word *thureos*, which was used by the Greeks to refer to *a door that was wide in width and long in length*. The Romans used this word for the shields they carried into battle because these shields were *shaped like a door*. In other words, they were wide in width and long in length, just like the door of a house.

The large battle shield was the very opposite of the first shield, which was far too small to protect a soldier from the slings and arrows of his adversary. The *aspis* shield never would have covered a soldier in the midst of the fray. Although beautiful and enjoyable to behold in public ceremonies and parades, such a small piece of armor would have left the soldier wide open to deadly blows. On the other hand, the second shield *completely covered* the man!

It is therefore very significant that the Holy Spirit selected this second shield (*thureos*) as the illustration of faith rather than the first shield (*aspis*). He is telling us that God has given us enough faith to make certain we are completely covered — just like a battle shield completely covered a Roman soldier!

Romans 12:3 says, "...God hath dealt to every man the measure of faith." How much faith has God given you? He has given you enough faith to make certain you are covered in life!

Don't ever worry or fret that God has given others more faith than He has given you. Rest assured in the fact that He has imparted enough faith to you to make sure you are covered from head to toe! Like a wide, long shield, the faith God has given you is adequate to cover every need that could ever arise in your life.

> Like a wide and long shield, the faith God has given you is adequate to cover every need that could ever arise in your life.

In the majority of cases, the Roman soldier's shield was composed of multiple layers — usually six layers — of thick animal hide that had been tightly woven together. These layers of animal hide were specially tanned and then woven together so tightly that they became almost as strong as steel.

One piece of leather is tough, but imagine how tough and durable six layers of leather would be! Because the shield of the Roman soldier was made from all these layers of animal hides, it was *extremely strong* and *exceptionally long-lasting and hard-wearing*.

Similarly, your faith is extremely tough and exceptionally durable — more so than you have ever realized! No matter how hard and how long the enemy beats against your faith, your faith can outlast his attack. The shield of faith that God has given you is a *strong, long-lasting,* and *durable* faith.

HOW TO CARE FOR YOUR SHIELD OF FAITH

Because the Roman soldier's shield was made of leather, it was important for the soldier to take good care of it.

Although the six layers of animal hide made the shield extremely strong and durable, that tough, thick leather could become stiff and breakable over a period of time if it wasn't properly taken care of. Therefore, it was necessary for Roman soldiers to know how to care for their shields.

> No matter how hard and how long the enemy beats against your faith, your faith can outlast his attack.

A soldier was given a daily schedule for maintaining his shield in excellent condition. Each morning when he woke up, he would reach for his shield and for a small vial of oil. After saturating a piece of cloth with this heavy ointment, he would thoroughly rub the oil into the leather of the shield to keep it soft, supple, and pliable. For a soldier to ignore this daily application of oil and to let his shield go without this kind of required care was essentially the equivalent of his inviting certain death.

Because this protective shield was made of leather, it would have become hard, stiff, and brittle without the proper care. If not correctly maintained, over time the leather would have hardened until, when put under pressure, it cracked and fell to pieces. This is why the end result of a soldier's failure to care for his shield was death on the battlefield.

If the Roman soldier wanted to live a long life, it was imperative for him to pick up that vial and apply the oil to his shield every single day of his military life.

Because the shield is representative of our *faith*, this analogy tells us that our faith requires *frequent anointings* of the Holy Spirit.

Without a fresh touch of the Holy Spirit's power on your life, your faith will become hard, stiff, and brittle. If you ignore your faith and allow it to go undeveloped, never seeking a fresh anointing of God's Spirit to come upon your life, your faith won't be soft, supple, and pliable enough to stand up under attack when a challenge comes your way. *Faith that is ignored nearly always breaks and falls to pieces during a confrontation with the enemy.*

Many believers make the incredibly tragic mistake of thinking they can keep moving forward in their Christian walk on the steam of their past experiences with the Lord. Thank God for those past experiences, but no believer can ever rest on his laurels from the past!

Regardless of how great your past experiences and victories are, if you stop developing your faith or fail to keep your faith freshly anointed by the Holy Spirit's presence, your shield of faith is in a hazardous position. So never assume that your faith is in top-notch shape. *Instead, play it safe and assume that your faith always needs a fresh anointing.* By taking this approach, you will always seek to do what is necessary to keep your faith alive, active, and well!

There was another reason the Roman soldier's shield was made out of animal hide. Before a soldier went out to war, he placed his shield in a tub of water; then he left it there soaking in the water until his shield was completely *saturated*.

Why did Roman soldiers saturate their shields with water? Because their enemies used arrows that carried *fire!* Even when those dangerous flaming arrows hit their target, the wet surface of the shields would extinguish them on impact! These water-saturated shields gave the soldier the upper hand in battle by putting out the enemy's fire.

> Play it safe and assume that your faith always needs a fresh anointing. By taking this approach, you will always seek to do what is necessary to keep your faith alive, active, and well!

In the same way, when we keep our faith completely saturated with "the washing of water by the word" (Ephesians 5:26), our "Word-saturated" shields have the power to extinguish all the flaming arrows of the adversary (Ephesians 6:16)!

> We must make certain that we are allowing the Holy Spirit to freshly anoint our lives on a daily basis as we regularly saturate our faith with the water of the Word.

So we see that in order for Roman soldiers to keep their shields in top-notch condition, it was required that their shields had daily applications of both *oil* and *water*.

Likewise, in order for us to keep our shield of faith in top-notch condition, we must give serious attention to the condition of our faith. We must make certain that we are allowing the Holy Spirit to freshly anoint our lives on a daily basis as we regularly saturate our faith with the water of the Word. Word-saturated faith will *always* extinguish the devil's attacks!

WHAT DOES 'ABOVE ALL' MEAN?

Some have mistakenly thought that faith is more important than any other piece of spiritual weaponry. This cannot be! The loinbelt of truth — the Bible, the written Word of God — is the most important piece of weaponry we possess.

How do we know that the Word of God is more important than faith? *Faith comes from the Word of God.* How then could the shield of faith be more important than the loinbelt of truth, the Word of God? Let's not get the cart before the horse!

Nevertheless, Paul does say, *"Above all,* taking the shield of faith...." What does that phrase "above all" mean?

This phrase is taken from the Greek phrase *epi pasin.* The word *epi* means *over.* The word *pasin* means *all* or *everything.* Rather than referring to being more important than the other pieces of armor, the phrase *epi pasin* describes *position over the other pieces of armor.* It could be better translated, *"out in front of all"* or *"covering all."*

This tells you that your faith is supposed to be *out in front* where it can *cover all.* Faith was never meant to be held next to your side or to be timidly held behind your back. Faith is designed to be *out in front* where it can *completely cover* you in every situation of life!

> Faith is designed to be out in front where it can completely cover you in every situation of life!

Keep in mind that the phrase "above all" describes *position*, not *importance*. Therefore, this phrase emphatically tells us that the shield of faith is meant to completely cover us and protect us from harm — especially when we are marching forward to take new ground for the Kingdom of God. It is a defensive weapon that is *out in front of all the other pieces of armor.*

When our shield of faith is in its proper *out-in-front* and *covering* position, it can do what God intended it to do! This is why Paul continues to say, "Above all, taking the shield of faith, *wherewith ye shall be able to quench all the fiery darts of the wicked.*"

Notice that Paul says, "...*taking* the shield of faith...." The word "taking" is from the word *analambano*, which is a compound of the Greek words *ana* and *lambano*.

The word *ana* means *up, back,* or *again,* and the word *lambano* means *to take up* or *to take in hand.* When compounded together into one word, it means *to take something up in hand* or *to pick something back up again.*

This plainly means that our shield of faith can be picked up or it can be laid down. The choice is ours to make. Moreover, it reassures us that if we've laid down our faith at some point along the way — if we've gotten discouraged and stopped believing God to work in our lives — it is not too late for us to "pick up" our shield and walk in faith again!

No well-trained Roman soldier would have gone to battle without his shield. That piece of weaponry was not optional! The shield was the soldier's guarantee that he would be guarded against deadly bombardments. Without that protective shield in front of him, there was absolutely nothing between him and his opponent. The soldier therefore understood that he would be walking into self-imposed destruction if he went forward into battle without a shield.

Sadly, many believers lack this same understanding when it comes to facing the enemy without their shield of faith. They mistakenly think that they can successfully live their Christian lives without giving attention to the development of their own faith. But that kind of thinking is utter foolishness! It was for this cause that Paul told Timothy, "…war a good warfare; holding faith, and a good conscience; which some having put away concerning faith have made shipwreck" (1 Timothy 1:18,19).

When a believer "puts away" his faith, it always leads to spiritual shipwreck. In other words, by ignoring and disregarding the significance of their faith, some of our brothers and sisters in the Lord have opted for a spiritual course that will eventually lead them to total exposure to the enemy's attacks.

> When a believer "puts away" his faith, it always leads to spiritual shipwreck.

In recent years, some have accused other believers of overemphasizing the importance of faith as compared to other aspects of the Christian life. But as we begin to understand the crucial nature of faith and its ramifications in our lives both physically and spiritually, we come to realize that it is *impossible* to overemphasize the necessity of a life of faith.

> It is impossible to overemphasize the necessity of a life of faith.

THE PURPOSE OF THE SHIELD OF FAITH

Paul continues in Ephesians 6:16, "Above all, taking the shield of faith, *wherewith ye shall be able to quench all the fiery darts of the wicked.*"

The word "wherewith" would be better translated, "by which." The phrase "shall be able" is taken from the word *dunamis*, which denotes *explosive power or dynamic power*. It is where we get the word "dynamite."

This phrase would thus be better translated, "...*By the use of this shield, you will have explosive and dynamic power....*"

What, then, is this part of the verse saying? When you hold your shield of faith in front of you — and when that shield of faith is both anointed by the Holy Spirit and saturated with the Word of God — your faith positions you to move in God's *explosive and dynamic power*!

The apostle Peter declares that we "...are kept by the power of God through faith..." (1 Peter 1:5). There is an unseen connection between the power of God and the operation of faith in your life. When these two are working hand in hand, they build a strong wall of defense against the enemy's tactics that is impenetrable.

In other words, when your strong faith activates the power of God in your life, those two forces combine to make a mighty, protective shield between you and every demonic onslaught that might come against you. To put it another way, power and faith working together in your life will spiritually equip you to hold an ironclad position against the enemy without taking any serious blows to yourself. The combination of these two elements will cause you to be *fortified*, *invulnerable*, and *armed to the teeth*!

> Power and faith working together in your life will spiritually equip you to hold an ironclad position against the enemy without taking any serious blows to yourself.

When the power of God and faith are operative in your life, you are like a huge army tank, with the ability to move your position forward without taking any losses!

This doesn't mean the devil won't *try* to stop you, because he *will*! This is why Paul says, "...that ye may be able to stand against *the fiery darts of the wicked*."

THE FIERY DARTS OF THE WICKED

You may ask, "What *are* the fiery darts of the wicked?"

The Greek word used to describe these particular "darts" is a very specific and historical word of warfare. Thucydides, the ancient Greek writer, used the identical Greek expression to depict *especially terrible arrows that were equipped to carry fire.*

The military of New Testament times used three types of arrows. First, there were regular arrows, similar to the arrows one would shoot from a bow today. Second, there were arrows that were dipped into tar, set on fire, and then shot through the air. Third, there were arrows containing combustible fluids that burst into flames upon impact.

The arrows in Ephesians 6:16 are called "fiery darts." Because Paul's word usage is identical to that of Thucydides, we know exactly what kind of arrows Paul has in mind.

Paul is thinking of *arrows that carry fire!* Specifically, he is referring to the third kind of arrows — those that were made from long, slender pieces of cane and filled with combustible fluids that exploded on impact.

These particular arrows were one of the greatest terrors of the day. To the natural eye, they looked minimally dangerous. But the natural eye couldn't see that these arrows had been filled with combustible fluids. Only after impact — when a great fire had begun — could one know for certain that these arrows had been equipped with the potential of explosive flames and disaster.

These fluid-filled arrows were not used in normal combat situations. Regular arrows were sufficient for those kinds of confrontations. Fire-bearing arrows were reserved to inflict damage on a fortified place or an encampment.

If the Roman army had fortified its position so that the enemy couldn't easily break in to destroy it, the opposing forces would then revert to using these deadly arrows of fire. The enemy soldiers would hold these long pieces of slender cane in an upright position and pour explosive fluids into them. Once they had filled these arrows to the brim with the death-dealing liquid, they sealed and disguised the arrows to look like normal, minimally dangerous ones.

Since the enemy could not physically break into the encampment and personally destroy the entrenched army, they shot these fire-bearing arrows over the walls of the army's fortified position. The arrows were disguised to *look* very harmless; as a result, those inside the encampment often made the fatal mistake of ignoring them — *at least until the first one hit its target.*

Troops were shocked and taken off guard when those arrows struck inside the fortress walls and burst into raging flames. (You might say these arrows were the *bombs* of the ancient world.) Then after the initial fiery conflagration, the enemy would continue to shoot more of these arrows, one after another, into the encampment — each equipped with the same deadly capabilities.

It is this very picture that Paul has in mind when he says, "Above all, taking the shield of faith, wherewith ye shall be able to stand against *the fiery darts of the wicked.*"

FIRE THAT STIRS THE VILEST PASSIONS

This is the kind of arrow the enemy wants to send your way. When Satan has no easy access into your life, he will try another, more covert way to come against you — shooting a fire-bearing arrow into your emotions. He launches fiery darts right smack into the middle of weak places in your mind and heart because he wants to make sure his darts have the greatest potential of arousing the worst and most vile of emotions in you!

When a flaming arrow from the enemy hits its target — *your emotions* — it can throw those emotions into a state of rage, anger, anxiety, unbelief, worry, and so forth. These flaming arrows are meant to do something destructive and horrendous in your mind and emotions. They are meant not only to *hit* you but also to *enflame* you like a fire that is hopelessly burning out of control.

Many believers are hit by the enemy's fiery arrows every day because they are not walking with their shield of faith held out in front of them where it belongs. Not only that, but they neglect their shield of faith, failing to keep it anointed by the Spirit and saturated with the water of the Word. If only they would do what they should to maintain and strengthen their faith, that invisible shield would keep those hellish arrows from getting through to harm them!

WHO IS RESPONSIBLE FOR FAILURE?

The devil and his hosts are *never* your real problem. The Lord Jesus Christ thoroughly spoiled them through His death and resurrection (Colossians 2:15)! If you continue to be controlled by habitual hang-ups and to struggle with the same hassles and emotional upsets, your primary problem may be that *you have not made the decision to submit your flesh and mind to the sanctifying work of the Holy Spirit.* If your shield of faith were properly anointed by the Holy Spirit and saturated in the Word of God, those arrows would be *extinguished* on impact!

If the devil's fiery arrows have been effective in throwing you into rage, anger, anxiety, unbelief, or worry, it is evident that there is a crack in your shield of faith. Regardless of how the crack got there in the first place, it is your responsibility to do something about it.

Often people have cracked shields due to wrong attitudes and thoughts in their minds. These cracks provide an open door through which the devil's arrows can potentially pass.

If you live in the presence of God on a daily basis, the Holy Spirit's anointing comes upon your faith. But if you don't, the absence of the Holy Spirit's "oil" causes your faith to become hard, stiff, and brittle. Sometimes the reason fiery arrows break through your shield of faith is that you don't do what is necessary to keep your faith supple, pliable, and durable. On the other hand, if you give the Word of God a place of priority in your daily schedule, your shield of faith is so saturated with the water of the Word that it extinguishes those flaming arrows!

As I stated earlier, human nature loves to shift the blame for failure to someone else. But the truth is, God has given us *everything* we need to stand against the wiles of the devil. If we have been wounded by the enemy's fiery darts, we must assume responsibility for repairing the cracks in our shield of faith and stop shifting the blame to someone else.

It is very important that you live the crucified life in the presence of God and give the Word of God a primary place in your daily schedule. By keeping your shield of faith anointed with the oil of the Spirit and saturated with the water of the Word, you will ensure that every fiery dart the enemy launches against you will miserably fail.

By dealing with the unseen areas of your life and mind (which may be known only to you, God, and the devil), you are ensuring that *there are no open doors through which the enemy's arrows can pass to pierce through your emotions and throw you into a fit of raging carnality!*

God has provided a way for us to avoid being hit by these fiery darts. He has provided a way for us to *escape* their destructive impact.

Paul said, "There hath no temptation taken you but such as is common to man: but God is faithful, who will not suffer you to be tempted above that ye are able; but will with the temptation also make *a way to escape*, that ye may be able to bear it" (1 Corinthians 10:13).

The shield of faith is your "way to escape" from the fiery darts of the adversary. When your faith is *out in front* and *covering all*, it quenches every temptation and every fire-bearing arrow that the enemy tries to send your way.

When you are carrying your well-maintained shield of faith, those deadly arrows lose their power and fall to the ground. *Thus, you escape, and the enemy's strategies against you are thwarted!*

QUENCHING, EXTINGUISHING, AND RICOCHETING FAITH

The enemy's goal is to lodge an arrow of unbelief in your mind that will eventually destroy you. Maybe that arrow is a thought that says, *"You are going to die of cancer!"* or *"Your marriage is going to fail!"* Perhaps the arrow that has lodged in your mind says, *"You are going to go under financially!"* If one of the devil's arrows lodges in your mind and you begin to *believe* its lie, your belief in that falsehood will most likely empower it to become a reality in your life!

For example, if an arrow of unbelief lodges in your mind and tells you that you are going to go broke, you may really go broke if you don't get rid of that lie.

If an arrow of unbelief lodges in your mind and convinces you that there is no hope for your marriage, your marriage may really begin to deteriorate as your negative faith empowers that demonic accusation to become a reality.

The shield of faith enables us to quench and extinguish every fiery dart of the enemy. This is why the Word of God commands us to cast down "...imaginations, and every high thing that exalteth itself against the knowledge of God" (2 Corinthians 10:5).

How much damage can Satan's fiery darts do to you if you by faith immediately cast them down? Those arrows *can't* harm you if they are lying on the ground around your feet. That's what the shield of faith does for you. It puts out the fire of the devil's hellish accusations and knocks them down to the ground, where their deceptive powers cease to influence you.

As you walk in faith, there will be times when you see another arrow from the evil one coming your way. But as you keep your shield of faith *up front* and *covering all*, that arrow will bounce right off you!

Because the Roman soldier regularly anointed his shield with oil, it was also *slippery*. Thus, when he walked with his shield held high, the fiery arrows that actually hit his shield would often slip right off it. Other times the arrow that hit the soldier's shield would ricochet back into the face of the enemy and explode in his own face!

Likewise, when you are walking in faith that is anointed by the power of the Holy Spirit, your faith will defend you. *Faith will quench, thwart, and extinguish anything the devil throws at you to harm and destroy!*

You may ask, "Just how bad would it be for me if the enemy's fiery darts succeeded in hitting me?" Ephesians 6:16 gives us a clue when it says, "...wherewith ye shall be able to quench all the fiery darts *of the wicked*."

The word "wicked" is taken from the word *poneros*. This word means *sorrow, pain, evil, malignant, malicious, ill,* or *vicious*.

This explicitly tells us that these are *vicious, evil* arrows. These are arrows that potentially carry unimaginable *sorrow* and *pain* in them — arrows that are actively involved in spreading the flame and fire of *wickedness, evil,* and *suffering*.

I hope you can see why it is so important that your faith is *out in front* where it belongs! If you ignore your faith and allow it to go undeveloped, you will soon discover for yourself that the devil's arrows have the capacity of producing great sorrow and pain. When they hit, they are *malicious*.

Furthermore, the lies that the devil shoots into your mind are not intended to merely wound you; they are intended to hit and then *explode* in your life with their full destructive force.

The devil's goal is to seize your mind, paralyze it with fear, and then flood it with allegations that are not true. If Satan can captivate your thinking and reasoning processes and then convince you to believe that his lying allegations are true, his fiery darts can then release their damnable destruction in your life and mind.

For example, some years ago we were ministering in a church where a prominent woman had died of cancer. Her death really shook the faith of that particular congregation. As a result, the entire congregation concluded, "Healing is not for us today!"

The enemy shot an arrow of cancer and suffering into that woman's body. From her, that deadly fire began to spread into the entire church body. Because the congregation's shield of faith was not *out in front* where it belonged, protecting and covering them, the people of that church were mortally wounded. When that arrow hit, it released its destructive powers. It didn't come just to kill one woman; it came to kill an entire church!

CORPORATE FAITH IN THE LOCAL CHURCH

Although a Roman soldier could carry a shield to fight individual enemy soldiers by himself, he and his shield were not big enough to take on an entire army. He could defend himself for a while and perhaps even make a little headway, *but what is one man against a whole army?*

Therefore, when Roman soldiers were threatened by a massive enemy army, they would walk very close to one another in one long line, side by side.

On the sides of their massive shields were small hinges. One at a time, each soldier would begin fastening his shield to the next soldier's shield, who would then fasten his to the next soldier's shield, and so on it would go down the entire long line.

After all the soldiers' shields were securely fastened to one another, they would begin marching in unison toward the opposing forces. To the enemy, the Roman army looked like one huge wall of armor moving across the field to meet them in battle!

Thus, with shield attached to shield, those soldiers had a massive wall of protection in front of them. When soldiers marched together like this with their shields connected, they were positioned to march right up to the enemy lines to do battle without losing any of their own.

Similarly, when we as believers learn how to walk with each other in unison, we position ourselves to make advances and inroads into the enemy's territory that we have never made before!

Thank God, our faith will work for us personally. But we must also thank God that when we join our faith to the faith of others, we position ourselves to make some significant gains as the corporate Body of Christ!

Believers are called to march together side by side, holding their closely connected shields of faith out in front of them just as the Roman soldiers did on their way to meet the enemy army. When there is that kind of unity among believers who walk in faith, it doesn't matter how many demonic forces are out there to oppose them. *Those unified believers will be able to steadily and aggressively move forward, putting hard pressure on the enemy and thwarting all his strategies with the power of their unified, corporate faith!*

DOES YOUR SHIELD HAVE CRACKS?

If you neglect your shield of faith — never receiving a fresh anointing of the Spirit's presence upon it and never soaking your faith in the Word of God — you had better not try to take on any big challenges. Your shield won't be in the best of shape!

Faith that is ignored becomes hard, stiff, and brittle. If you run out to challenge the adversary with a hard, stiff, and brittle faith, it will crack in the midst of conflict. If you wave a cracked shield in the enemy's face, you're going to end up in a heap of trouble!

If, however, your faith is intact — if the presence of God's Spirit is active upon your faith and your faith is saturated in God's Word — then you can wave your faith like a shield in the face of the enemy, and every dart he tries to use against you will fall to the ground.

IF YOUR FAITH NEEDS AN ANOINTING

Does your faith need a fresh anointing? If so, you must go before the Great Anointer and allow *Him* to give you a fresh anointing of the Holy Spirit.

This is precisely what David was referring to when he said, "...I shall be anointed with *fresh oil*" (Psalm 92:10).

The word "anoint" comes from the Greek word *chrio*. It was originally a medical term. When a patient with sore muscles came to see his physician, the physician would pour oil on his own hands and then begin to rub that oil into the patient's sore muscles.

Technically, then, the word "anoint" has to do with *the rubbing or smearing of oil on someone else*. I call the anointing *a hands-on situation*!

Thus, when we speak of a person who is anointed, we are actually saying that the hand of God is upon that person and that God is rubbing the strong presence of the Holy Spirit into that man or woman's life or ministry. If a person's sermon is anointed, it is anointed because the hand of God is upon it. If a person sings an anointed song, the song is anointed because the hand of God is upon it.

The anointing is the result of God's hand personally imparting the strong presence of the Holy Spirit into something. Therefore, if you need a fresh anointing of the Holy Spirit upon your faith, you must come before the Great Anointer! He alone can give you what you need. Open your heart to the Spirit of God, and allow Him to lay His hand upon your life and your faith in a fresh, new way. As you do, a strong anointing will follow — this is *guaranteed*!

In Conclusion

When you walk with your shield of faith *up front* and *covering all*, you are in position to storm the enemy's lies and allegations without fear of getting hurt.

Perhaps you've tried to act in faith in the past and were disappointed with the results. Maybe you were believing God for your healing but instead began to feel worse, and this discouraged you into thinking that your faith doesn't produce results. Because of experiences like this, you may be afraid to step out to believe God again.

But perhaps you felt the stab of the enemy's evil arrows in the past because your faith wasn't *out in front* where it belonged. Those malignant arrows may have brought sorrow, pain, suffering, or mental distress. They may have assaulted your soulish realm, hitting your mind and emotions.

Remember, the devil knows that the mind is the strategic control center of your life. If he can seize your mind, he can then begin to wage warfare against the other parts of your being.

In order to keep your mind from being struck in the future by those vicious fiery darts that come to deceive and destroy, it is imperative that you *pick up your shield of faith once again*. But you can't stop there. You have to keep your faith strong with a daily soaking in the presence of the Holy Spirit and in the water of the Word. Then you have to hold your shield up before you continually so that it covers and protects every area of your life.

As you do all these things and begin to walk in strong faith, you can be assured of this: *You will not be affected mentally, emotionally, or physically by the fiery darts of the enemy!*

QUESTIONS FOR PERSONAL GROWTH OR GROUP DISCUSSION

1. What two things must you apply on a daily basis to your shield of faith in order to keep your faith strong and ready for any challenge?

2. Why do some believers lay aside their shield of faith, and what happens to their spiritual walk when they do?

3. What is an example of a fiery dart that Satan has thrown your way in the past? Did you allow that fiery arrow to enflame your emotions, or was your shield of faith covering you from head to toe, protecting you from the devil's attack?

4. What must you do if you find a crack in your shield of faith, whether it was caused by your own wrong attitude or by someone else's wrong actions?

5. Have you laid aside your shield of faith because you were disappointed in the lack of results from past prayers? What must you do to get back in the fight and prepare yourself for future faith challenges?

Notes:

_____

_____

_____

_____

_____

_____

_____

_____

_____

_____

_____

_____

_____

_____

_____

_____

_____

_____

_____

_____

_____

_____

_____

_____

_____

CHAPTER FOURTEEN

THE HELMET OF SALVATION

*B*efore we go on in our discussion of each piece of our spiritual armor, I want to take a moment to consider the perfect balance that exists in the armor of God. God has given us three *offensive* weapons, three *defensive* weapons, and one *neutral* weapon.

The breastplate, the shield, and the helmet are *defensive* weapons. These are weapons that protect you and give you confidence and assurance so you can move forward in your spiritual growth.

The three *offensive* weapons are the shoes, the sword, and the lance. These are weapons that enable you to enforce and demonstrate Satan's already secured defeat.

The neutral weapon is the loinbelt, which is representative of the Word of God. It is the central piece of weaponry that holds all of these other pieces together. Without this central piece of spiritual armor, the written Word, the other pieces of armor cannot function properly in your life.

Let me remind you that all these pieces of weaponry come *from God*. To walk in them and to see them work in your personal life mandates that you *live* in the presence of God.

Just as you draw your power and your nature *from God*, so also you must draw your spiritual weaponry *from Him*. He is the Source of origination for everything you have — *including spiritual armor*.

THE HELMET OF SALVATION

In Ephesians 6:17, Paul continued with his list of spiritual armor by saying, "And take *the helmet of salvation*...."

The Roman soldier's helmet was a fascinating and beautiful part of his armor. It was a flamboyant piece of weaponry, very ornate and intricate. In fact, it looked more like a piece of artwork than a helmet! Rather than being a simple piece of metal formed to fit his head, the Roman soldier's helmet was highly decorated with all kinds of engravings and etchings.

> Just as you draw your power and your nature from God, so also you must draw your spiritual weaponry from Him.

It was not uncommon for pastoral farm scenes with animals to be depicted on the helmet of a Roman soldier. Frequently the entire helmet of the Roman soldier was fashioned to look like the head of an elephant, a horse, or another animal. Other helmets had ornate engravings and etchings of fruit all over them.

Think of how odd some of these helmets must have been to behold. The Roman soldier's helmet often looked more like a piece of sculpture than a piece of armor!

Furthermore, as if these fabulous engravings and etchings were not enough, a huge plume of brightly colored feathers or horsehair stood straight up out of the top of the helmet. If the helmet was one to be used in a public ceremony or parade, this brightly colored plume could be very long — long enough to hang all the way down the soldier's back.

The helmet was made of bronze and equipped with pieces of armor that were specifically designed to protect the cheeks and jaws. It was extremely heavy; therefore, the interior of the helmet was lined with a spongy material in order to soften its weight upon the soldier's head. This piece of armor was so strong, so massive, and so heavy that nothing could pierce it — not even a hammer or a battleaxe.

It would be very hard to walk past one of these soldiers without noticing him. You would definitely take note of a man who had a piece of sculpture on his head! And certainly your eyes would follow a man who had a brightly colored plume standing straight up on the top of his helmet. *These helmets undoubtedly made the Roman soldier noticeable.*

GOD'S MOST GORGEOUS GIFT

Why would the Holy Spirit compare a piece of weaponry like this to salvation? *Because your salvation is the most gorgeous, most intricate, most elaborate, and most ornate gift God ever gave you!*

Paul calls this marvelous gift "the helmet of salvation." Moreover, he used the example of a Roman soldier's helmet to make his point. He likened salvation to the flamboyant helmet that was worn on a soldier's head where everyone would notice it. And just to make *sure* everyone noticed his helmet, the soldier had a plume of feathers or horsehair standing straight up at the top!

By using this example, Paul is telling us something very important. When a person is confident of his salvation — and when he is walking in the powerful reality of all that salvation means for him — that person is *noticeable*!

> When a person is confident of his salvation — and when he is walking in the powerful reality of all that salvation means for him — that person is noticeable!

The word "helmet" is taken from the Greek word *perikephalaia*. The word *peri* means *around*, and the word *kephalaia* is the Greek word for *the head*. When these two words are compounded together, the new word *perikephalaia* denotes *a piece of armor that fits very tightly around the head*.

Why did a Roman soldier need a helmet? Because his opponent carried a short-handled axe called a battleaxe — and when battleaxes were used, heads rolled! If the Roman soldier didn't have his helmet on when he went out to fight, he could be absolutely certain that he would lose his head. So the Roman helmet was not merely a beautiful piece of weaponry; it was something intended to save a man's head!

That's exactly what salvation will do for you when you wear it like a protective helmet on your head. On the other hand, if you *don't* walk in your salvation and all that your salvation entails, you may feel the brunt of the enemy's battleaxe coming to attack your mind and steal your victory.

If your salvation — like a helmet — is not worn tightly around your mind, the enemy will come to chop the multiple benefits and blessings of your salvation right out of your belief system. He will whack away at your spiritual foundation, trying to tell you that healing, deliverance, preservation of mind, and soundness are not really a part of Jesus' redemptive work on the Cross. By the time the enemy is finished with your mind, the only thing he will leave you with is Heaven!

By exposing your unprotected mind to the devil's lying insinuations, you are placing yourself in a position to be deceived. In fact, to face the adversary without your helmet of salvation is the equivalent of *spiritual suicide*!

> To face the adversary without your helmet of salvation is the equivalent of spiritual suicide!

Many believers try to do the work of God without making it a personal goal to walk in the full knowledge of their sal- vation — and as a result, they are spiritually slaughtered. A believer *must* have this helmet on if he is going to be useful to the Kingdom of God.

How is the enemy going to attack you? How is he going to try to wage warfare against you? How is he going to try to do you in? *The devil comes to attack the mind.*

Satan knows that your mind is the control center for your life. He knows that if he can seize control of your thought life, he can then begin to extend his influence to other areas. From this position of control, he will try to manipulate your emotions, send sickness and disease to attack your body, and so on.

To protect us from such attacks, God has given us a helmet of salvation. The fact that Paul likens salvation to a helmet means that we must learn about our salvation and find out all that it includes, inside and out.

- We must spend time studying what the Bible has to say about healing.

- We must spend time studying what the Bible has to say about our deliverance from evil powers.

- We must spend time studying our redemption and its beneficial consequences in our lives.

Our intellectual understanding and comprehension of salvation and all that it encompasses must be *ingrained* in our minds. When our minds are convinced of these realities — when our minds are trained and taught to think correctly in terms of our salvation — that knowledge becomes a protective helmet in our lives!

Once the knowledge of our salvation and all that it is becomes a part of us, it won't matter how hard the devil tries to hit and whack away at us. We will know — *beyond a shadow of a doubt* — what Jesus' death and resurrection purchased for us. At that point, the enemy will no longer be able to attack our minds as he did in the past, because he won't be able to get past our impenetrable helmet of salvation.

ARMED AND DANGEROUS

Remember, Paul's command is to "put on the whole armour of God, that ye may be able to stand against the wiles of the devil" (Ephesians 6:11).

When God sends you forth to reinforce the victory of Jesus Christ over Satan in various areas of your life, He doesn't send you out naked and defenseless. He gives you armor! Specifically, for our subject right now, He gives you the helmet of salvation. Without that helmet, you will be open for attack by the "wiles of the devil" (Ephesians 6:11).

Because it is so important to understand how the wiles of the devil work against us, we must quickly review the words "wiles," "devices," and "deception." (For more on this subject, *see* Chapter Eight.) These three words are foundational to our understanding of how the devil successfully defeats believers.

In review, the word "wiles" is taken from the word *methodos*. This word is a compound of the word *meta*, which means *with*, and the word *odos*, the word for *a road*. The word *odos* is where we get the word *odometer*, which is the instrument in your car that measures how many miles you have driven on the road. Taken as one word, *methodos* literally means *with a road*.

What is God's Word saying? It is saying that when the devil works against a believer, he does it *with a road*.

In other words, there is no creativity or variety with the devil. He uses only one road, one avenue, or one lane of attack into the life of a Christian. The enemy has only one way to work, and he always attacks believers in that same way.

However, we know that all roads go *somewhere*. So where do you suppose the devil's "road" goes?

Playing Mind Games With the Devil

This question leads us to the second word that has to do with how the devil works in the life and mind of a believer — the word "devices." Paul said, "...For we are not ignorant of his [Satan's] *devices*" (2 Corinthians 2:11).

What is a "device"? The word "device" comes from the Greek word *noemata*, which is from the root word *nous*, the word for *mind*. However, the form *noemata* could be translated as *a scheming of the mind*.

A modern-day translation of this verse could read: *"We are not ignorant of the mind games that the devil tries to pull on us."* Have you ever experienced one of the devil's mind games?

When we put these first two words together, we see that the devil works with a "wile," or he works *with a road*. Where is that road headed? *It is headed for your brain!* And if the devil can get a foothold *inside* your brain, he is going to pull a "device" on you and start messing around with your mind!

Now we come to the third word that has to do with the way the devil works in the life and the mind of a believer. It's the word "deception," which is taken from the word *dolios*. The word *dolios* doesn't mean to deceive accidentally or haphazardly; it means *to deceive with purpose*. This word can be found throughout the New Testament in verses that are connected with the devil's deceptive abilities.

In its most literal sense, the word *dolios* means *to bait someone*, as in setting bait in front of a fish. By putting these three words together, we see exactly how the devil works in a believer's life and mind. Again, the enemy comes with a "wile," which means *with a road*. That diabolical road is headed for the mind.

If the devil can beat down a believer's resistance, he can then begin to wage warfare in the person's mind with a "device" or a *mind game*.

Once the mind games are in full motion, Satan then *baits* the believer with lying accusations and slanderous allegations. If the believer perceives these lies to be true and bites the bait, the process of "deception" is then fully implemented in his or her life.

WHAT IS A STRONGHOLD?

It was for this cause that Paul said, "(For the weapons of our warfare are not carnal, but mighty through God to the pulling down of strong holds;) casting down imaginations, and every high thing that exalteth itself against the knowledge of God, and bringing into captivity every thought to the obedience of Christ" (2 Corinthians 10:4,5).

Especially notice that Paul says spiritual weapons are effective at pulling down "strongholds." There is a lot of talk today in the Body of Christ about strongholds. In light of this, we must ask, "What *is* a stronghold?"

The word "stronghold" comes from the Greek word *ochuroma*. It is one of the oldest words in the New Testament and was originally used to describe *a fortress*. By New Testament times, this same word depicted *a prison*.

A more accurate rendering of the word *ochuroma* would be *"...to the pulling down of fortresses."* Or you could even translate it *"...to the pulling down of prisons."* Both of these are correct and convey two powerful messages to us about strongholds.

In the first place, this tells us that a stronghold is like a *fortress*, which is *a fortified place* — such as a citadel, a fort, or a castle. Fortresses have exceptionally thick, impregnable walls to keep outsiders from breaking in. To ensure that outsiders didn't scale the walls and break in, people built the walls of their fortresses very high. Those high walls were designed for one primary purpose — to keep intruders *outside*.

The word "stronghold" was later translated as the word "prison." What does a prison do? It serves the opposite purpose of a fortress. Whereas a fortress keeps *outsiders* from *getting in*, a prison keeps *insiders* from *getting out*!

Prisons are places of detention or holding tanks — places such as dungeons or jails. Like fortresses, prisons also have fortified walls. Furthermore, prisons have bars of steel to keep prisoners in captivity.

The fact that the word "stronghold" can be translated as both the words "fortress" and "prison" tells us some important things about strongholds.

In the first place, this emphatically means that when a person has a mental or emotional "stronghold" in his life, he has walls around him that are so thick, others cannot seem to break through that barrier to help him. *Those invisible walls keep outsiders from getting in!*

Like impregnable, invisible walls, strongholds are rooted in people's minds and emotions to keep others from getting too close to them. This is a trick of the devil to keep people isolated and far removed from those who could help bring freedom to their lives and their minds.

> Like impregnable, invisible walls, strongholds are rooted in people's minds and emotions to keep others from getting too close to them.

Please understand that these strongholds do not suddenly pop up in a person's life overnight. You can be sure that when the adversary first begins to attack a believer's mind and to fill it with immobilizing fear, the Holy Spirit tries to warn that person about it.

But suppose that person allows those lies to go unresisted in his mind. Suppose he permits wrong thinking and wrong believing to go unchallenged hour after hour and day after day.

The devil will begin to use those lies, insinuations, and unrealistic fears to build thick, impregnable walls around that individual's life. Finally, the person will become besieged and taken captive mentally and emotionally by the lying allegations of the enemy.

How do these kinds of destructive strongholds affect your life?

- Unrealistic fears of rejection will keep you from developing healthy relationships in your life.

- Unrealistic fears about the future of your marriage will hinder you from functioning in the marital relationship as God intended.

- Unrealistic fears about potential failure will keep you from stepping out to obey God and do something worthwhile with your life.

In such cases, you must *command* the devil in the name of Jesus to release his claim on your mind and emotions. However, there is another step that you must take first. *The first step to eradicating strongholds in your life is to recognize YOUR responsibility in the matter.*

You permitted your mind and emotions to get into this mess! Therefore, repentance for allowing the mental and emotional strongholds to develop in your life is absolutely essential — *before all else*! Until you have taken this first step, no further progress will occur. But once you have repented, the power of God will cooperate with you as you seek to daily renew your mind to right thinking and right believing with the Word of God.

> Repentance for allowing the mental and emotional strongholds to develop in your life is absolutely essential — before all else!

A stronghold acts not only like a *fortress* but like a *prison*. In other words, those same walls that keep other people from *getting in* will also keep a person from *breaking out* and becoming all that God meant for him to be. Like the steel bars of a prison, those mental strongholds hold that person captive by making him believe the lie that he will fail, that no one wants him, that he isn't worth anything, and so on.

Individuals who have these kinds of strongholds in their lives are in bondage both *mentally* and *emotionally*. Sometime in the past, the enemy located an open door in their lives. Then after passing through that entrance into their minds, he began the process of taking their thoughts captive through his lies. The result is always the same: Strongholds are built that act as a prison, preventing these individuals from breaking free to fulfill their God-ordained purpose on this earth.

TWO KINDS OF STRONGHOLDS

There are two kinds of strongholds: *rational* and *irrational*. The rational strongholds are the hardest to deal with because they usually make sense!

Paul refers to these rational strongholds when he says, "Casting down *imaginations*...." The word "imaginations" is taken from the word *logismos*. It is where we get the word "logic," as in *logical thinking*.

Thank God for a good, sound mind — but even a good, sound mind must be submitted to the sanctifying work of the Holy Spirit. Otherwise, that mind will begin to dictate your life from a stronghold of natural reason.

I wonder how many people have been called by God to go into the ministry but then did *not* go because they rationalized away that divine call. I wonder how many have been bombarded with thoughts such as, *You can't go into the ministry! You have a wife, three children, and monthly house and car payments to make. You can't obey God!*

People who call themselves "thinkers" are prone to fall prey to such rational strongholds. Because they are rational thinkers anyway, they are naturally inclined to allow their minds to dominate them and to conquer their faith.

> The logical mind, although necessary and wonderful, will work against your spiritual life unless it is submitted to the control of the Holy Spirit.

The logical mind, although necessary and wonderful, will work against your spiritual life unless it is submitted to the control of the Holy Spirit. The unsubmitted rational mind will always try to talk you out of doing things God's way. That means if you don't take charge of your mind, it will begin to completely dominate and control your will to obey God!

In addition to rational strongholds, there are *irrational* strongholds. Everyone has fallen prey to these irrational strongholds from time to time.

Irrational strongholds primarily have to do with fears and worries that are completely unrealistic. These include such strongholds as a fear of disease, a fear of dying early in life, an abnormal fear of rejection, a fear of financial collapse, and so forth.

These irrational strongholds in the mind, emotions, and imagination will often play their course and eventually dissipate. After a time, it becomes apparent that such fears are ridiculous and unfounded, even to those who are dominated by them. Frequently these ridiculous yet captivating thoughts lose their power as soon as a person tells a friend or spouse what he or she has been thinking.

Irrational strongholds are so ridiculous that you finally wake up to the realization that this is a trick of the enemy to enslave you and keep you from functioning normally. But if these harassing thoughts persist in your mind and insist on controlling you mentally and emotionally, you must obey the Word of God and deal with them straightforwardly.

This is why Paul says, "...bringing into captivity every thought to the obedience of Christ" (2 Corinthians 10:5). Notice that Paul doesn't say one thing about the devil in this verse! Paul doesn't say, "and bringing *the devil* into captivity...." Rather, he says, "and bringing into captivity *every thought* to the obedience of Christ."

The truth is, if you don't take your thoughts captive, your thoughts will take *you* captive!

Let me draw your attention to the phrase "bringing into captivity" for a moment. This phrase is taken from the Greek word *aichmalotidzo*. It is a brutal word that means *to take one captive with a spear pointed into his back.*

By electing to use this word, Paul lets us know that our thoughts are not going to be taken captive easily. We must determine to take them captive regardless of the opposition we face. *We must be brutal with ourselves and forcibly seize control of our minds.* If our minds and our emotions try to get away from us, we must *grab hold* of them and *force* them into subjection!

And guess what! The word "thought" in this verse is taken from the word *noema*, which has the same meaning as the word "devices" (*noemata*) that we saw in Second Corinthians 2:11. Paul is talking about mind games again!

Paul continues to tell us that these mind games must be brought "to the *obedience* of Christ." The word "obedience" is from the word *hupakoe*, which is a compound of the words *hupo* and *akouo*.

The word *hupo* means *under*, and the word *akouo* means *I hear* or *I listen*. The word *akouo is* where we get the word *acoustics.* This is the picture of *forcing someone into a subordinate position and then making him listen to you.*

Remember, Paul is talking about mental strongholds and mind games that the devil uses to attempt to manipulate and control you. Rather than listen to these lying emotions and slanderous accusations, you must lay hold of your mind and tell it to submit and listen to what the Word of God has to say!

> You must lay hold of your mind and tell it to submit and listen to what the Word of God has to say!

When you choose to do this, this is the very moment that the renewing of the mind begins to work wonders in your life. This is when real *mental renovation* begins!

WHAT IS OPPRESSION?

On the other hand, if we choose to let our minds and our emotions continue to dominate and control us, we will inevitably become *oppressed*.

What is oppression? The word "oppression" is found in Acts 10:38. In Peter's sermon to the household of Cornelius, he says, "How God anointed Jesus of Nazareth with the Holy Ghost and with power: who went about doing good, and healing all that were oppressed of the devil; for God was with him."

This word "oppression" is taken from the Greek word *katadunasteuo*, which is a compound of the words *kata* and *dunamis. Kata* denotes *something that is dominating or manipulating. Dunamis* refers to *a power that is explosive.*

Oppression is therefore *a force that comes to powerfully dominate and manipulate*. It was technically used to portray a wicked tyrant or an evil king who forcibly imposed his will on his subjects. The tyrant told the people what they would eat, where they would live, and what kind of money they would make. He imposed his will on them against their wishes.

Therefore, when a person is oppressed, his mind and emotions are manipulated and dominated by an outside source. The devil, like a wicked tyrant, comes to oppress the person by telling him what his future will or will not hold, what his self-image is, and whether or not he has any hope of advancement in life.

> When a stronghold in the mind remains unchallenged, it will eventually turn into a serious case of oppression.

When a *stronghold* in the mind remains unchallenged, it will eventually turn into a serious case of *oppression*. And when oppression sets in, the end result is *hopelessness*.

SALVATION PROTECTS YOUR MIND

When the helmet of salvation is wrapped tightly around your mind, the devil's strategies to take you captive *cannot work*! That is why salvation is depicted in Ephesians 6 as a defensive weapon. It's a weapon that protects your mind from such hellish assaults.

When a strong knowledge of your salvation is wrapped around your mind, you will never again fall prey to the devil's deceptive tactics. With the helmet of salvation fitted tightly in place, your mind is in safekeeping. You are protected.

> When a strong knowledge of your salvation is wrapped around your mind, you will never again fall prey to the devil's deceptive tactics.

Remember, the devil knows that if he is going to attack you, he must begin his attack in your mind, since it's the strategic control center of your entire being. If the enemy can get a foothold in your mind, he can get a foothold in your body. But if he has no say-so in your mind, then he has no say-so in your body, in your family, or in your finances. *That mind of yours is extremely important!*

God gave you a brain, and He didn't give it to you so you could set it on the back burner. God wants you to *use* your mind. That's why First Peter 1:13 tells you to "gird up the loins of your mind." God is saying, "Gather up the loose ends of your mind, and get your mind into good shape!"

If the devil can wear you out in your mind, you will lose out in the long run. If he plants a seed of unbelief in your mind and you allow it to grow, you will end up in a dismal condition. That mind of yours is vitally important, and God did not leave it unprotected. He gave you a helmet, and He called that gorgeous, elaborate, ornate, intricate piece of defensive weaponry *salvation*.

Your helmet of salvation provides you with all kinds of God-given attributes and benefits. It gives you *deliverance from sin, salvation from hell, divine protection, preservation, healing, wholeness,* and *complete soundness of mind.* In other words, God has given you all that you need to withstand every assault of the great deceiver, Satan himself!

WHAT IS A SOUND MIND?

A primary emphasis of this chapter is to see what the helmet of salvation does for us. In Second Timothy 1:7, the Word of God says, "For God hath not given us the spirit of fear; but of power, and of love, and of a *sound mind.*"

What is a sound mind? One translation says, "sensible thinking." The word for "sound mind" or "sensible thinking" is taken from the Greek word *sophroneo.* It is a compound of the word *sodzo,* which means *saved or delivered,* and the word *phroneo,* which refers to *intelligent thinking.*

Put the two words together, and the new word means to have *a saved mind* or *a delivered mind.* In other words, this describes a mind that has been set free and is thinking correctly. You might say that this is a picture of *saved brains!*

When your mind is guarded and renewed by the Word of God, you will think saved thoughts. When you have a renewed mind, *it seems perfectly rational to walk by faith.* When you think with a renewed mind, *it sounds perfectly logical to obey God with your money.*

It is as though Paul is saying, "Timothy, why are you allowing fear to control your mind and emotions? God hasn't given you this spirit of fear, but of love and of power — and He has given you a mind that has been delivered!"

- When you are walking in the full knowledge of your salvation, *you think and talk like a saved man or woman.*

- When your mind is renewed with the Word of God concerning all the blessings contained in your salvation, *you think and talk like a saved man or woman.*

- When your mind is filled with the goodness of God because salvation is tightly wrapped around your mind, *you think and talk like a saved man or woman.*

Some people have been saved for years, but they do not think or talk like saved people. Some Christians have more unbelief about what they think God *can't* do than they have faith in what He *can* do. This is what happens when saved people don't walk in the knowledge of their salvation.

On the other hand, when a believer meditates on the Word of God and begins to comprehend the multitude of blessings contained in his salvation, all he can think or talk about is what God *can* do!

You think differently when you wear your helmet of salvation. Why is this important? Because when you begin to live a life of faith — when you reach out to do the impossible —

the enemy will try to assault you mentally and emotionally in an attempt to stop your progress.

The devil may speak to your mind and say, *"You can't do this! You can't do that! This doesn't make sense! Don't you know that you have a car payment to make? What will your family and friends think of this?"* He may try to pave a road into your mind so he can play mind games with your head and ultimately succeed in deceiving you.

That's why it is so important to make certain that you are growing in the knowledge of your salvation. Take care to guard your mind with the Word of God, and wear your helmet of salvation by filling your mind with the Word of God. When you "walk" in your helmet of salvation, you think like God thinks, you reason like God reasons, you believe like God believes, and you act like God acts!

> When you "walk" in your helmet of salvation, you think like God thinks, you reason like God reasons, you believe like God believes, and you act like God acts!

In Romans 8:6, Paul says, "For to be carnally minded is *death....*" In Titus 1:15, he restates this when he says, "...Unto them that are defiled and unbelieving is nothing pure; but even their mind and conscience *is defiled.*" Although these verses are about a lost man's mind, there are plenty of believers out there who still walk around with their natural, carnal minds controlling them.

It doesn't matter how many years you have been saved. If you take off your helmet and stop walking in the knowledge of your salvation, you will end up with a mind that is contaminated and defiled.

Do not underestimate the importance of filling your mind with the proper understanding and knowledge of your salvation. Salvation is a powerful piece of weaponry. If it is allowed to function correctly in your life, it will defend your mind from every mental attack the enemy might wage against you!

However, the moment you take off your helmet of salvation, the devil is going to start hitting your mind and emotions and toss you here and there. And if you don't put that helmet back on, you will eventually start habitually vacillating — believing God one moment and doubting Him the next!

In a very real sense, you will become spiritually deformed if you do not walk through life wearing your helmet of salvation. Do you want to live life spiritually deformed? If not, you'd better place your helmet of salvation tightly around your mind and make sure it *stays* there!

WHAT DOES THE WORD 'SALVATION' MEAN?

Now let's look at the word "salvation." This word literally means *saved* or *delivered*. In the broadest sense of the word, it means *to be brought into a safe place*. It is taken from the Greek word *soterios*, which means *to be saved, to be delivered from danger*, and *to be brought into a safe place*.

So we see that when a person is "saved," he is *delivered from danger* and *brought into a safe place*. He is *rescued from a place of danger*.

Being spiritually lost is a dangerous condition to be in, for a lost person is under the dominion of Satan. But when he is saved, he is brought *out of* that dangerous place and brought *into* a place of safety. And the knowledge of the Gospel message sets his mind free!

A TRANSFORMED MIND

It is very pertinent that Paul viewed your salvation as a helmet upon your mind. After all, when you were saved, God rescued you — not just spiritually, but *mentally*.

Prior to our salvation, we were members of Satan's slave market and our minds were accustomed to thinking just like the rest of the world. (For more on Satan's slave market, *see* Chapter Three.) "By nature," the Bible says, we were all "the children of wrath" (Ephesians 2:3). That word "wrath" means we were *bent out of proportion*. What a plight we were in!

What the devil had done to us was incredible. He left his marks and scars all over our minds and emotions during the time we were under his control. But now that God "...hath delivered us from the power of darkness, and hath translated us into the kingdom of his dear Son" (Colossians 1:13), we must allow His power to work in our minds and renew them to right thinking — to *saved* thinking.

God doesn't want even one area of your mind to think like the world — the way it used to think. God doesn't want one cell in your brain to have unbelief in it. That is not His will. Instead, God intends for every cell in your mind to be dominated by your new birth. He intends for your mind to think like a mind that is controlled by the Holy Spirit!

> God intends for every cell in your mind to be dominated by your new birth.

You may ask, "How do I get my mind into that kind of condition?"

First, get in touch with the power of God. That's the prerequisite to walking in spiritual armor. Ephesians 6:10 says, "Be strong in the Lord." When that strength comes to you, it will clothe you with spiritual armor.

But there is a second thing you have to do. In Ephesians 6:17, Paul says, "And *take* the helmet of salvation...." The word "take" is translated as the word "receive" 40 times in the New Testament. Thus, the verse would be better translated, "And *receive* the helmet of salvation."

God is not going to force a renewed mind on you; you have to *receive* this helmet of salvation. That means *you* have a part to play in the saving of your mind.

How do you do that? You *put on* salvation. You put the helmet of salvation on your head by studying what the Bible has to say about salvation. Know what the Bible teaches about Jesus' redemptive work to deliver, heal, preserve, and give a sound mind to you. Never stop meditating on those truths, even *after* you know all that your salvation includes, inside and out!

Wrap that knowledge of salvation around your brain, and let it protect your mind. As you do, you will begin to be transformed.

- You will no longer think and talk like an individual who is constantly sick.

- You will no longer think and talk like an individual who is poor.

- You will no longer walk through life like an individual who is continually defeated.

What will make the difference? Your mind will be filled with the knowledge of salvation, and *that new knowledge will begin to change not only the way you think and talk, but also the way you experience life!*

The devil wants to rob you of every blessing that God has prepared for you. Satan wants to take every good thing from you that he can. So it's up to you to fill your mind with all that God has done for you. Let that knowledge of salvation and all of its benefits become like a helmet of bronze on your head to protect your mind from the "battleaxe" of the enemy.

As you faithfully meditate on the Word of God and allow it to work in your thought life, your mind *will* be renewed. Salvation will become so *real* to you — you will become so convinced of your salvation and of all its benefits — that your mind will be able to rest securely in God, no longer capable of being penetrated by doubt and unbelief.

Those questionable areas in your mind that the enemy used to attack regularly will no longer be attackable! With the helmet of salvation firmly in place, you will be completely surrounded — both *mentally* and *emotionally* — by the unassailable truth of all that is yours in Jesus Christ.

QUESTIONS FOR PERSONAL GROWTH OR GROUP DISCUSSION

1. How does a solid knowledge of all that your salvation provides for you act as a protective helmet around your mind? What does that helmet protect you from, and how does it affect the way you think?

2. How does an area of deception become a stronghold in your mind? How can you prevent that process from ever reoccurring in your life ?

3. In what way does a mental stronghold act as both a fortress and a prison in your life?

4. Have you ever been held in bondage by an irrational stronghold, such as the fear of flying or the fear of failure? If so, how did that irrational stronghold affect your walk of faith and your fellowship with God?

5. What is the first step to breaking out of the prison created by a stronghold? What must you do after taking that first step?

NOTES:

_____

_____

_____

_____

_____

_____

_____

_____

_____

_____

_____

_____

_____

_____

_____

_____

_____

_____

_____

_____

_____

_____

CHAPTER FIFTEEN

THE SWORD OF THE SPIRIT

*S*piritual battles are just like natural battles. Nations don't constantly engage in warfare; they fight when a problem comes along. Afterward, their soldiers return home, experience a time of peace and refreshing, and don't fight again until there is a reason to fight.

The same is true with biblical spiritual warfare. Battles *will* come, but they won't come every day. God has given us spiritual weaponry so that when battles do come, we will be prepared to maintain our victorious position over Satan.

This book was written with this principle in mind. The teaching contained within these pages is not designed to make you run around looking for the devil behind every door. Rather, it is designed to help equip you so that when battles do come, you will be prepared to stand against them.

> God has given us spiritual weaponry so that when battles do come, we will be prepared to maintain our victorious position over Satan.

In this chapter, we are going to look at one of the most aggressive, offensive weapons that God has given to the Body of Christ — the "sword of the Spirit." Our text is Ephesians 6:17, which says, "And take the helmet of salvation, and the sword of the Spirit, which is the word of God."

THE SWORDS OF THE ROMAN SOLDIER

Of the five different kinds of swords that Roman soldiers used in their confrontations with enemy forces, the Holy Spirit carefully selected one of them to illustrate our "sword of the Spirit." Let's look at each of these swords individually.

The *first sword* of the Roman soldier was called the *gladius* sword. It was an extremely heavy, broad-shouldered sword with a very long blade. Of all the swords used by the Romans, the *gladius* was the most aesthetically beautiful. However, because of its weight, it was also the most cumbersome and awkward to use.

This massive sword was referred to as a *two-handed sword*. In other words, it was so heavy that the soldier had to use both hands and swing it with all his might in order to wield it against the enemy.

Furthermore, this first sword was sharpened only on one side. The other side of the sword was blunt and dull. After suffering a terrible defeat at the hands of the Carthaginians, the Romans abandoned these large swords, adopting another version similar to the ones the Carthaginians had used to defeat them.

The *second sword* was shorter and narrower. It was approximately 17 inches long and about two and one half inches in width; hence, it was lighter than the swords Roman soldiers had previously used. This newer version rapidly grew in popularity throughout the empire because it was so much easier to carry and swing.

The *third sword* used by the Roman army was even shorter than the second sword. In fact, it was so short that it looked more like a dagger than a sword. This dagger-like sword was carried in a small, hidden scabbard beneath the soldier's outer coat and was used to inflict a mortal wound into the heart of an enemy or an aggressor.

The *fourth sword* Roman soldiers used was a long and very slender sword. This sword was primarily used by the cavalry, as opposed to the more durable swords carried by the infantry. In addition, this long, slender sword was used in a sport that was similar to modern-day fencing. No soldier would have wanted to enter into combat with this sword, for it wasn't an effective sword to use in battle.

The *fifth sword* was the type of sword that Paul had in mind when he wrote about this piece of spiritual armor in Ephesians 6:17, saying, "...and the sword of the Spirit, which is the word of God."

The word for "sword," as used in this text, is taken from the Greek word *machaira*. This brutal weapon of murder was approximately 19 inches long. Both sides of its blade were razor sharp, making this sword much more dangerous than the other four. In addition, the tip of the sword turned upward, causing the point of the blade to be extremely sharp and deadly.

This two-edged blade inflicted a wound far worse than the other swords. Before a Roman soldier withdrew this particular sword from the gut of his enemy, he would hold his sword very tightly with both hands and give it a wrenching twist inside his enemy's stomach. This would cause the opponent's entrails to spill out as the soldier pulled the sword from his enemy's body.

Of all the swords available, this *machaira* sword was the most dangerous of all. Although the other swords were deadly, *this one was a terror to the imagination!* This sword was not only intended to kill, but to completely rip an enemy's insides to shreds. It was *a weapon of murder!*

WHAT IS A *RHEMA*?

Because Paul uses the word *machaira* in Ephesians 6:17 to describe our "sword of the Spirit," he declares that God has given the Church a weapon that is just that brutal against *our* enemy! This weapon, called the "sword of the Spirit," has the potential to rip our foe to shreds!

Paul goes on to give us more information about this sword. He says, "...the sword of the Spirit, *which is the word of God.*" The term "word" is taken from the Greek word *rhema*, which is one of the most familiar Greek words used in the New Testament. It describes something that is *spoken clearly; spoken vividly*; *spoken in undeniable language*; or *spoken in unmistakable, unquestionable, certain, and definite terms.*

In the New Testament, the word *rhema* carries the idea of *a quickened word*, such as a word of Scripture or a "word from the Lord" that the Holy Spirit supernaturally drops into a believer's mind, thus causing it to supernaturally come alive and impart special power or direction to that believer.

These *rhema* words are *powerful*. When the Holy Spirit supernaturally quickens such a word or Bible verse to a believer's heart and mind, that believer *knows that he knows* he has heard from the Lord! There is no doubt about it!

Jesus referred to this quickening work of the Holy Spirit in John 14:26 when He said, "But the Comforter, which is the Holy Ghost, whom the Father will send in my name, he shall teach you all things, and *bring all things to your remembrance, whatsoever I have said unto you.*"

The Holy Spirit might drop a *rhema* word into our hearts, supernaturally remind us of a scripture, or put us in remembrance of a Bible promise. When this happens, that word, scripture, or promise floods our entire being with faith because *the Holy Spirit has spoken to us in a way that is clearly spoken, unmistakable, undeniable, unquestionable, certain, and definite.*

Thus, a *rhema* is a specific word or message that the Holy Spirit quickens in our hearts and minds at a specific time and for a special purpose. So when Paul says, "...the sword of the Spirit, *which is the word of God,*" he is referring to the Holy Spirit's

> A *rhema* is a specific word or message that the Holy Spirit quickens in our hearts and minds at a specific time and for a special purpose.

ability to make such a divine "word" vividly come alive in our hearts and minds at a moment of need.

One expositor translated this scripture, *"...the sword that the Spirit wields as He draws forth a special word from God."* This kind of word from the Lord gives you *"sword power"* in the spirit realm.

THE SWORD AND THE LOINBELT

Like the other pieces of armor that God has given us, *the sword and the loinbelt are inseparable.*

Just as the shield rested on a clip on the right side of the loinbelt, the sword hung from a clip on the *left* side of the loinbelt. The loinbelt thus served as both a support for the shield and a resting place for the soldier's sword.

As we have seen before, the loinbelt is representative of the written Word of God, the Bible. This written Word of God is the primary source for a *rhema* from God.

A genuine *rhema* — a word or verse that the Holy Spirit quickens in your heart at a specific time and for a specific purpose in your life — is so strong and powerful that it is as if God has put a supernatural sword in your hand. With that sword in hand, you have a powerful weapon with which to repel Satan's attacks against you. These *rhema* words are both given and supernaturally empowered by the Holy Spirit to enable you to withstand the adversary's spiritual, mental, emotional, and physical attacks. They are the Holy Spirit's powerful rebuff to the devil's attempt to penetrate your mind with slanderous lies and accusations!

> Rhema words are both given and supernaturally empowered by the Holy Spirit to enable you to withstand the adversary's spiritual, mental, emotional, and physical attacks.

Have you ever experienced the "sword of the Spirit" before?

When you faced a precarious situation, has the Holy Spirit ever reached into that reservoir of scriptures you have stored up in your heart through study, prayer, and meditation and quickened a verse to your mind that helped you in your time of need?

Have you ever been empowered by a verse from the Bible that seemed to drop from out of nowhere into your mind at just the right moment? Naturally speaking, you weren't even thinking of that verse, yet it seemed to suddenly pop into your mind. And the moment that verse was quickened to you, you just *knew* on the inside that everything was going to be all right.

A verse that leaps off the pages of the Bible and into your heart carries a special measure of power in your life. It is as though God is speaking *only to you* through those life-transforming words.

You might say the written Word, the Bible, is like the *gladius* sword of a Roman soldier — a broad-shouldered and extremely heavy blade. This huge blade is capable of making a sweeping blow against the enemy. On occasion, however, we need a specific *rhema* word — a smaller, two-edged sword — to deal the enemy a fatal blow!

You need to stab the enemy! This will require a *rhema*, or a "specifically quickened word" from the scriptures that the Holy Spirit has placed into your heart. With a *rhema* from God like this placed into your heart and hand, you will have deadly *sword power* to wield against the devil when he attacks!

Vegetius, the famous fourth-century Roman historian, said, "...A stroke with the edges, though, made with ever so much force, seldom kills, as the vital parts of the body are defended by both the bones and armor. *On the contrary, a stab, though it penetrates but two inches, is generally fatal.*"[1] (For more of Vegetius' historical description of Roman soldiers, *see* Chapter Six of *Living in the Combat Zone*.)

It is not the sweeping action of a sword that kills. On the contrary, it is the stabbing action of a sword that mortally wounds a foe. Vegetius tells us a stab that penetrates two inches is all that is required to kill an adversary.

Many people mistakenly think they must memorize the entire Bible before God can use them or speak to them. Certainly the memorization of the Bible is good, and believers

[1] Flavius Vegetius Renatus, *The Military Institutions of the Romans*, trans. by Lt. John Clarke. (Text written in 390 A.D. British translation published in 1767. Copyright expired.) E-text version by Mads Brevik, 2001: http://www.pvv.ntnu.no/~madsb/home/war/vegetius/dere03.php#10.

should commit as many scriptures to memory as possible. However, it is *not* necessary for a person to know the entire Bible in order to have the "sword of the Spirit" at his disposal.

Please understand this point: It is not necessary to receive a ten-page prophecy in order to have the "sword of the Spirit" in your hand! I have received numerous so-called "words from the Lord" from people over the years. I will never forget one man who wrote and asked me to verify that his "word from the Lord" for his personal life was accurate.

> It is not necessary for a person to know the entire Bible in order to have the "sword of the Spirit" at his disposal.

As I looked at this "word," I saw that it was nearly 20 pages long! It was so outrageous that I wondered how anyone could have led himself to believe it was actually a valid word from the Spirit of God!

A specific *rhema* word from the Lord does *not* have to be long and complicated in order to be valid. I meet many people who have pages and pages of prophecies and "words from the Lord" concerning their ministries, their businesses, or their families. Most of these lengthy prophecies are so complex and difficult to follow that these individuals wouldn't be able to obey them if they tried. Most of the time, they can't even figure out what their "words" mean!

It is true that the Spirit of God can speak a lengthy personal word to our hearts about our lives. However, this is the *exception* and not the *rule*. On the contrary, when you study history, it becomes clear that most great men and women of God who have earned a place in the pages of history have done so by obeying *a single, simple word from God.*

Consider these examples from the Bible:

Noah received a very relatively short word from God that saved him and his family from destruction (Genesis 6:13-7:4).

> Most great men and women of God who have earned a place in the pages of history have done so by obeying a single, simple word from God.

Considering the ramifications of the flood and the history-making consequences of Noah's obedience, the Lord's word to him was quite brief and simple. This history-making and life-saving word from the Lord probably lasted no more than ten minutes!

Likewise, when God called Abraham to leave Mesopotamia and to start his walk of faith, his word of instruction from the Lord was a whole three verses long and a mere 75 words (Genesis 12:1-3)! This extremely brief word from God led to the establishment of the Jewish people and, ultimately, to the walk of faith we all now enjoy.

Joseph received a word from God about his personal life through two short dreams. Through these dreams, the Holy Spirit vividly spoke to Joseph and revealed his future to him (Genesis 37:6-9). These two encounters with God eventually put Joseph in a position to care for his family and the entire nation of Israel.

While Moses was tending sheep on Mount Horeb, the angel of the Lord appeared to him in a burning bush, unmistakably revealing that Moses had been chosen by God to lead Israel out of Egyptian captivity (*see* Exodus chapters 3 and 4). By obeying this relatively short word from the Lord, Israel's captivity was reversed and Moses became one of the greatest prophets of all time.

Mary, the mother of Jesus, received a word from God that is still working wonders in the world today. The angel Gabriel delivered a very brief, yet life-changing word to Mary. *That supremely important word from the Lord was only eight verses long* (Luke 1:28,30-33,35-37)! Because Mary's heart was receptive to this word from God, she was chosen to give birth to the Son of God.

The ministry of the apostle Paul was constantly influenced by supernatural words from the Lord.

- A word from God was spoken to Paul at the time of his conversion (Acts 9:4-6).

- A special word from God was given to Ananias concerning Paul's salvation (Acts 9:10-16).

- Another word was spoken to Paul by the Holy Spirit at the time of his "sending forth" into public ministry (Acts 13:2).

- A word from the Lord was given to Paul to prepare him for a period of persecution that he would experience in Jerusalem (Acts 21:11).

- Likewise, Paul received a word from the Holy Spirit concerning his ministry in the city of Rome (Acts 23:11).

If I tried to name the modern-day men and women whose obedience to a simple, succinct word from the Holy Spirit affected multitudes for the Kingdom of God, the list would be too long to cover in this book. Suffice it to say that, by obeying these simple words from the Lord, these men and women of God altered history. Indeed, the reason we enjoy many of our spiritual blessings today is that godly men and women obeyed the simple, specially spoken *rhema* words they received from the Lord.

Without exception, these historical figures received words from the Lord that were simple to understand and right to the point. These *specially spoken, vividly given, unmistakable, undeniable* words from God changed the history of mankind!

> The reason we enjoy many of our spiritual blessings today is that godly men and women obeyed the simple, specially spoken *rhema* words they received from the Lord.

You might say these men and women lethally stabbed the domain of darkness by responding to a *rhema* word they had heard from God concerning the purpose of their lives. Although these words from the Lord were brief and straight to the point, they did great damage to Satan's dark kingdom, mortally wounding the enemy's strategy to keep these individuals from fulfilling their God-ordained destiny in life.

Remember, a two-inch penetration by a sword is all that is required to fatally wound an enemy. When the Holy Spirit puts a sword — a *rhema* — in our hands, it will probably be short, concise, and succinct. The Lord knows that a long word would be confusing to the majority of us. Therefore, He speaks clear, vivid, unmistakable, undeniable, certain, definite, and easy-to-understand words to us.

In the majority of cases, the *rhema* you desperately need will come right out of the Bible as the Holy Spirit supernaturally makes a verse leap right off the pages of the written Word and into your heart. As you respond in faith to that freshly given, freshly spoken *rhema* word from the Holy Spirit, it will act like a mighty blade in your hand, releasing a mighty force of divine power that is capable of destroying the work of the devil in your life.

WHAT IS A TWO-EDGED SWORD?

Two-edged swords, such as the sword Paul refers to when he writes about the "sword of the Spirit" in Ephesians 6:17, are mentioned throughout the New Testament. For instance, when the apostle John received his vision of Jesus on the isle of Patmos, he said, "And he had in his right hand seven stars: *and out of his mouth went a sharp two-edged sword...*" (Revelation 1:16).

A "two-edged sword" came out of Jesus' mouth!

The phrase "two-edged" is taken from the Greek word *distomos*, and it is unquestionably one of the oddest words in the entire New Testament.

Why is the phrase "two-edged" so odd? Because it is a compound of the word *di*, meaning *two*, and the word *stomos*, which is the Greek word for one's *mouth*. Thus, when these two words are compounded into the word *distomos*, the new word describes something that is *two-mouthed*.

John is telling us that this was a sword that had *"two mouths"*! Therefore, you could accurately translate Revelation 1:16 to read, *"...and out of his mouth went a sharp two-mouthed sword...."*

A similar statement is found in Revelation 2:12, which says, "And to the angel of the church in Pergamos write; These things saith he which hath the sharp sword with two edges."

The phrase "two edges" is once again taken from the Greek word *distomos*. As before, the word *distomos* would be better translated as "two mouths." Thus, Revelation 2:12 could be translated, *"...a sharp sword with two mouths."*

The identical phrase is also found in Hebrews 4:12, a verse that is very crucial to this chapter on the "sword of the Spirit." The writer of Hebrews said, "For the word of God is quick, and powerful, and sharper than any twoedged [*distomos*] sword [*machaira*, the same word Paul uses in Ephesians 6:17 to describe the "sword of the Spirit"]...."

Why is the Word of God repeatedly referred to as a "two-edged sword"? Or even more correctly, why does the original

Greek text actually say that the Word of God is a "two-mouthed sword"?

Keep in mind that the Romans had previously used a very large sword that was sharpened only on one side. The other side of the blade was dull and blunt. To use this *gladius* sword effectively, a soldier had to swing it perfectly, making certain that he was swinging with the correct side of the blade exposed toward his foe. If the soldier hit his foe with the blunt side of that blade, the blow would certainly lay a bruise on his opponent, but it would not kill him. Thus, this kind of sword was not entirely effective in battle.

The *machaira* sword, however, was sharp on both sides of its murderous blade. And because the blade of this special sword was sharpened on both sides, it made deeper gashes and wounds than the *gladius* sword. It was also terribly sharp and pointed at the tip. Hence, if the soldier wrenched the blade just right inside his opponent's stomach, it would pull the man's entrails out of his body when the sword was withdrawn.

When a soldier used this deadly, two-edged sword correctly, it always left the enemy lying on the ground in a puddle of his own blood — a position that guaranteed he would never bother the soldier again! Now the Holy Spirit tells us that the Word of God is just like that! It is like a sword that has two edges, cutting both ways and doing terrible damage to an aggressor.

One sharpened edge of this sword came into being when the Word of God initially proceeded from the mouth of *God*. The second edge of this sword is added when the Word of God proceeds out of *your* mouth! This is the reason the original text calls the Word of God a *"two-mouthed sword."*

When God first spoke His Word and inspired biblical writers to record it, it was a *one-mouthed* sword. In other words, it had only come out of one mouth at that time. Yes, it was the Word of God, and, yes, it was a mighty sword. However, since it had only come out of God's mouth at that time, it was only a *one-mouthed sword*.

You might say that the written Word of God is like a *gladius* sword — sharp on one side but dull on the other. However, when you willfully plant that Word into your spirit, meditating on it and giving it a place of top priority in your life, you take the first necessary step toward giving the Word of God a second edge in your life.

That step gets you ready for the next time you are confronted by a challenge from the demonic realm. The Holy Spirit will be able to reach down into that reservoir of God's Word you have stored up on the inside of you and pull one of those scriptures up out of your inner man. Then as that verse or divine promise begins to fill your mind and come out of your mouth, it becomes *a two-mouthed sword*!

First, that powerful Word passed through the mouth of God, thus giving it one sharp edge. Second, that same power-packed Word rose up from your spirit, invaded your understanding, and then proceeded out of your mouth. When that *rhema* Word came out of your mouth, a second edge was added to that "sword," making it a lethal weapon to wield against the enemy!

MEDITATION AND CONFESSION

I hope you can now see why it is so important to meditate on the Word of God and why it is vital for you to confess the Word with your mouth!

By meditating on God's Word, you allow the Word to do its marvelous work in you. Hebrews 4:12 goes on to say, "For the word of God is quick, and powerful, and sharper than any twoedged sword, piercing even to the dividing asunder of soul and spirit, and of the joints and marrow, and is a discerner of the thoughts and intents of the heart."

When God's Word begins to work inside of you, it cuts through the muck and mire of your mind and emotions and goes straight to the heart of the matter. In other words, it divides between soul and spirit to discern your innermost thoughts, attitudes, desires, and motives.

You could figuratively say that *the Word of God has eyes*! It sees what the human eye cannot see; it knows what no human knows. And once received into the heart, the Word immediately begins working to renovate those areas of your mind, will, and emotions that are off base and wrong.

> Once received into the heart, the Word immediately begins working to renovate those areas of your mind, will, and emotions that are off base and wrong.

This is precisely the reason the writer of Hebrews continues to say, "Neither is there any creature that is not manifest in his sight:

but all things are naked and opened unto the eyes of him with whom we have to do" (Hebrews 4:13).

Ignoring the Word of God will allow old patterns of wrong thinking and bondages from our past to continue exerting authority over us. On the other hand, meditating on the Word of God releases its dividing and discerning work inside us.

When we willfully take the Word of God into our lives and allow it to do its supernatural work in us, *that Word acts like a divine blade, slicing right to the heart of the matter.* It does what no spouse, friend, pastor, teacher, psychologist, or psychiatrist could ever do — dividing asunder the soul and the spirit and correctly discerning the thoughts and intents of the heart.

When the Word has done this extraordinary work in us, *we are inwardly changed.* Furthermore, we become *filled with faith* when we allow the Word of God to work in our lives. Why? Because "faith cometh by hearing, and hearing by the word of God" (Romans 10:17).

Once that Word has taken root in your heart, and once your mind and emotions have been changed by its power, you are then in a position to speak the Word of God from deep down inside of your being. Finally, your renewed mind will cooperate with your faith, and you'll be able to speak the Word of God boldly with no doubt whatsoever!

One reason people don't experience results when they confess God's Word is that they speak before the Word has personally done its life-transforming work inside of *them.* They hastily begin to mimic what someone else confessed or what someone else did before the Word has had time to take root in their hearts and to renew their minds. But because the Word of God hasn't yet become personal revelation to *them*, it produces no lasting results.

Do not underestimate the importance of studying, meditating, and praying over the Word of God. The vital work of studying, meditating, and praying releases the Word to become a part of your own inner being. When the truth of God's Word takes root in your heart like this and begins to release its transforming power in your mind, you are then in position to confess the Word of God in a manner that will release tremendous amounts of spiritual power. This kind of confession is truly the equivalent of stabbing a two-edged sword into the heart of your adversary!

> The vital work of studying, meditating, and praying releases the Word to become a part of your own inner being.

When the Holy Spirit reaches into that reservoir of Scripture inside of you and quickens one of those verses to your memory — you are ready to wield that verse like a mighty sword as it rises up from your inner man to your mind and then is spoken forth through your mouth! *As it proceeds from your mouth, a second deadly edge is miraculously added to it!* At that very moment, that Word becomes a "two-edged" or a *"two-mouthed"* sword!

Some have said, "I have the Word down in my spirit. There's no need for me to confess the Word of God with my mouth. I'll just keep the Word to myself."

But stopping short of confession will keep you from the victory you desire.

It's good to meditate on the Word — that's how your mind is renewed. You *should* meditate on God's Word as much as you possibly can, for the Word will make you inwardly rich! However, if this is all you do, you have only a *single-edged*, not a *two-edged* sword. Because the Word has only passed from the mouth of God into your heart and has not yet come out of *your* mouth, it will be like a blade with only one sharpened edge.

> Stopping short of confession will keep you from the victory you desire.

To be sure, that Word will work in you *personally*. However, it will never release its full power until it comes out of your mouth (the second mouth), thus adding *a second fatal edge to that sword*.

It is interesting to note that the Bible describes Jesus, who *is* the Word of God, as having a two-edged sword coming out of His mouth. Notice that the sword is not in His hand but *in His mouth*!

Likewise, when the Word that God has quickened in your spirit rises up to your mind and you speak it out, you are wielding a powerful sword with two edges on it. That sword has already had the opportunity to produce faith in you. Hence, when you speak forth that special word from the Lord, it comes out of your mouth with *force*!

HOW TO HEAR FROM GOD

The sword of the Roman soldier hung down from the loinbelt in a beautiful scabbard that was made of either leather or specially tooled metal. The sword hinged entirely on the soldier's loinbelt.

Likewise, your *rhema* — that word you need from God today — hinges entirely on the presence or absence of the written Word of God in your life. In other words, you will receive the *rhema* you need from God because you have the written Word at your disposal.

> Your *rhema* — that word you need from God today — hinges entirely on the presence or absence of the written Word of God in your life.

Some people go out and sit on a rock, waiting for God to speak to them. Some have been sitting on that rock for years and years, wondering why they have never heard from God!

But God speaks through His Word! The sword of the Spirit hangs from the loinbelt! So if you want a sword of the Spirit, *get in God's Word.* Until you have planted the Word in your heart and mind, there will be no sword of the Spirit available to you. Let me repeat it again for the sake of emphasis: *The sword and the loinbelt are inseparable.*

If you are in the Word — if you are walking with the loinbelt of truth firmly affixed to your life — you are in position to hear from God. It doesn't matter what problem you are facing, the

Spirit of God will provide you with the exact word you need at the exact time you need it!

That *rhema* is going to come directly up out of the Word you have been studying, meditating on, and praying over. After you have meditated on a portion of the Word and permitted it to become a part of you, the Holy Spirit will exercise His option to use those scriptures as a mighty sword against the enemy. But you will *not* be given a sharp, two-edged sword that puts the devil on the run simply by sitting on a rock somewhere, waiting for God to mysteriously speak to you!

Psalm 119:130 says, "The entrance of thy words *giveth light....*" Isaiah 8:20 has more to say along this line: "...If they speak not according to this word, *it is because there is no light in them.*" These two verses explicitly teach that when people do not have the Word of God, they have no light and sit in darkness. Why? Because it is *the entrance of God's Word* that gives light.

When the Word of God gets in your heart and mind, that Word begins to impart light and direction to you. It will rise up from within as a sword — a specific word of divine guidance. It doesn't matter how dark the situation is that you're facing, *when this sword of the Spirit comes up from YOUR spirit, it will show you the way to go.*

The devil may try to use all kinds of lies, accusations, and allegations against you. But when the divine light of the Word is working in your spirit and mind, that light will come forth like a mighty blade out of your mouth, giving you the very words and direction you need to overcome the devil's attacks at that precise moment.

A believer's ability to walk in this kind of supernatural direction and revelation is completely determined by *how much Word* he has inside of him. People who receive frequent *rhema* words from the Lord are people who have made the *logos*, the written Word, a central part of their lives.

WHEN JESUS NEEDED A SWORD

In Matthew 4, we find the story of Jesus' temptation in the wilderness. For 40 days and 40 nights, Jesus was inordinately and intensely tested by Satan. Because this testing of the devil was so extreme and intense, the Lord Jesus Christ needed a *rhema*, a "sword of the Spirit," to withstand these attacks from the evil one.

> People who receive frequent *rhema* words from the Lord are people who have made the *logos*, the written Word, a central part of their lives.

> **Then was Jesus led up of the Spirit into the wilderness to be tempted of the devil. And when he had fasted forty days and forty nights, he was afterward an hungred. And when the tempter came to him, he said, If thou be the Son of God, command that these stones be made bread.**
>
> Matthew 4:1-3

Jesus faced the enemy in the same way *we* face the enemy in life. In this portion of Scripture, the devil was saying to Jesus, *"If You are who You say You are, show me!"*

How did Jesus answer Satan? Verse 4 says, "But he answered and said, *IT IS WRITTEN*...." The Holy Spirit, in all of His power and might, provided a verse in due season! He drew a scripture right up out of Jesus' spirit, who then spoke it forth with great power and authority. Jesus wielded that *rhema* word like a mighty blade — and the enemy could not stand against it!

Why was the Holy Spirit able to pull a sword up and out of Jesus' inner man? Because the Lord Jesus Christ had spent time studying, meditating, and praying over the Word of God! As a Child, He had been reared in the synagogue and had heard the Word of God week after week. Over a period of time, Jesus, in His humanity, had taken the Word deep into His soul.

Thus, when Jesus needed a "sword of the Spirit," the Holy Spirit reached directly into that reservoir of Scripture stored up inside of Jesus and quickened one of those verses to His mind. When that Word passed through Jesus' memory and out of His mouth, it became a *two-edged, two-mouthed* sword that the enemy could not withstand, no matter how hard he tried!

Notice that Jesus said, *"...It is written...."* What scripture was Jesus quoting? He was quoting from Deuteronomy 8:3 — *a verse He had obviously committed to memory at some earlier point in His life*! Because this scripture was already a part of Jesus, the Spirit of God could simply bring that Word to the forefront of His mind when He needed that particular two-edged sword to repel the adversary's attack.

Notice what happened next in verse 6. The devil attempted to pull a mind game on Jesus, just as the enemy tries to pull mind games on you! The devil said, "...*If* thou be the Son of God, cast thyself down: for it is written...."

Keep in mind that Jesus had just stabbed the enemy with the Word of God! Jesus had just said, "*It is written....*" How did the devil react to the stabbing action of that sword of the Spirit? He threw the Word of God right back into Jesus' face, saying, "*It is written....*"

Talk about a mind game! The devil started quoting Scripture! He said, "...For it is written, He shall give his angels charge concerning thee: and in their hands they shall bear thee up, lest at any time thou dash thy foot against a stone" (v. 6).

But Jesus knew exactly what to do with the devil's mind game. Verse 7 says, "Jesus said unto him, *It is written AGAIN....*"

Jesus had to know the Word of God; otherwise, He would have been deceived by this deceptive ploy. After all, the devil can quote the Bible better than any believer on the face of the earth! But Jesus *knew* the written Word, and its discerning power was continually at work in Him. This is the key that kept Him on course when dealing with the devil's temptations.

In the same way, the Word of God had better be in you — *living, active, and powerful*! Moreover, it had better be more than mere head knowledge. If all you have is head knowledge of God's Word, the devil will be able to confuse you and ultimately pull you down into defeat.

Satan knows how to use the Bible! He is a very cunning Bible teacher. He knows how to teach you the Bible the way *he* wants you to know it, filled with error and misunderstanding that will rob you of the blessings of God. The devil will tell you everything that is *not* in the Bible; then he will send someone along to supposedly "scripturally prove" every one of his lies!

Don't be deceived! The devil is well able to declare, *"It is written...."* That is why you must allow the Word of God to get deep down inside of you. Plant the Word deep in your heart, and renew your mind with that Word. Then you will be able to discern the lies and mind games that the devil will try to use against you — because *the Word of God is a discerner of the thoughts and intents of the heart*!

The devil tried to pull a mind game on Jesus by incorrectly quoting the Bible to Him. But Jesus knew that these scriptures had been misquoted, and He said, *"...IT IS WRITTEN AGAIN...."* It was as if Jesus said, "Now *you* listen to what the Word of God *really says*, Satan!"

Jesus told the devil, "...It is written again, Thou shalt not tempt the Lord thy God" (Matthew 4:7). How did Jesus know to quote that scripture from Deuteronomy 6:16? This was clearly another verse that He had committed to memory at some earlier point in His life. Because Deuteronomy 6:16 was already stored up inside of Jesus, the Spirit of God could draw it out of Him like a deadly blade!

The story continues: "Again, the devil taketh him up into an exceeding high mountain, and sheweth him all the kingdoms of the world, and the glory of them" (v. 8).

The Gospel of Luke records this same scenario, giving us more details regarding what the devil said to Jesus: "...All this power will I give thee, and the glory of them: for that is delivered unto me; and to whomsoever I will I give it" (Luke 4:6).

Talk about an invitation! The devil gave Jesus the most inviting invitation anyone has ever been offered! Satan offered Jesus the glory and authority of the earth — all that had been handed over to him by Adam!

That's why the devil said all of this has been "delivered" to him. The word "delivered" is taken from the word *paradidomi*. It describes *the act of handing something over to someone else*. By disobeying God, Adam transferred to Satan the authority of this earth that God had earlier delegated to Adam.

Now Jesus had come to seize the control of the earth and of mankind from Satan's hands. The apostle John refers to this in First John 3:8: "...For this purpose the Son of God was manifested, that he might destroy the works of the devil."

The Lord Jesus Christ knew He was going to face the Cross. He knew He was going to take sin and sickness upon Himself and die a sacrificial death. In an effort to appease Jesus' flesh, the devil said, "Hey, Jesus! You can skip every bit of that, and I'll give You this whole place — *if You will just worship me*. I'll give You authority over this earth without Your ever having to be crucified! I'll give it to You without Your ever having to go to the grave! I'll give it without Your ever knowing what sin is!"

Talk about a mind game! That would be an invitation hard to refuse! But how did Jesus respond to Satan's seducing temptation? Jesus said, *"...Get thee behind me, Satan...."* (Luke 4:8).

What empowered Jesus to resist this profound temptation? *The Word of God!* Jesus went on to say, "...For it is written, Thou shalt worship the Lord thy God, and him only shalt thou serve." Once again, Jesus told the devil, *"...It is written...."* The Spirit of God gave Jesus another deadly sword to wield in answer to the devil's evil offer.

Finally, the devil ended his temptations. The Spirit of God had continually drawn on the reservoir of Scripture that was stored up in Jesus, causing those *rhema* words to come alive and raising up that Word like a terribly dangerous sword. But now the devil, admitting defeat, "...departed from him for a season" (v. 13).

A SURE-FIRE GUARANTEE!

You might as well get ready for your own "testing in the wilderness," because when you begin to take new territory for the Kingdom of God, the devil will try to stop you! As soon as you begin to grow in your knowledge of God's Word and make spiritual progress, Satan will try to slow you down. The enemy doesn't *want* you to make any progress in your spiritual life!

Most believers just passively sit back and let the devil batter them to pieces. They forget that they don't just have *defensive armor* at their disposal. They also have *offensive* weapons to destroy every strategy that the enemy throws at them!

So remember — like the Roman soldier of old, your "sword of the Spirit" hinges on the presence or absence of God's Word in your life. God has given you a sword, but it will not work for you until you've taken the first step of planting the written Word of God in your heart.

If you permit the written Word to have an authoritative role in your life *today*, you will be ready when you face the wiles of the enemy *in the future*. The Spirit of God will have a vast reservoir of Scripture within you from which to draw the exact "sword" you need to repel every attack.

Therefore, in order to guarantee that you have a "sword of the Spirit" in your hand to answer the devil's mental assaults, begin today to attach the "loinbelt of truth" firmly to your life. Study the written Word — praying over it and meditating on it continually — for it is the source from which your sword will be drawn.

> If you permit the written Word to have an authoritative role in your life today, you will be ready when you face the wiles of the enemy in the future.

Refuse to allow the devil to beat you down in defeat any longer with his lies and accusations. Instead, allow the Holy Spirit to wield a powerful *rhema* word — *like the blade of a mighty, two-edged sword* — through the faith-filled words of your mouth. Then *the enemy* will be the one who leaves the scene defeated and demoralized, while *you* keep moving forward, walking victoriously in the light of God's Word!

QUESTIONS FOR PERSONAL GROWTH OR GROUP DISCUSSION

1. What is a *rhema* word? How do you know when you receive one from God?

2. What makes a *rhema* word inseparable from a *logos* word?

3. When you receive a *rhema* word from God, what do you have to do to wield it like a sword against the enemy's attacks?

4. Think back to a time when you received a very definite *rhema* word from God. What was the outcome of the specific word, either because of your obedience or your disobedience?

5. What did Jesus do when the enemy tempted Him in the wilderness? How can you follow His example the next time you are faced with temptation, doubt, fear, etc.?

NOTES:

CHAPTER SIXTEEN

THE LANCE OF PRAYER
AND SUPPLICATION

*U*p to this point, we have covered the "loinbelt of truth," the "breastplate of righteousness," the "shoes of peace," the "shield of faith," the "helmet of salvation," and the "sword of the Spirit." Now we come to the last piece of weaponry Paul lists in Ephesians 6.

Paul finishes his discussion on spiritual armor in verse 18, when he says, "Praying always with all prayer and supplication in the Spirit, and watching thereunto with all perseverance and supplication for all saints."

As I studied these verses about spiritual armor, I was perplexed when I came to the end of this text. I was particularly puzzled by what most commentators and expositors had to say at this point. Although all of them agreed that the Roman soldier had seven pieces of weaponry in his suit of armor, they all said Paul's list of armor was incomplete, stopping short of mentioning one more weapon — the Roman soldier's *lance*.

I was perplexed by the absence of the lance because Paul commanded us, "Put on the *whole* armour of God...." I thought,

If it's true that the lance is not a part of our armor as these commentators and expositors claim, then it isn't possible for us to put on the whole armor of God, because the lance was a strategic part of a Roman soldier's weaponry!

I concluded that although the lance is not specifically mentioned by name in these verses, it *has* to be in this text; otherwise, we do not have the *whole* armor of God. Then I came to realize that the lance *is* included as a part of this set of spiritual equipment. It's found in Ephesians 6:18: "Praying always with all prayer and supplication in the Spirit...." I call this last weapon "the lance of prayer and supplication."

> When you wield "the lance of prayer and supplication," this powerful prayer tool is thrust forward into the spirit realm against the malevolent works of the adversary.

When you wield "the lance of prayer and supplication," this powerful prayer tool is thrust forward into the spirit realm against the malevolent works of the adversary. By forcibly hurling this divine instrument into the face of the enemy, you exercise the power God has given you to stop major obstacles from developing in your personal life.

VARIOUS KINDS OF LANCES

When Paul came to the conclusion of this text about spiritual armor, he had the images of Roman lances and spears in his mind. It is quite possible that Paul was able to look over to the other side of his prison cell and see where his Roman guard had propped up against the wall several kinds of lances and spears of different sizes.

The lances used by the large and diverse Roman army varied greatly in size, shape, and length. Over the course of many centuries, these various lances had been modified substantially, so the Roman soldier had all kinds of lances at his disposal.

The old Greek lances, used during Homer's time, were normally made of ash wood and were about six to seven feet long with a solid iron lance-head at the end. Like the lance itself, the iron head of the lance varied tremendously in form. Often it resembled a leaf, a bulrush, a sharp barb, or simply a jagged point like the lance-heads used on spears today.

Some lances were small; others were extremely long. The smaller, shorter lances were used for gouging and thrusting at an enemy up close, whereas the longer lances were used for hurling at an enemy from a distance.

Most Roman soldiers carried both lances, short and long. With the shorter lance, they were able to thrust through the bodies of enemy soldiers at close range — and what a morbid death this was! With the longer lance, they would strike their adversary with a deadly blow from afar. After successfully hitting an enemy with this longer lance, the Roman soldier would draw his sword and run to finish off the opponent — cutting off his head while he lay wounded on the ground.

In addition to these, there were many other kinds of lances. For instance, during the time of Greek historian Xenophon, the armed forces carried a whole myriad of lances — short lances, long lances, narrow lances, wide lances, pointed lances, dull lances, jagged lances, multiple-blade lances, and so forth. The average soldier in the infantry carried five short lances and one long lance.

Of all the lances in the ancient world, the Macedonians used the longest. The lance they used in battle was 21 to 24 feet long, or the length of a telephone pole! Imagine the awkwardness of using such a lengthy weapon of war. Such a lance would require the user to be amazingly strong! However, this was not the only lance the Macedonians used. The Macedonian cavalry used other lances that were much shorter.

The Roman army used a lance called the *pilum*, which was primarily used for throwing at an enemy from a distance. These *pilum* lances were used when an opposing force came to attack the Romans' fortified position or encampment. Rather than wait for the enemy to come upon them before commencing the battle and thus take many losses, the Roman soldiers would hurl these extremely heavy lances through the air toward their foes. By doing this, the Romans could strike many of the enemy soldiers to the ground before they were able to penetrate their army encampment.

The length of the *pilum* by New Testament times was about six feet long, with the iron lance-head at the top of the lance and the iron shaft at the bottom each approximately three feet in length. This means that all six feet of these *pilum* were made of solid iron! Many of these lances have survived to this day and can be viewed in museums of antiquity around the world.

Vegetius, the Roman historian who wrote about the military institutions of the early Romans, told of another lance that the Roman soldier used. This lance, Vegetius says, was about five and a half feet long, with a three-pointed lance-head that was between nine and twelve inches long. It was later modified to be three and a half feet long, with a lance-head that was five inches in length.

If the soldier desired to inflict a massive and terrible wound upon his enemy, he made sure to load his lance-head with extra iron. The heavier the instrument was, the more deadly was the wound. Furthermore, this heavier load of iron helped carry the lance farther when the soldier had to throw it a great distance.

There were many different kinds of lances and many variations of each one of them. In fact, there were so many shapes, sizes, and lengths of lances during that time in history that I could keep writing on this subject for many pages to come!

Various Kinds of Prayer

What does all of this have to do with spiritual armor? Why am I taking the time to stress the various shapes, sizes, and lengths of lances?

Here is the point: Paul is imagining the entire range of lances and spears as he comes to the issue of prayer. Now by revelation, he begins to compare these various lances to the various kinds of prayer that God has made available to us. This is why Paul said, "Praying always, *with all prayer* and supplication...."

Especially notice the middle portion of this verse, where Paul says, "with all prayer." The phrase "all prayer" is taken from the Greek phrase *dia pases proseuches*, and it would be better translated *"with all kinds of prayer."*

So as Paul moves toward the end of this text on spiritual weaponry, he urges us to pick up our final weapon — *prayer* — and utilizes the imagery of these different kinds of lances to portray different kinds of prayer. Just as Roman soldiers used all different types of lances in battle, Paul now begins to enlighten us to the fact that God has made many kinds of prayer available to us for different purposes in our fight of faith. Now Paul instructs us to use each of these forms of prayer as it is needed. (We'll discuss six of these various forms of scriptural prayer later.)

> God has made many kinds of prayer available to us for different purposes in our fight of faith.

Just as the Roman soldier had a short lance for thrusting an enemy at close range, nothing can compare to a believer's prayer of faith that is filled with authority! A prayer like this is well able to deal a mortal wound to an unseen foe who has come too close within range.

Similarly, just as the Roman soldier had a long lance to hurl at his opponent from afar, we have the weapon of intercession that allows us to thwart an enemy attack in our lives or in someone else's life before it ever occurs. Like a lance loaded with deadly weight, intercession can deal a wound so fatal to the domain of darkness that it hinders the devil's lethal devices from becoming a reality in others' lives or in our own lives, families, businesses, churches, and ministries.

Unseen spirits continually seek to bombard the flesh and hassle the minds of believers. These wicked spirits hate the presence of Jesus Christ and His Church on the earth, making prayer an indispensable offensive weapon for believers to use to ward off the enemy's attacks.

Yes, it is true that our victory has already been won through Jesus' death and resurrection. But regardless of how skilled, bold, and courageous we think we are when it comes to the issue of spiritual conflict, we simply cannot maintain a victorious position apart from a life of prayer. In fact, without this vital spiritual weapon, we can be sure of absolute and total defeat! On the other hand, as we seek God in prayer to receive His direction and His power for our daily living, we get ourselves in position to victoriously reinforce Jesus Christ's triumphant victory over Satan and gloriously demonstrate Satan's miserable defeat.

> We simply cannot maintain a victorious position apart from a life of prayer.

To assist us in maintaining this victorious position, God has given the Church various kinds of powerful prayer. That's why this phrase in Ephesians 6:18 can be translated:

- *"Pray with all manner of prayer."*

- *"Pray with all kinds of prayer."*

- *"Pray with all the kinds of prayers that are available for you to use."*

There is no doubt about it. As Paul writes about the different kinds of prayer, he sees a mental picture of the various types of lances available to the Roman soldier. In his mind's eye, Paul sees long lances, short lances, wide lances, narrow lances, sharp lances, dull lances, multiple-blade lances, and so on. Then he tells us, *"Pray with all the kinds of prayers that are available for you to use...."*

This means that no one kind of prayer is better than the others. Rather, each serves a different purpose and is necessary for the life of faith.

HOW OFTEN SHOULD WE PRAY?

Before we get into a discussion about the wide range of prayers that have been made available to us, we must first back up for a moment and ask, "How often should we pray?"

Notice how Paul begins at the very first of Ephesians 6:18. He says, *"Praying always...."*

The word "always" is taken from the Greek phrase *en panti kairo*. The word *en* would be better translated *at*. The word *panti* means *each and every*. It is an all-encompassing word that embraces *everything, including the smallest and most minute of details*. The word *kairo* is the Greek word for *times* or *seasons*.

When all three of these words are used together in one phrase (*en panti kairo*), as Paul uses them in Ephesians 6:18, they would be more accurately translated, *"at each and every occasion."* This phrase could also be translated to read, *"at every opportunity," "every time you get a chance," "at every season,"* or *"at each and every possible moment."*

The idea Paul is trying to get across to us is this: *"Anytime you get a chance, no matter where you are or what you are doing, at every opportunity, every season, and every possible moment —* SEIZE *that time to pray!"*

This clearly tells us that prayer is not optional for the Christian who is serious about his spiritual life. Unfortunately, however, prayer is the most ignored piece of weaponry the Body of Christ possesses today. People find it more exciting to talk about the shield of faith, the sword of the Spirit, or the breastplate of righteousness than to talk about prayer.

> **Prayer is the most ignored piece of weaponry the Body of Christ possesses today.**

Yet the lance of prayer and supplication is equal in importance to these other pieces of armor. Prayer is a part of our spiritual equipment. In fact, this piece of weaponry is so crucial that Paul urges us to use it continually and habitually — *at every possible moment.*

SIX KINDS OF PRAYER FOR THE BELIEVER

Paul says, "Praying always with *all* prayer and supplication in the Spirit...." The New Testament uses six different Greek words for prayer that are available for our use. Some sources may list more than these six; however, these additional words primarily have to do with worship or are prayer words that were used only by the Lord Jesus Christ. God has given six specific kinds of prayer that pertain to us as believers.

Each one of these six forms of prayer is different from the others, just as the multiple types of Roman lances varied from each other. Each form of prayer is also continually at our disposal to use in our fight of faith.

The basic types of prayer found in the New Testament can be categorized as follows:

1. Prayer of Consecration

2. Prayer of Petition

3. Prayer of Authority (or the Prayer of Faith)

4. Prayer of Thanksgiving

5. Prayer of Supplication

6. Prayer of Intercession

Let's look more in depth at each one of these different forms of prayer.

PRAYER OF CONSECRATION

The most common word for "prayer" in the New Testament is taken from the Greek word *proseuche*. This particular word in its various forms is used approximately 127 times in the New Testament. It is this very word that Paul uses in Ephesians 6:18, when he says, *"Praying always with all prayer...."* In both instances, the word "prayer" is taken from the Greek word *proseuche*.

The word *proseuche* is a compound of the words *pros* and *euche*. The word *pros* is a preposition that means *face to face*. We have already seen this word once before, used in John 1:1 to portray the intimate relationship that exists between the Members of the Godhead.

This verse says, "In the beginning was the Word, and the Word was *with God....*" The word "with" is taken from the word *pros*. By using this word to describe the relationship between the Father and the Son, the Holy Spirit is telling us that theirs is an *intimate* relationship. One translator has translated the verse, "In the beginning was the Word, and the Word was *face to face* with God...."

The word *pros* is also used in Ephesians 6:12 to picture our *close contact* with unseen, demonic spirits that have been marshaled against us. Nearly everywhere it is used in the New Testament, the word *pros* carries the meaning of *a close, up-front, intimate contact with someone else*.

The second part of the word *proseuche* is taken from the word *euche*. The word *euche* is an old Greek word that describes *a wish, desire, prayer,* or *vow*.

The word *euche* was originally used to depict a person who made some kind of a vow to God because of a need or desire in his or her life. This individual would vow to give something of great value to God in exchange for a favorable answer to prayer.

A perfect example of this can be found in the story of Hannah, the mother of Samuel. Hannah deeply desired a child but was not able to become pregnant. Out of great desperation and anguish of spirit, she prayed and made a solemn vow to the Lord.

> **And she vowed a vow, and said, O Lord of hosts, if thou wilt indeed look on the affliction of thine handmaid, and remember me, and not forget thine handmaid, but wilt give unto thine handmaid a man child, then I will give him unto the Lord all the days of his life, and there shall no razor come upon his head....**
>
> **And they** [Hannah and her husband, Elkanah] **rose up in the morning early, and worshipped before the Lord, and returned, and came to their house in Ramah: and Elkanah knew Hannah his wife; and the Lord remembered her. Wherefore it came to pass, when the time was come about after Hannah had conceived, that she bare a son....**
>
> 1 Samuel 1:11,19,20

In exchange for receiving the precious gift of this son, Hannah vowed that her young boy would be devoted to the work of the ministry. Technically, this was a *euche*, for by making this commitment, Hannah gave her most valued and prized possession to God in response to His answering her prayer.

Quite frequently, people seeking an answer to prayer would offer God a gift of thanksgiving in advance. This was their way of releasing their faith in the goodness of God and of thanking Him for His favorable response to their prayer requests.

Before a person verbalized his prayer, he would set up a commemorative altar and offer a sacrifice of thanksgiving on that altar. Such offerings of praise and thanksgiving were called "votive offerings" (derived from the word "vow"). This votive offering was similar to a pledge, for it was the person's promise that once his prayer was answered, he would be back to give additional thanksgiving to God.

All of this information sets the backdrop for the word *proseuche*, used more than any other word for "prayer" in the New Testament. Keep in mind that the majority of Paul's readers were Greek in origin; hence, they understood the full ramifications of this word.

What a picture this paints of prayer! Certainly it tells us several important things about the subject. First, the word *proseuche* tells us that prayer should bring us *face to face* and *eyeball to eyeball* with God in an intimate relationship. Prayer is more than a mechanical act or formula to follow. It is a vehicle that lifts us to a place in the Spirit where we can enjoy *a close, intimate relationship with God!*

> Prayer should bring us face to face and eyeball to eyeball with God in an intimate relationship.

The idea of *sacrifice* is also associated with this word for "prayer." This word portrayed an individual who so desperately desired to see his prayer request answered that he was willing to surrender everything he owned in exchange for answered prayer.

Clearly this describes an altar of sacrifice and consecration in prayer, where a person's life is yielded entirely to God.

Although the Holy Spirit may convict our hearts of areas that need to be surrendered to His sanctifying power, He will never forcibly take these things from us. Thus, this particular word for prayer points to a place of decision and consecration — an altar where we freely vow to give our lives to God in exchange for *His* life.

Because the word *proseuche* has to do with these concepts of surrender and sacrifice, this tells us that God obviously desires to do more than merely bless us. *He wants to change us!*

Thanksgiving was also a vital part of this common word for prayer. We therefore know that when we offer a genuine prayer in faith, we should never stop short of thanking God in advance for hearing and answering our prayers.

> We should never stop short of thanking God in advance for hearing and answering our prayers.

Thus, this Greek word *proseuche* refers to much more than making a simple prayer request. It is also the act of *surrender*, *consecration*, and *thanksgiving*.

This form of prayer is the first "lance of supplication and prayer" that God has placed into our hands. By learning to use this powerful prayer tool, we place our lives into His hands in an act of consecration.

The idea behind *proseuche* is this: *"Come face to face with God, and surrender your life in exchange for His, consecrating your life on an ongoing basis. And be sure to give Him thanks in advance for moving in your life!"*

The possible references for the word *proseuche* are far too many to list here. I suggest that you study many of the 127 occurrences of this word in the New Testament.

PRAYER OF PETITION

The second most often used word for "prayer" in the New Testament is taken from the word *deesis*. The word *deesis* and its various forms are translated "prayer and petition" more than 40 times in the New Testament.

Paul uses this word in Ephesians 6:18, when he says, "Praying always with all prayer and *supplication*...." In this verse, the word *deesis* is translated as the word "supplication."

Deesis is taken from the verb *deomai*, which most literally describes *a need* or *a want*. This is the picture of a person with some kind of need or desire in his or her personal life.

As time passed, the word "need" began to take on the meaning of *prayer* — the kind of prayer that expresses one's basic needs and wants to God. This word, however, has to do with *very basic needs*, not desires for tangible things such as larger homes, more expensive cars, etc. Rather, the word *deesis* has to do with *the basic needs that must be met in order for a person to continue in his or her existence.*

You could therefore say that a *deesis* is *a petition or a cry for God's help that exposes a person's insufficiency to meet his or her own needs.*

We find that Jesus prayed in this manner in Hebrews 5:7: "Who in the days of his flesh, when he had offered up *prayers and supplications* with strong crying and tears unto him that was able to save him from death, and was heard in that he feared."

The word "prayers" in this verse is taken from the word *deesis*. This plainly tells us that the Lord Jesus Christ was very aware of the weakness of His humanity. Recognizing His need and the Father's ability to provide strength for Him, Jesus prayed deeply from His heart and soul, asking the Father to provide divine assistance to help Him in His humanity.

Jesus was so aware of His own need that He prayed (*deesis*) with "strong crying and tears." Some have tried to use this phrase "strong crying and tears" as the scriptural basis for a new method of prayer; then they have attempted to teach this "new method" as doctrine to others. This verse, however, does *not* provide a new formula for prayer. This was the cry of Jesus' heart to the Father, crying out for God to empower Him and to meet His most basic needs of strength and power.

The word *deesis* is used again in James 5:17, where it says, "Elijah was a man subject to like passions as we are, and *he prayed earnestly....*" The phrase "prayed earnestly" is also taken from the word *deesis*. This means that although Elijah was a great and mighty man of God, he recognized his own inability to do anything significant for God. Out of this deep sense of need, he prayed earnestly (*deesis*), asking God to intervene on his behalf.

This kind of prayer stems from someone who is very aware of his or her own great need in life. The word *deesis* almost always portrays a cry for help. A person praying this kind of prayer appeals to God from a position of humility as he or she asks God to grant some kind of special petition — such as a request for spiritual power to minister, for strength to resist temptation or to be sustained in a crisis, etc.

Whereas the word *proseuche* has to do primarily with *surrender* and *consecration*, the word *deesis* has to do with *humility*. Again, this word paints the picture of a believer who recognizes his utter dependence on God, and, therefore, his inability to meet his own need. Relying completely on God's ability to meet his need — whether it be spiritual, mental, or emotional — this person prays earnestly and sincerely, beseeching God from the depths of his spirit and soul to graciously move on his behalf.

Now we see that this word *deesis* is used in Ephesians 6:18 and translated "supplication." The *King James Version* says, "Praying always with all prayer and supplication [*deesis*]...." A better rendering would be, *"Praying always, with all prayer and with all earnest, sincere, and heartfelt petition...."*

This intense form of prayer stems from one's awareness of his own human frailty. *The prayer of petition is therefore prayer that exposes a person's insufficiency and his continual need for God.*

> The prayer of petition is therefore prayer that exposes a person's insufficiency and his continual need for God.

(For other examples *of deesis, see* Second Corinthians 8:4 and First Thessalonians 3:10.)

PRAYER OF AUTHORITY

The third form of prayer used in the New Testament is taken from the word *aiteo*. The word *aiteo* is used approximately 80 times in the New Testament, making it the third most common word for prayer.

The word *aiteo* means *I ask* or *I demand*. At first glance, this Greek word seems to be a strange word for prayer because it doesn't refer to one who humbly requests something from God. Rather, this word *aiteo* describes someone who prays authoritatively, almost demanding something from God! This person knows what he needs, and he isn't afraid to boldly ask to receive it!

Unlike the word *deesis*, which has more to do with spiritual needs and wants, the word *aiteo* primarily has to do with *tangible* needs, such as food, shelter, money, and so forth.

But how can one approach God with such frankness, commanding and demanding that his needs be met by God? Jesus gave us the key to understanding this word *aiteo* in John 15:7. He said, "If ye abide in me, and my words abide in you, ye shall *ask* what ye will, and it shall be done unto you."

The word "ask" in this verse is taken from the word *aiteo*. This phrase could therefore be translated, "...ye shall *demand* what ye will...."

Some are disturbed by this notion of "demanding" something from God. However, it is not so disturbing when you keep it in context with the entire verse. At the first of the verse, the Lord Jesus said, "If ye abide in me, and my words abide in you...." Notice the word "abide" is used twice in this verse. In both instances, the word "abide" is taken from the word *meno*, which means *to stay, to dwell, to lodge, to remain, to indwell, to continue, to remain in constant union with*, or *to take up permanent residency*.

In light of this definition, you could translate the verse, *"If you permanently and habitually lodge, dwell, abide, and remain continually in Me, and if My words permanently and habitually lodge, dwell, abide, and remain continually in you, you will be able to strongly ask for whatever you wish and it will be done for you."*

The Lord Jesus knew that if His words took up permanent residency in our hearts and minds, we would never ask for something that was out of line with His will for our lives. Hence, when we allow the Word of God to permanently and habitually lodge in our hearts, that Word so transforms our minds that when we pray, we do so in accordance with God's will.

> When we allow the Word of God to permanently and habitually lodge in our hearts, that Word so transforms our minds that when we pray, we do so in accordance with God's will.

When you know you are praying according to the will of God, you don't have to sheepishly utter your requests. Instead, you can boldly assert your faith and expect God to move on your behalf! As the writer of Hebrews states, "Let us therefore come boldly unto the throne of grace, that we may obtain mercy, and find grace to help in time of need" (Hebrews 4:16).

The word *aiteo* is also found in First John 5:14,15. In these verses, John says, "And this is the confidence that we have in him, that, if we ask any thing according to his will, he heareth us: and if we know that he hear us, whatsoever we ask, we know that we have the petitions that we desired of him."

Notice the first part of verse 14, where John says, "And this is the *confidence*...." The word "confidence" is derived from the word *parresia*, and it always depicts someone who is *exceedingly bold or courageous*. It is as though John says, "*If you want to know why we are so bold, courageous, and outspoken when we pray, here is the reason....*"

The verse goes on to say, "...that, if we ask any thing *according to his will*, he heareth us: and if we know that he hear us, whatsoever we ask, we know that we have the petitions that we desired of him."

Notice especially that John says, "...that if we *ask* any thing according to his will...." The word "ask" is once again taken from the word *aiteo*. It must be pointed out that this word is once again used in connection with knowing the will of God for one's life. This verse could thus be paraphrased to say, "...If we strongly request anything that is according to His desire for our lives...."

Echoing Jesus' words in John 15:7, John makes a similar assertion: If the Word of God permanently dwells in us, and if we pray according to that indwelling Word, we can come into the presence of God and make our requests known with great boldness, courage, and confidence.

God is clearly not offended by this type of outspoken prayer. John continues, "And if we know that he hear us, whatsoever we *ask*, we know that we have the petitions that we desired of him." That word "ask" is once again taken from the word *aiteo*.

If the Word of God dwells in you — if the Word has lodged in your heart and mind and has taken up residency in your life — then you will not pray prayers that are out of line with God's plan. Thus, when you pray, your prayers will be accurate and in line with His predetermined plan for your life. *You will be praying God's will!*

When you have stored in your heart a strong foundation of accurate knowledge based in God's Word, you can be very bold and courageous in your prayer life, which is exactly what God wants you to do. His desire is that you move forward boldly and courageously in prayer in order to seize His will for your life and bring it into manifestation!

By allowing God's Word to take an authoritative role in your heart and mind, you are giving that Word the freedom to transform your thinking. And the more that your mind is renewed to God's Word, the more your prayers will be in accordance with His plan for your life.

> God's desire is that you move forward boldly and courageously in prayer in order to seize His will for your life and bring it into manifestation!

When you are in this position, you are ready to experience this *aiteo* kind of prayer. With this "lance of supplication and prayer" at your disposal, you can boldly, courageously, and confidently move into higher realms of prayer to obtain the petition you desire of God!

(For other examples of the word *aiteo, see* Ephesians 3:20, James 1:5,6 and First John 3:22.)

Prayer of Thanksgiving

The fourth most common form of prayer in the New Testament is taken from the word *eucharistia.* The word *eucharistia* and its various forms are used 15 times throughout the New Testament.

The word *eucharistia* is a compound of the words *eu* and *charistia.* The word *eu* describes something that is *good* or *well.* It denotes *a general good disposition or feeling about something.* The word *charistia* is from the word *charis,* the word for *grace.*

When compounded together into one word, the new word *eucharistia* refers to *wonderful feelings and good sentiments that freely flow up out of the heart in response to something.* It is primarily used in Paul's epistles when he joyfully thanks God for someone or for a group of individuals.

For instance, when Paul wrote to the Ephesian church, he was so overwhelmed with the grace of God in their midst that he spoke freely from the depths of his heart, saying, "[I] cease not *to give thanks* for you, making mention of you in my prayers" (Ephesians 1:16). This is the idea carried in these words: *"My feelings concerning you cannot be contained. I can't help but thank God for you!"*

In Colossians 1:3, Paul prays the same way for the Colossian church, saying, "We *give thanks* to God and the Father of our Lord Jesus Christ, praying always for you."

Paul prayed in a similar manner for the Thessalonian believers: In First Thessalonians 1:2, he said, "We give thanks to God always for you all, making mention of you in our prayers." Likewise, he later prayed, "We are bound *to thank* God always for you, brethren..." (2 Thessalonians 1:3).

Furthermore, Paul used the word *eucharistia* in First Thessalonians 5:18, when he tells us, "In every thing *give thanks*: for this is the will of God in Christ Jesus concerning you."

According to this verse, it is God's will that we use the prayer of thanksgiving in every aspect of our lives. Paul says, "In every thing...." The Greek could be better rendered, *"On every occasion and in every way possible...."* This plainly means a spirit of thanksgiving should play a dominant role in our lives.

Especially when you are praying for others, you should stop for a moment and reflect on all that God has done in those individuals' lives. You will probably realize that, although they may still have flaws that are disturbing to you, they have made great progress from where they used to be. As you remind yourself of what God's grace has already accomplished in the people you're praying for and how much they have changed, you will be able to freely, joyfully, and unreservedly thank God for His transforming work in their lives.

This particular "lance of supplication and prayer" is extremely important in our spiritual lives. Although most would prefer to talk about supplication, intercession, and other forms of prayer, the prayer of thanksgiving is also a vital part of our spiritual weaponry.

(For other examples of the word *eucharistia*, *see* 2 Corinthians 4:15; 9:11,12; Philippians 4:6; Colossians 2:7; 4:2; 1 Timothy 4:3,4; and Revelation 7:12.)

PRAYER OF SUPPLICATION

The fifth form of prayer used in the New Testament is taken from the word *enteuxis*. This word *enteuxis* and its various forms are used only five times in the New Testament.

The word *enteuxis* is taken from the root *entugchano*, which is a compound of the word *en* and *tugchano*. The word *en* means *in* or *into*. The word *tugchano* means *to happen upon*. When these two words are compounded into one, it means *to fall into a situation* or *to happen into a circumstance* with someone else.

This word *enteuxis* and its various forms (such as *entugchano*) are usually translated as the word "intercession" in the New Testament. However, *enteuxis* does not necessarily refer to intercession as most people think of intercession (i.e., prayer for other people). The word *enteuxis* rather carries the idea of *one who comes to God in simple, childlike faith, to freely enjoy fellowship in the presence of the Lord*. One expositor has said that this is prayer in its most individual and simple form.

It literally means *to fall into* or *to happen upon*. The idea is *to fall into the presence of the Lord* or *to come into wonderful relationship in prayer*. In some places, it has been translated as the word "supplication."

Indeed, this is the idea reflected in this word *enteuxis* — to *supplicate* with the Lord. This word was used in some classical writings to depict a love relationship between two lovers — two individuals who had happened upon each other — who had found or discovered each other — and now were sharing their lives together.

The word *enteuxis* denotes a wonderful, intimate form of prayer whereby we learn to come before God in childlike faith to freely express ourselves and our desires and to unreservedly enjoy His wonderful presence. Furthermore, the prayer of supplication refers to those special times in prayer when God by His Spirit showers us in love and fills us with the knowledge of His life-transforming acceptance.

> The prayer of supplication refers to those special times in prayer when God by His Spirit showers us in love and fills us with the knowledge of His life-transforming acceptance.

Thank God for the glorious privilege He has extended to us to enjoy this kind of intimate fellowship with Him!

(For other examples of the word *enteuxis, see* Romans 11:2; 1 Timothy 2:1; 4:5.)

PRAYER OF INTERCESSION

The sixth word for prayer used in the New Testament is taken from the word *huperentugchano*. This Greek word is found only one time in the entire New Testament, making it the rarest of the words that denote different forms of prayer.

The only usage of *huperentugchano* in the New Testament is found in Romans 8:26. However, it is not used in connection with believers; rather, it is used in connection with the *Holy Spirit*. Romans 8:26 says, "Likewise the Spirit also helpeth our infirmities: for we know not what we should pray for as we ought: but the Spirit itself [Himself] maketh intercession for us with groanings which cannot be uttered."

Did you notice who was doing this particular work of intercession? *The Holy Spirit!* Paul says, "...but the Spirit itself [Himself] maketh intercession...." Therefore, this word for intercession, *huperentugchano*, is not an intercessory work that we do, but a work that the Holy Spirit does *on our behalf*.

The word "intercession" (*huperentugchano*) is an old word that means *to fall in on behalf of someone else*. It is what we would call a word for *rescue*. For instance, if someone fell deep into a cavern, you would have to descend down into that cavern along with that person in order to get him out and rescue him.

This is precisely the idea behind this word for "intercession." By using this word, Paul tells us that this is a special work of intercession, done by the Holy Spirit Himself. It speaks of those times when the Spirit of God supernaturally joins us in our circumstances, shares our emotions and frustrations, and then begins working a plan that will ultimately get us out of that mess!

> The true intercessory ministry of the Holy Spirit occurs when you are at a loss for words and don't know how to pray.

The true intercessory ministry of the Holy Spirit occurs when you are at a loss for words and don't know how to pray. Suddenly and supernaturally, the Holy

Spirit falls into that place of helplessness and joins with you in the rhythm of prayer.

With all His wonderful attributes and personality traits, the Holy Spirit still feels everything you feel. He empathizes with your feelings of complete inadequacy. He understands the battles you are facing. He willingly falls into each difficult circumstance along with you, feeling your emotions of fear, anger, or frustration. Then He begins a plan of rescue!

Thus, even though the word "intercession" means *to fall in with someone else*, the purpose is not to have Someone with whom you can share your experience of being down in the dumps. Rather, the purpose of intercession is so you can be *rescued*, *renewed*, and *delivered* from the predicament you're facing. That is exactly what the intercessory ministry of the Holy Spirit is all about.

Who experiences this type of supernatural intercession and divine intervention? Romans 8:26 begins, "Likewise, the Spirit also helpeth our infirmities...." Especially pay heed to the word "infirmities." One great expositor has said this could be translated, *"Likewise, the Spirit helps those who know they are weak and infirm...."* This is exactly the idea Paul had in mind!

In other words, it is when we finally recognize our own human weakness that we begin to open our hearts and souls to this intercessory ministry of the Holy Spirit. Until we admit our utter need for His work in us, the Holy Spirit is limited in His ability to move freely in our lives.

However, the moment we come to grips with our need for supernatural assistance — the moment we open our hearts to the Holy Spirit and cry out for His help — we liberate Him to release His power on the inside of us. That's when the Spirit of God can begin His supernatural, intercessory ministry in our lives — throwing His deadly lance into the heart of the enemy's strategies to destroy them before they can ever be manifested in our lives!

> Until we admit our utter need for His work in us, the Holy Spirit is limited in His ability to move freely in our lives.

A FINAL WORD

In this book, we have thoroughly searched the Scriptures to grasp a fuller understanding of spiritual weaponry. We have studied God's Word to see what it has to say about our victorious position over Satan.

Now that you have finished this book, you may decide to pass it on to someone else to read. But don't allow yourself to forget the basic principles contained within these pages. Especially remember these two truths, and never stop applying them to your life:

- Real spiritual warfare has to do with taking authority over your mind and your flesh, as well as taking authority over the works of darkness.

- If you are living a holy and consecrated life, the bulk of spiritual warfare in your life has already been settled. To deal with the other attacks that the enemy brings against you, you must learn to apply the Word of God on a daily basis to the circumstances you face.

No matter what challenge you encounter, your ultimate victory depends on whether or not you use the spiritual weapons God has provided for you. Therefore, if you want to live as more than a conqueror in this life, Paul's words in Ephesians 6:13 must define the way you face every situation: "Wherefore take unto you the whole armour of God, that ye may be able to withstand in the evil day, and *having done all, TO STAND*"!

> No matter what challenge you encounter, your ultimate victory depends on whether or not you use the spiritual weapons God has provided for you.

QUESTIONS FOR PERSONAL GROWTH OR GROUP DISCUSSION

1. What does it mean to "pray without ceasing"? How can you obey that command in your everyday life?

2. What are the characteristics of the prayer of consecration? Can you think of a landmark moment in your spiritual walk when you prayed this particular kind of prayer to the Father? How did your life change as a result of that prayer?

3. What is the primary element of the prayer of petition? In what type of circumstances might a person pray this kind of prayer?

4. What is the vital prerequisite that you must fulfill before you can pray the prayer of authority?

5. Why is it so important to obey the scriptural command to give thanks in *everything* through the prayer of thanksgiving?

NOTES:

_____

_____

_____

_____

_____

_____

_____

_____

_____

_____

_____

_____

_____

_____

_____

_____

_____

_____

_____

_____

_____

_____

_____

WORKS CITED

Bingham, Jane, Fiona Chandler, Jane Chisholm, Gill Harvey, Lisa Miles, Struan Reid, and Sam Taplin. *The Usborne Internet-Linked Encyclopedia of the Ancient World*. London: Usborne House, 2003.

Bunson, Margaret. *Dictionary of the Roman Empire*. New York: Oxford UP, 1991.

Clayton, Peter. *Treasures of Ancient Rome*. New York: Crescent Books, 1995.

Collins, Michael, and Matthew A. Price. *The Story of Christianity*. New York: DK, 1999.

Connolly, Peter. *Greece and Rome At War*. London: Greenhill Books, 1998.

Conti, Flavio. *A Profile of Ancient Rome*. Los Angeles: Getty Publications, 2003.

Cornell, Tim, and John Matthews. *Atlas of the Roman World*. New York: Checkmark Books, 1982.

Gabucci, Ada. *Ancient Rome: Art, Architecture and History*. Great Britain: The British Museum P, 2002.

Goldsworthy, Adrian. *The Complete Roman Army*. London: Thames and Hudson Ltd., 2003.

Guhl, E.. and W. Koner. *Everyday Life of the Greeks and Romans*. New York: Crescent Books, 1989.

Klucina, Petr. *Armor From Ancient to Modern Times*. New York: Barnes & Noble Books, 1997.

Liberati, Anna Maria, and Fabio Bourbon. *Ancient Rome: History of a Civilization That Ruled the World*. New York: Barnes & Noble Books, 2000.

Matyszak, Philip. *Chronicle of the Roman Republic: The Rulers of Ancient Rome From Romulus to Augustus*. London: Thames and Hudson Ltd., 2003.

Scarre, Chris. *Chronicle of the Roman Empires: The Reign-by-Reign Record of the Rulers of Imperial Rome*. London: Thames and Hudson Ltd., 1995.

Stambaugh, John E. *The Ancient Roman City*. Baltimore: The John Hopkins UP, 1988.

Stephens, William H. *The New Testament World in Pictures*. Nashville: Broadman P, 1987.

PHOTO/ILLUSTRATION ACKNOWLEDGMENTS

(**NOTE:** Pages below refer to photos and illustrations in center-fold insert.)

All coin images (pages 1-16), *except* Valerian I, *from:*
Sear, Donald R. *Roman Coins and Their Values.* London: B.A. Seaby Ltd., 1981.
© Spink & Son Ltd. Used by permission.
Historical order of coins obtained from *Roman Coins and Their Values.*

AKG-Images, London:
Peter Connolly, 2, 3-l, 3-r, 4-b, 6-t, 6-bc, 7-l, 7-r, 8, 9-b, 10-tl, 10-br, 11, 13-r, 13-b, 14, 15-c, 16.

The Art Archive:
Archaeological Museum Instanbul/Dagli Orti, 12; Bardo Museum Tunis/Dagli Orti, 4-tl; Musée du Louvre Paris/Dagli Orti, 1; Museo Capitolino Rome/Dagli Orti, 15-tr.

Corbis:
Bettmann, 5

FotoLibra:
Miles Kelly, 6-bl, 6-br, 9-t.

Rick Renner Ministries:
Valerian I coin, 9.

REFERENCE BOOK LIST

1. *How To Use New Testament Greek Study Aids* by Walter Jerry Clark (Loizeaux Brothers).

2. *Strong's Exhaustive Concordance of the Bible* by James H. Strong.

3. *The Interlinear Greek-English New Testament* by George Ricker Berry (Baker Book House).

4. *The Englishman's Greek Concordance of the New Testament* by George Wigram (Hendrickson).

5. *New Thayer's Greek-English Lexicon of the New Testament* by Joseph Thayer (Hendrickson).

6. *The Expanded Vine's Expository Dictionary of New Testament Words* by W. E. Vine (Bethany).

7. *Theological Dictionary of the New Testament* by Geoffrey Bromiley; Gephard Kittle, ed. (Eerdmans).

8. *The New Analytical Greek Lexicon*; Wesley Perschbacher, ed. (Hendrickson).

9. *The New Linguistic and Exegetical Key to the Greek New Testament* by Cleon Rogers Jr. (Zondervan).

10. *Word Studies in the Greek New Testament* by Kenneth Wuest, 4 Volumes (Eerdmans).

11. *New Testament Words* by William Barclay (Westminster Press).

12. *Word Meanings* by Ralph Earle (Hendrickson).

13. *International Critical Commentary Series*; J. A. Emerton, C. E. B. Cranfield, and G. N. Stanton, eds. (T. & T. Clark International).

14. *Vincent's Word Studies of the New Testament* by Marvin R. Vincent, 4 Volumes (Hendrickson).

15. *New International Dictionary of New Testament Theology*; Verlyn D. Verbrugge, ed. (Zondervan).

ABOUT THE AUTHOR

Rick Renner is a prolific author and a highly respected Bible teacher and leader in the international Christian community. Rick is the author of more than 30 books, including the bestsellers *Dressed To Kill* and *Sparkling Gems From the Greek*, all of which have sold more than 3 million copies combined. In 1991, Rick and his family moved to what is now the former Soviet Union. Today he is the senior pastor of the *Moscow Good News Church*; the founder and director of the *Good News Association of Pastors and Churches*, with a membership of several hundred churches; and the founder of *Media Mir*, the first Christian television network in the former USSR that today broadcasts the Gospel to a potential audience of 100 million people and to countless Russian-speaking viewers around the world via multiple satellites. Rick's wife and lifelong ministry partner, Denise, and their three sons — Paul, Philip, and Joel — lead this amazing work with the help of their committed leadership team. Rick and Denise, along with their sons and families, all reside in Moscow.

A WORD ABOUT OUR WORK

From inception to its current role in the Body of Christ, *RENNER Ministries'* purpose and vision has been to teach, strengthen, and rescue people for the Kingdom of God. Although the Renners' ministry began much earlier, in 1991 God called Rick and Denise Renner and their family to what is now the former Soviet Union. Since that time, millions of lives have been touched by the various outreaches of *RENNER Ministries.* Nevertheless, the Renners' ever-increasing vision for this region of the world continues to expand across 9 time zones to reach 300 million precious souls for God's Kingdom.

The *Moscow Good News Church* was begun in September 2000 in the very heart of Moscow, right next to Red Square. Since that time, the church has grown to become one of the largest Protestant churches in Moscow and a strategic model for pastors throughout this region of the world to learn from and emulate. Today outreaches include ministry to families, senior citizens, children, youth, international church members, specialized ministry to businesspeople, and an outreach to the poor and needy. Rick and Denise also founded churches in Riga, Latvia, and in Kiev, Ukraine, both of which continue to thrive.

Part of the mission of *RENNER Ministries* is to come alongside pastors and ministers and take them to a higher level of excellence and professionalism in the ministry. Therefore, since 1991 when the walls of Communism first collapsed, this ministry has been working in the former USSR to train and equip pastors, church leaders, and ministers, helping them attain the necessary skills and knowledge to fulfill the ministries that the Lord has given them.

To this end, Rick Renner founded both a ministry training center and a ministerial association. The *Good News Training Center* operates as a part of the *Moscow Good News Church.* It specializes in training leaders to start new churches all over the former Soviet Union. The *Good News Association of Pastors and Churches* is a church-planting and church-supporting organization with a membership of pastors and churches that numbers in the hundreds.

Rick and Denise Renner also oversee *Media Mir*, the first and one of the largest TV outreaches within the territory of the former USSR. Since its inception in 1992, this television network has become one of the strongest instruments available today for declaring the Word of God to the 15 nations of the former Soviet Union, reaching 100 million potential viewers every day with the Gospel of Jesus Christ. The network also reaches an untold number of Russian speakers on almost every continent of the world via satellite.

The Renners also founded the *"It's Possible"* humanitarian foundation, which is involved in various outreaches in the city of Moscow. The *"It's Possible"* foundation uses innovative methods to help different age groups of people who are in great need.

In addition to conducting their work in the former Soviet Union, Rick and Denise Renner continue to expand their outreach throughout the world. They are teaching God's Word to people in the United States through a variety of means: producing books and audio resources; conducting meetings in churches, seminars, and conferences throughout the country; and appearing frequently on nationwide TV programs, such as *Believer's Voice of Victory* with Kenneth Copeland, *Enjoying Everyday Life* with Joyce Meyer, *700 Club* with Pat Robertson, and *Life Today* with James Robison. The Renners also reach out to English-speaking people around the globe through their eBooks and MP3 audio teachings; their online IMPART network, designed to help ministers; their various Internet video programs; and the meetings they conduct in other nations around the world.

If you would like to learn more about the many aspects and outreaches of *RENNER Ministries*, please visit our website at www.renner.org, or call 918-496-3213.

A NOTE TO BOOKSELLERS

*For all wholesale book orders,
please contact:*

TEACH ALL NATIONS

A book company anointed to take God's Word
to you and to the nations of the world.

A Division of
Rick Renner Ministries
P. O. Box 702040
Tulsa, OK 74170-2040
Phone: 877-281-8644
Fax: 918-496-3278
Email: tan@renner.org
Website: www.tanpublish.com

FOR FURTHER INFORMATION

For additional copies of this book
or for further information
about this ministry and other Renner products,
please contact the RENNER Ministries office nearest you,
or visit the ministry website at **www.renner.org**.
(**Note:** For online orders, digital downloads are available.
All physical product orders are available only in the U.S.
If outside the U.S., please contact
a RENNER Ministries office near you.)

ALL USA CORRESPONDENCE:
RENNER Ministries
P. O. Box 702040
Tulsa, OK 74170-2040
(918) 496-3213
Or 1-800-RICK-593
Email: renner@renner.org
Website: www.renner.org

MOSCOW OFFICE:
RENNER Ministries
P. O. Box 53
Moscow 109316, Russia
7 (495) 727-1470
Email: mirpress@umail.ru
Website: www.mgnc.org

RIGA OFFICE:
RENNER Ministries
Unijas 99
Riga LV-1084, Latvia
(371) 780-2150
Email: info@goodnews.lv

KIEV OFFICE:
RENNER Ministries
P. O. Box 146
Kiev 01025, Ukraine
380 (44) 246-6552
Email: mirpress@rrm.kiev.ua

OXFORD OFFICE:
RENNER Ministries
Box 7, 266 Banbury Road
Oxford OX2 7DL, England
44 (1865) 355509
Email: europe@renner.org

A LIGHT IN DARKNESS
VOLUME ONE

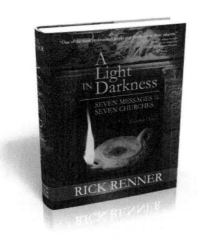

$79.95 (Hardback)
ISBN 978-0-9779459-8-6

Step into the world of the First Century Church as Rick Renner creates a panoramic experience of unsurpassed detail to transport you into the ancient lands of the seven churches of Asia Minor. Within the context of this fascinating — and, at times, shocking — historical backdrop, Rick outlines challenges early believers faced in taking the Gospel to a pagan world. After presenting a riveting account of the apostle John's vision of the exalted Christ, Rick leads you through an in-depth study of Jesus' messages to the churches of Ephesus and Smyrna — profoundly relevant messages that still resonate for His Church today.

Rick's richly detailed historical narrative, enhanced by classic artwork and superb photographs shot on location at archeological sites, will make the lands and the message of the Bible come alive to you as never before. Parallels between Roman society of the First Century and the modern world prove the current relevance of Christ's warning and instructions.

A Light in Darkness is an extraordinary book series that will endure and speak to generations to come. This authoritative first volume is a virtual encyclopedia of knowledge — a definitive *go-to* resource for any student of the Bible and a classic *must-have* for Christian families everywhere.

Faced with daunting challenges, the modern Church *must* give urgent heed to what the Holy Spirit is saying in order to be equipped for the end of this age.

For more information, visit us online at: **www.renner.org**
Book Resellers: Contact Teach All Nations at 877-281-8644,
or email **tan@renner.org** for quantity discounts.

MINING THE TREASURES
OF GOD'S WORD

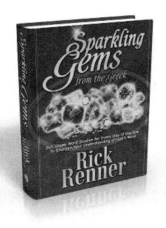

Author Rick Renner unearths a rich treasure trove of truths in his remarkable devotional, *Sparkling Gems From the Greek.* Drawing from an extensive study of both the Bible and New Testament Greek, Rick illuminates 365 passages with more than 1,285 in-depth Greek word studies. Far from intellectualizing, he blends his solid instruction with practical applications and refreshing insights. Find challenge, reassurance, comfort, and reminders of God's abiding love and healing every day of the year.

$34.95 (Hardback)
ISBN: 978-0-9725454-2-6

Sparkling Gems From the Greek Electronic Reference Edition

Now you are only a few short clicks away from discovering the untold riches of God's Word! Offering embedded links to three exhaustive indices for ultimate ease in cross-referencing scriptures and Greek word studies, this unique computer study tool gives you both convenience and portability as you read and explore Rick Renner's one-of-a-kind daily devotional!

$29.95 (CD-ROM)
ISBN: 978-0-9725454-7-1

For more information, visit us online at: **www.renner.org**
Book Resellers: Contact Teach All Nations at 877-281-8644,
or email **tan@renner.org** for quantity discounts.

EVERY DREAM IS TARGETED BY A THIEF – ARE YOU ON GUARD?

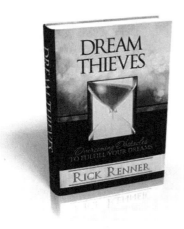

$24.95 (Hardback)
ISBN: 978-0-9779459-3-1

In his revised and updated classic, ***Dream Thieves***, Rick Renner identifies thieves lurking along the road to your destiny and reveals the strategies that you must adopt to ensure that you achieve your God-given dreams. He explains that every dream God plants in your heart has a significant purpose, leading ultimately to a specific destination. That's why dream thieves show up early and repeatedly along your journey to shift your focus from opportunities to obstacles. Their goal is to overwhelm and intimidate you until you're either immobilized and stuck or moving in a direction that's ineffective. These thieves try to make you challenge your call, doubt your dream, and question your capacity to deliver on the vision that consumes you — until eventually the fire in your heart flickers and fades away.

Whether your dream has been delayed — or even if it seems to be dead — this book will revitalize your vision, steering you back on track with renewed momentum to see it through to its fulfillment. You can — *you must* — fulfill your unique purpose in life by walking in your God-ordained calling. Too many abandoned dreams litter the road of life. Don't let *your* dream be one of them.

BOOKS BY RICK RENNER

<u>Books in English</u>

Dream Thieves*

Dressed To Kill*

The Dynamic Duo

If You Were God, Would You Choose You?*

Insights to Successful Leadership

Let It Go*

A Light in Darkness, Volume One

Living in the Combat Zone*

Merchandising the Anointing

Paid in Full*

The Point of No Return*

Seducing Spirits and Doctrines of Demons

Sparkling Gems From the Greek Daily Devotional*

Spiritual Weapons To Defeat the Enemy*

Ten Guidelines To Help You Achieve
  Your Long-Awaited Promotion!*

365 Days of Power*

Turn Your God-Given Dreams Into Reality*

*Digital version available for Kindle, Nook, iBook, and other eBook formats.

Note: For audio and video teaching materials by Rick Renner, please visit **www.renner.org**.

BOOKS IN RUSSIAN

Dream Thieves

Dressed To Kill

The Dynamic Duo

Good News About Your New Life

If You Were God, Would You Choose You?

Insights to Successful Leadership

Let It Go

Hell Is a Real Place

How To Test Spiritual Manifestations

A Light in Darkness, Volume One

Living in the Combat Zone

Merchandising the Anointing

Paid in Full

The Point of No Return

Seducing Spirits and Doctrines of Demons

Sparkling Gems From the Greek Daily Devotional

Spiritual Weapons To Defeat the Enemy

Ten Guidelines To Help You Achieve
     Your Long-Awaited Promotion!

365 Days of Power

What the Bible Says About Healing

What the Bible Says About Tithes and Offerings

What the Bible Says About Water Baptism

What To Do if You've Had a Failure

Study Notes

Study Notes

Study Notes

Study Notes

Study Notes

Study Notes

Study Notes

Study Notes

Study Notes